POE'S LITERARY BATTLES

POE'S LITERARY BATTLES

---

*The Critic in the Context of
His Literary Milieu*

Sidney P. Moss

Durham, North Carolina
DUKE UNIVERSITY PRESS
1963

© 1963, Duke University Press

Library of Congress Catalogue Card Number 63–9010

Cambridge University Press, London N.W.1, England

*This book is published with the assistance
of a grant to the Duke University Press
by the Ford Foundation*

Printed in the United States of America by
the Kingsport Press, Inc., Kingsport, Tenn.

Preface

In going over the ground of Poe's first battle, I found that a significant portion of Poe's essays, reviews, lectures, and editorial comment was concerned with matters that we do not ordinarily associate with literary critics—namely, a preoccupation with the policies and practices of publishers, editors, and reviewers; and that this battle was fought over such policies and practices. A more exhaustive study of Poe as a working critic convinced me that much of Poe's criticism and comment was written under and shaped by the exigencies of attack and defense. Concerned as I was with Poe's critical career, I would have been dull not to see these battles as related campaigns, since the battles were made coherent by the recurrence of common issues, common principles, and common practices. I would have been even duller had I not recognized that these battles might serve as a kind of stereoscopic viewer by which I could see Poe's criticism in its contemporary and therefore three-dimensional context.

Although such a frame does not admit of an exhaustive analysis of Poe's reviews, it provides a means—the most dramatic one I could find—for discussing his characteristic critical views and the typical responses he made to his literary times, and therefore a way of getting at the essence of Poe as a working critic.

In writing this book, I have sought to satisfy two major conditions: first, to collect, assemble, and present every piece of available evidence pertinent to Poe's literary battles; second, to interpret that evidence, however that interpretation may differ from current opinion, not so much with the object of defending Poe as a critic but of understanding him in that capacity. In satisfying the first condition, I have received so many kindnesses from so many librarians that merely to list their names in acknowledgment of their services is prohibitive. I have tried in each case to thank them personally, and here I thank them again collectively. The very numerous debts I owe to scholars whose works I consulted or whose information I solicited, I have sought to acknowledge whenever possible in my notes.

But there are some people to whom I owe a special debt of gratitude which must be acknowledged here. Among them are the editors of *American Literature* and the *American Book Collector* for their double kindness to me—first, in publishing my articles; second, in granting me permission to draw upon them in writing this book; Dr. Hensley C. Woodbridge, Head Librarian at Murray State College, who assisted greatly in putting library materials at my disposal; Professor Clell T. Peterson who had the patience to listen to certain inchoate ideas; Mr. Carroll G. Bowen who gave me encouragement at a crucial time; Mr. and Mrs. David A. Page—for sentimental reasons; and my family—Rita, Laura, Colleen, and Philip—without whose presence there would have been little pleasure in the work.

Contents

Introduction

Poe's literary battles had a singleness of purpose: to prepare the ground for writers of genuine talent and, in consequence, for a respectable American literature. At a time when America had nothing that could be called a significant native criticism, Poe formulated the highest critical standards and provided models of criticism in his own essays and reviews. At a time when American authors imitated English writers, he had the boldness to denounce this "colonial sin" and charge that imitation was a certain sign of mediocrity. At a time when the divine afflatus represented an explanation of the creative process, he insisted upon conscious art, even exaggerating the consciousness of the process in "The Philosophy of Composition." At a time when American critics, as well as American writers, confused a moralistic intent with literary value, Poe condemned didacticism both as a critical principle and as an aesthetic purpose, and insisted upon Beauty—a cant term, it is true, but one that becomes clear in such contexts as "The Poetic Principle." At a time when critics judged by provincial and ephemeral standards, Poe proclaimed that standards needed to be universal and eternal. And at a time when criticism was subjective at best and logrolling at worst, Poe insisted upon an analytic and impartial criticism. Moreover, and scarcely the least of his accomplishments, Poe concerned himself with exposing and censuring those conditions of publishing, reviewing, and merchandising that militated against talented writers in favor of mediocre ones—those forces whose position has since been usurped by book clubs, culled prepublication blurbs, large-scale advertising, and TV puffs, though the cliques and the claquers are still with us.

One hears at times, even from the mouths of scholars, the wistful remark that Poe should have left the task of exposing the fool and lashing the knave to his betters—the same admonition given to Swift, which he properly satirized. Unfortunately, Poe's "betters" were above that sort of thing; and even assuming that they had the hardihood and intelligence for the task, they disqualified themselves by their squeamishness at becoming involved in journalistic give-and-take. To deplore Poe's splenetic critical temper, or the personalities he introduced into his articles, or his inability to maintain an indifference to abuse as weaknesses is as ridiculous under the circumstances as to deplore a general's aggressive tactics as weaknesses. Without these qualities, Poe would no more have entered the critical arena than a Longfellow, a Hawthorne, or a Lowell; nor, having entered it, could he have survived the cutthroat journalism of his time. These "weaknesses," to speak the truth, constituted his strength—something that his contemporaries recognized, even if we do not.

What lies behind such wistful remarks is a refusal to recognize that Poe's criticism had a context, the context of journalism, and that he had causes at stake, victories for which could not be wrested in a study. His was not the ivory tower criticism that we find moldering in Lowell's *Among My Books* and *My Study Windows* or the disengaged criticism of the academic critics that lies buried in the *North American Review*. If his criticism had been of that order, a resurrection would be called for, not an analysis. Once this is understood, that Poe's criticism was a form of journalism, we can see why Poe, forced to compete with the "scholar critics," feigned an erudition he did not always have; why, in cutthroat competition with rival magazinists—a rivalry upon which depended his livelihood and the maintenance of his principles—he became vitriolic on occasion, or defiantly contemptuous, or savagely ironic; and why, as a means of enlisting allies in his cause or of strengthening his personal position, he was occasionally inconsistent and favoritistic in his critical judgments. In saying this, however, let it also be said that Poe *was* widely and well read; that his prose *was*, by and large, elevated and brilliant; that his intellectual reach *was* great; that, for the most part, he *was* consistent and impartial in his judgments; that no one can read his critical works without recognizing in him a high seriousness and an essential integrity; and that, finally, as Edmund Wilson tells us in *The Shock of Recognition*, his "literary articles and lectures ... surely constitute the most remarkable body of criticism ever produced in the United States."

POE'S LITERARY BATTLES

BACKGROUND
FOR BATTLE

We are perpetually misled in our judgment by the
impossibility of identifying ourselves with the writers
—of inducing a full sympathy with the circumstances that impelled them, and thus with the objects for which they wrote. . . .——*Edgar A. Poe*

From 1835 to 1849, the period that spans Poe's critical career, Poe was engaged in literary battles that involved such
celebrities of the day as Theodore Sedgwick Fay, associate
editor of the popular *New York Mirror,* Colonel William Leete
Stone, co-owner and editor of the powerful *New York Commercial Advertiser,* Lewis Gaylord Clark, editor of the widely
circulated *Knickerbocker Magazine,* and Henry Wadsworth
Longfellow, Harvard professor and well-known poet. These
battles had two related objectives, a fact that accounts for some
of Poe's reviews being destructive and others constructive.
First, he wanted to smash the power of the literary cliques
intrenched in Boston and New York City that could make the
reputations and fortunes of those authors, editors, and publishers with whom they were in league, and that could ruin
those who were outside the pale or who threatened their interests. Second, he wanted to establish conditions favorable for
authorship and attractive to men of creative power. To this
end he insisted that books be literature, not merely literary
wares. To this end he argued for critical and literary standards
other than those associated with the market place. To this end

he formulated principles of literary art. And to this end he sought to purify the taste of the reading public. One may have reservations about Poe's methods; one may want to take issue with some of his aesthetic principles; one may find it difficult to condone his lapses—his favoritism, his occasional poor literary taste, his desire for reputation, even if that amounted only to notoriety. But to fail to recognize that Poe *was* a literary reformer; that his battles *were* related campaigns in his total war on what he called "our general editorial course of corruption"; in short, to read Poe's criticism outside the context of his literary milieu is seriously to misread him. This may explain the embarassment, disdain, or confusion that some commentators on his criticism have expressed. It may also explain why other readers have interpreted Poe's actions principally in psychological terms, assigning his captiousness to inward sources such as spite and envy, and not to outward sources such as corrupt publishing and editorial practices.

To understand the issues involved and which, in fact, gave shape and coherence to Poe's critical career, it is necessary to sketch the economic-literary background that existed about the time that Poe took command of the *Southern Literary Messenger,* the first magazine he edited, and began to assault the literary cliques. The discussion will serve not only to remove the stigma of spite and envy that has become gratuitously attached to much of Poe's criticism; it will also make intelligible certain phenomena that are more often labeled than explained —mainly, the *economic* bases for literary sectionalism and for the so-called American Renaissance with its characteristic exploitation of the American past, the American landscape, and the American experience.

A national literature, defined merely as works written by Americans and published in America, was still a fairly novel idea as late as 1835, and one that was being trumpeted by native writers who wanted to assure themselves of a market for and an income from their writings.[1] Without this assurance,

---

1. The most elaborate work on the subject of national literature is by Benjamin T. Spencer, *Quest for Nationality: An American Literary Campaign*

they contended, authors could not hope to survive and, instead of devoting their talents to risky literary ventures, would enter other professions in which remuneration was less uncertain, to the detriment of our national literature.[2] Poe himself might have abandoned literature as a profession had the chance been offered him. Despite a considerable if, in some quarters, notorious reputation, he sought a custom-house appointment in 1842, as Nathaniel Hawthorne earlier and Herman Melville later sought and gained such appointments, for, as he said, "Literature is at a sad discount. There is really nothing to be done in this way. Without an international copyright law, American authors may as well cut their throats."[3]

American publishers, whatever deference they paid to the idea of a national literature, were far from sympathetic to it in practice. The copyright law then operative in the United States protected only works written by Americans, and firms that published such works were obliged, though by no means bound, to give their authors a nominal share of the profits, if any, or buy the copyright to those works outright—either of which procedures threatened their potential gains. Being as a group far more interested in earning profits than in encouraging a national literature, publishers were reluctant to engage in such patently poor business practices. Thus, unless an American

---

(Syracuse, 1957). At a booksellers' dinner held in New York City on March 30, 1837, which was attended by some three hundred people, including such prominent editors as James Bennett and Lewis Gaylord Clark, such leading publishers as Mathew Carey and James Harper, and such celebrated authors as Washington Irving, James K. Paulding, and William Cullen Bryant (not to mention Poe), William L. Stone, "as the senior of the editorial corps of New York City," had this to say: "A great deal has been said . . . about the duty of encouraging native literature. . . . It is but a few years since we began to think of having native authors." (See the *New York American*, XIX, April 3, 1837, for a detailed report of this event.) And William Ellery Channing in *The Importance and Means of a National Literature* (London, 1830, p. 13) asked even earlier: "Do we possess, indeed, what may be called a national literature? . . . We regret that the reply . . . is so obvious. The few standard works which we have produced, and which promise to live, can hardly, by any courtesy, be denominated a national literature."

2. In *Notions of the Americans* (Philadelphia, 1828), II, 108, for instance, James Fenimore Cooper asserted that "Talent is sure of too many avenues to wealth and honors, in America, to seek, unnecessarily, an unknown and hazardous path [of authorship]."

3. Letter to Frederick W. Thomas dated Aug. 27, 1842. See John Ward Ostrom, ed., *The Letters of Edgar Allan Poe* (Cambridge, Mass., 1948), I, 210.

author was popular and the sale of his work assured, he was asked to underwrite the publication of his work, guaranteeing the publisher full compensation for all losses resulting from such publication, for which he usually received 10 per cent of the net profits, if profits accrued. When Poe, to touch upon one case, submitted his second work,[4] *Al Aaraaf, Tamerlane, and Minor Poems* (Baltimore, 1829) to Carey, Lea, and Carey, that firm refused to publish the manuscript unless Poe furnished $100 to cover all possible loss—a sum that Poe was unable to raise at the time.[5] The way Poe finally managed to have his *Poems* (New York, 1831) published in a purported second edition by Elam Bliss was by subscription, raising seventy-five cents from each of his fellow cadets at West Point, for which, in gratitude, he dedicated the volume to them.

Poe had even worse luck in attempting to publish his first collection of short stories in 1836, since, apparently, he declined to pay for publication out of his own pocket. Carey and Lea rejected the collection, as did Harpers, despite James K. Paulding's intercession with that company,[6] and it was not until September 28, 1839—when Poe had earned a wide reputation as a critic and magazine contributor—that Lea and Blanchard agreed to publish an edition of 750 copies of the two-volume *Tales of the Grotesque and Arabesque,* provided they keep all the profits and Poe only the copyright and a few copies. When Poe, later in the year, sought to get some money from the work by offering to sell the copyright to that firm, Lea and Blanchard refused, saying that they had no expectation of even

---

4. Next to nothing is known about the circumstances of the publication of his first work, *Tamerlane and Other Poems* (Boston, 1827). Calvin F. S. Thomas, who was a job printer, not a publisher, may have agreed to print this work out of friendship for Poe (Poe and he were nearly the same age). On the other hand, Poe may have saved enough out of his army pittance to defray the cost of the estimated forty-copy edition. Thomas, of course, had no way of distributing the book. Even if he had, it is doubtful that anyone would have bought the poems "By a Bostonian."

5. See Poe's letter to his guardian, John Allan, dated May 29, 1829 (Ostrom, *Poe's Letters,* I, 20). Poe regretfully recalled the manuscript on July 28, 1829 (*ibid.*, p. 27), and submitted it to Hatch & Dunning, Baltimore publishers. Some time before November 18 Poe received $80 from John Allan (*ibid.*, p. 34), a sum that may have gone to those publishers to guarantee them against loss.

6. Arthur Hobson Quinn, *Edgar Allan Poe: A Critical Biography* (New York, 1941), pp. 250–251.

regaining the capital they had invested in the book, let alone any hope of realizing a profit. Their final and humiliating comment was that, if they had to do it again, they would not undertake to publish the tales at all, and if Poe knew of someone who would take over the copies at cost, or even below cost, they would be happy to rid themselves of the edition.[7]

Though details concerning Poe's transactions with other publishers are disappointingly vague, it is certain that none of his publishers ever treated him generously. The year 1845 saw Poe's first satisfactory publishing venture, for he was then at the height of his fame: he was given a royalty of eight cents a copy for his *Tales* (New York, Wiley and Putnam). The work sold about 1,500 copies by October of that year, a figure that Poe flaunted in the *Broadway Journal*,[8] and fetched him at least $120.

Poe's was not an exceptional case. Nathaniel Hawthorne as a beginning author had to pay for the publication of *Fanshawe* (1828) himself. And even after he had earned an enviable reputation in the magazines, he was told by Samuel Goodrich, the publisher to whom he submitted his second work, the *Twice-Told Tales* (1837), that he had to put up $250 in cash as a guarantee against loss. Fortunately, Hawthorne had a prosperous friend in Horatio Bridge, a former classmate of his at Bowdoin College, and Bridge furnished the money, for which Hawthorne reimbursed him when the thousand-copy edition was sold.[9] And though *Mosses from an Old Manse* (1846) was Hawthorne's ninth published work, no more than 750 copies had been sold by 1848.[10]

This fairly standard practice of American publishers de-

7. George E. Woodberry, *Edgar Allan Poe* (Boston, 1885), pp. 116–117. When Poe broached that company again in 1841 to publish a new collection of his tales, he received a letter from Mathew Carey remarking that the *Tales of the Grotesque and Arabesque* had, as predicted, failed to earn expenses and that he was bound to reject the new manuscript. See Earl L. Bradsher, *Mathew Carey, Editor, Author and Publisher: A Study in American Literary Development* (New York, 1912), p. 92.
8. II (Oct. 4, 1845), 200.
9. Randall Stewart, *Nathaniel Hawthorne: A Biography* (New Haven, Conn., 1948), p. 35.
10. George Haven Putnam, *George Palmer Putnam: A Memoir* (New York, 1912), p. 195.

manding protection against loss was by no means short-lived.
In 1847 Henry David Thoreau reported that "Wiley & Putnam, Munroe, the Harpers, and Crosby & Nichols have all
declined printing it [*A Week on the Concord and Merrimack
Rivers*, 1849] with the least risk to themselves; but Wiley &
Putnam will print it . . . at *my* risk."[11] Thoreau finally had a
thousand-copy edition of the *Week* published at his own expense, 75 copies of which were given away, 219 sold, and 706
remaindered to him. Almost five years after the *Week* was
printed, Thoreau made this wry observation in his journal under the date of November 28, 1853: "Settled with J. Munroe &
Co. . . . I have paid him directly out of pocket since the book
was published two hundred and ninety dollars. . . . This does
not include postage on proofsheets, etc., etc. I have received
from other quarters about fifteen dollars. This has been the
pecuniary value of the book."[12] *Walden* (1854), the only other
book that Thoreau saw through the press, was published by
Ticknor and Fields, and Thoreau received a royalty of fifteen
cents a copy, which netted him more than a year later the sum
of $51.60.[13] And in 1848 Poe advised a woman who sought his
counsel about publishing her poems: "The Appletons will publish them, leaving you the eventual copyright, but binding you
to supply all loss resulting from the publication:—and they
will allow you ten per cent on all values effected after all ex-
pences are paid . . . . No publisher will make better terms
with you than these—and even these will be more advantageous
to you than printing on your own account."[14]

The reason American publishers (most of whom doubled as
booksellers) had no need to make concessions to American authors was that they did not need American manuscripts to
feed their presses. They could and did reprint books published

    11. Letter to Emerson dated Nov. 14, 1847. See Walter Harding and Carl
Bode, eds., *The Correspondence of Henry David Thoreau* (New York, 1958),
p. 191.
    12. Quoted by Joseph Wood Krutch, *Henry David Thoreau* (New York,
1948), pp. 98–99.
    13. See the letter from Ticknor & Co. dated Sept. 29, 1855 (Harding and
Bode, *Thoreau's Correspondence*, p. 387).
    14. Letter to Anna Blackwell dated June 14, 1848 (Ostrom, *Poe's Letters*, II,
370).

by non-Americans anywhere in the world because works by foreigners, barred from copyright in the United States, were free to them. Better still, such republication minimized risk because the salability of such works had been pretested abroad. Thus, unless a publisher wanted to scoop his competitors and thereby increase his sales;[15] or unless he wanted to give the public an authorized or author's edition, which promised to be free from mutilation and which, therefore, might sell better;[16] or unless he had scruples about piracy, as some few publishers had; unless, in short, he wanted to increase his profits or satisfy his conscience, he really had no reason to pay for manuscripts. What a literary agent for Harpers remarked about that company in 1843 was generally true for the entire publishing business in America: "Publishing for American authors forms but an inconsiderable part of their business. . . ."[17]

The urge to be first on the American book market with pirated works led publishers to some fantastic practices, if one can credit the reports. An almost incredible story is told about Mathew Carey, one of the most successful publishers of his day, who stole a march on his piratical competitors by securing either uncorrected advance sheets or even galley proofs of Scott's manuscripts. He accomplished this feat, we are told, either by a secret transaction with Ballantyne, the printer for Archibald Constable, Scott's publisher; or by bribing one of Ballantyne's employees; or by planting one of his own agents in Ballantyne's office. As soon as Carey got these sheets, he

15. See the letter from M. Carey & Sons dated Jan. 31, 1823, to John Miller, their English agent, which contains detailed instructions regarding the profit to be made in "scooping competitors" (Bradsher, *Carey,* p. 130).

16. The so-called authorized or author's edition was at times desired not only by American publishers but British ones as well. For example, Cooper's *The Spy* (1821) was brought out in England in an author's edition, even though a pirated version was already on the British market. See Henry Walcott Boynton, *James Fenimore Cooper* (New York, 1931), p. 98. An anonymous American (generally thought to be Grenville A. Sackett) urged American publishers—and he might have admonished British ones too—that if they "will not prevent this cruel injustice, that makes a spoil of every literary work cast upon our shores, let them at least preserve them from wanton and undeserved mutilation." *Plea for Authors and the Rights of Literary Property* (New York, 1838), p. 27.

17. John Lloyd Stephens' letter to Prescott dated March 25, 1843. Roger Wolcott, ed., *The Correspondence of William Hickling Prescott, 1833–1847* (Boston, 1925), p. 19.

farmed them out piecemeal to printing houses in Philadelphia, where his company was located, thereby managing to put a complete Scott novel in type in a matter of days and the book itself in the hands of waiting booksellers all over the country. Not only was he able to scoop all American reprinters in this way, but, we are told, he turned this trick for every Scott novel published from 1822 on. However unlikely, there is the possibility that in one or two instances at least Scott was published in America before he was published in England.[18] Though I have not collated American and English versions of Scott's novels, there is reason to believe that such versions differ, for Scott never revised his prose except on galley or page proof.[19]

If this instance seems too unusual, we do know that an American journalist was able to bribe a pressman in the employ of Bradbury and Evans, the printers of Dickens' *American Notes,* and managed in this way to steal proof sheets of that work so that three or four publishers could hurriedly begin printing editions that "flooded the country at six cents a copy."[20]

This is not to suggest that *all* American publishers engaged in such nefarious practices as this. In many instances, as has been stated, publishers were quite willing to buy sheets printed in England and publish them under their own firm names; or, in other instances, to buy proof sheets or manuscripts from which to set their own editions.[21] The fact that at times American publishers were willing to clog their presses with works of obscure native authors which had little likelihood of selling was, if anything, to their credit. Nor is this

18. The details of this story are reported by David A. Randall, "Waverley in America," *The Colophon,* New Series, I (Summer, 1935), 35–55. Constable and Company did, in fact, accuse Carey & Son of the theft of one of Scott's novels, but the accusation was withdrawn when Mathew Carey insisted upon his innocence in the affair. See Bradsher, *Carey,* pp. 87, 130–131.

19. James T. Hillhouse, *The Waverley Novels and Their Critics* (Minneapolis, Minn., 1936), p. 11 n. 13, and John Gibson Lockhart, *Memoirs of the Life of Sir Walter Scott* (Boston, 1910), III, 421.

20. Edgar Johnson, *Charles Dickens: His Tragedy and Triumph* (New York, 1952), I, 441.

21. Pure altruism on the part of at least one American publisher was not manifested until 1842, if we can believe Caroline Ticknor (*Hawthorne and His Publisher,* Boston, 1913, p. 3), when W. D. Ticknor began to pay English authors for the American publication of their works.

intended to suggest that *all* American authors suffered financially from the national copyright law. Once an author was certain that his books would sell in quantity, he could turn the existing situation to his advantage. Washington Irving in 1836, for example, accepted $4,000 from Mathew Carey for the right to publish five thousand copies of *Astoria*.[22] And William Hickling Prescott, instead of accepting Harpers' offer to share half the net profits from the sale of his *Conquest of Mexico* (1843), preferred to sell the American copyright to that history to Harpers for $7,500.[23] Longfellow and Emerson were no less shrewd than Prescott in such business. After 1845 Longfellow, as well as Prescott, paid at times to have stereoplates to his own books manufactured so that he could sell publishers the printing rights to them. Though allowance must be made for his burgeoning reputation, Longfellow in this way was almost able to double his net royalty rate—from an average of roughly 10 to 18 per cent. And Emerson, once he was assured of the sales of his books, used still another method to increase his returns: he paid for the publication of his books himself so that he needed to give his publisher-bookseller only a commission for selling them.[24]

Yet even this sounds better than it actually was. As Poe observed on several occasions, American writers, if they wanted to exploit the American book market, had to establish an English reputation first, for if Americans "were induced to read at all the productions of our native writers, it was only after repeated assurances from England that such productions were not altogether contemptible."[25] Alexis de Tocqueville also ob-

22. Bradsher, *Carey*, p. 90.

23. See the letter dated March 25, 1843, from John Lloyd Stephens to Prescott (Wolcott, *Prescott's Correspondence*, p. 339). For a case study of one author's relations with his publishers, see C. Harvey Gardiner, *Prescott and His Publishers* (Carbondale, Ill., 1959).

24. The information regarding Longfellow and Emerson appears in William Charvat's article, "Longfellow's Income from His Writings, 1840–1852," *Papers of the Bibliographical Society of America*, XXXVIII (First Quarter, 1944), 9–21.

25. *Southern Literary Messenger*, II (April, 1836), 326. See also the same volume of the *Messenger* (Dec., 1835), p. 57, and (Feb., 1836), p. 192, for similar statements. Urged by Thomas W. White, the proprietor of the *Messenger*, Edward Johnston, a New York writer, tried to interest Saunders and Otley, Eng-

served that before Americans "can make up their minds upon the merit of one of their authors, they generally wait till his fame has been ratified in England . . . ."[26] Longfellow, to avoid the fate that awaited *Hyperion* (1839)—a net profit of $72.50 —sought to get the two-volume work noticed abroad. He wrote to George W. Greene, who was then in Italy, to do him a *"very great favor;*—namely by getting these books noticed in the foreign journals . . . . You know what *cursed sharps* [*sheep?*] our countrymen are, and how they follow everything that comes from the other side of the sea."[27] As for Prescott's *Conquest of Mexico,* Poe said only what was true, that this work was usually cited in defense of the liberality of American publishers. But, he added with only slight exaggeration, if one inquired further he would discover that Prescott had been "engaged for many years at his work, and that he expended for the necessary books and other materials a large sum:—the compensation thus afforded him, amounting in the end to little more than any common scavenger might have earned in the same period, upon our highways."[28] Moreover, Emerson, by paying the Boston publishers, Munroe and Company, a commission to sell his books, was forced to confine his sales to New England in order to assure himself of greater profit than if he had published in the regular way and enlarged his market —a dilemma that he himself recognized.[29]

Cooper in 1828 aptly described the situation existing between American authors and American publishers, a situation that with some few modifications was to prevail until the International Copyright Act of 1891:

lish publishers, in Poe's first collection of tales so that Poe could establish an English reputation, but nothing came of the attempt (Quinn, *Poe,* p. 251).

26. *Democracy in America* (New York, 1843), II, 58.

27. Letter dated Oct. 1, 1839. Luther S. Livingston, *A Bibliography of the First Editions in Book Form of the Writings of Henry Wadsworth Longfellow* (New York, 1908), pp. 24–25.

28. *Broadway Journal,* II (Nov. 29, 1845), 321.

29. George Edwin Mize, "The Contributions of Evert A. Duyckinck to the Cultural Development of Nineteenth Century America," unpublished Ph.D. dissertation (New York University, 1954), pp. 68–69. William Charvat in *Literary Publishing in America, 1790–1850* (Philadelphia, 1959), p. 27, observed: "It is safe to say that Emerson's influence was restricted and delayed because he did all his publishing in Boston."

A capital American publisher has assured me that there are not a dozen writers in this country, whose works he should feel confidence in publishing at all, while he reprints hundreds of English books without the least hesitation. The preference is by no means so much owing to any difference in merit, as to the fact that, when the price of an original author is to be added to the uniform hazard, which accompanies all literary speculations, the risk becomes too great. . . . The publisher on this side of the Atlantic has the advantage of seeing the reviews of every book he wishes to print, and, what is of far more importance, he knows, with the exception of books that he is sure of selling, by means of a name, the decision of the English critics before he makes his choice. Nine times in ten, popularity, which is all he looks for, is a sufficient test of general merit. . . .[30]

To cite one or two statistics regarding the publication of American and foreign works: in 1834, 114 titles, grouped together as novels and tales, were published in the United States. Of this number, only 19 had been written by American authors; the remaining 95 had been published abroad first.[31] Having to compete with foreign writers whose works were available to American publishers and whose salability had been established, these few American authors were fortunate if they did not have to finance the publication of their books themselves. Cost, of course, was the major concern of publishers. They had to compete, not only among themselves, but in the 1840's with the so-called mammoth papers such as the New York *Brother Jonathan* and *The New World* which, without the binding and distribution problems of book publishers, could not only scoop book publishers by reprinting a new Dickens novel as an extra or supplement, but could sell the novel at a few cents a copy. Such republishing competition served to glut the market with foreign reprints and aggravate a situation already detrimental to the rise of a national literature.

In an effort to halt a situation that made professional authorship in America all but impossible, observers, either for selfish or altruistic reasons, made all sorts of appeals and charges.

---

30. *Notions of the Americans,* II, 107.
31. These statistics are taken from those given by William L. Stone at the booksellers' dinner held in New York City (see n. 1 above). Needless to say, perhaps, the statements made here apply to literary works rather than to works dealing with education, theology, law, and the like, which managed to compete quite successfully with their British rivals.

Mathew Carey, whose larcenous activities have been noted, charged with unconscious irony that the mammoth weeklies were responsible for preventing American authors from being published. He said that there was little hope for American writers so long as those papers continued to saturate the market with reprints of English novels.[32] William Tudor, editor of the *North American Review* from 1815 to 1817, laid the blame on the cupidity of the American public as well as on the avarice of American publishers who, together, "connive at this proscription of domestic talent . . . since if the author receives any thing for his labours, American books must be dearer than foreign ones . . . ."[33] Cooper contended that so long as America refused copyright to foreigners, so long would England continue to dominate America morally.[34] Poe, though he recognized the advantage of getting "more reading for less money," was unhappy with what he considered the wholesale dishonesty and hypocrisy engendered by piracy and with the "democracy in general which permits its perpetration." Moreover, he made the telling point that piracy injures "our national literature by repressing the efforts of our men of genius; for genius, as a general rule, is poor in worldly goods and cannot write for nothing."[35] And English writers, dismayed that their popularity in America earned them nothing except what might be given to them by courtesy or charity, also opposed American piracy. A typical English opinion stated:

. . . it is a matter of regret, and not of censure, that America should be destitute of a national literature. . . . With the literature of England pouring in upon her, relieved of the charges of copyright and taxation, it is impossible there can be any effectual encouragement for native talent. Literature is, consequently, the least tempting of all conceivable pursuits. . . . Even were [Americans] . . . purer,

---

32. Carey's letter to William Gilmore Simms dated Dec. 16, 1841 (Bradsher, *Carey*, p. 93). Carey also noted: "We do not see much hope in the future of the American writer in light literature—as a matter of profit it might be abandoned."

33. *Letters on the Eastern States* (New York, 1821), pp. 161–162. Tudor regarded "the publishing booksellers of the United States [as] . . . the natural enemies of our authors; they whose intervention is a matter of necessity, either refuse it altogether, or offer it with reluctance and as a favour."

34. James Grossman, *James Fenimore Cooper* (New York, 1949), p. 54.

35. *Godey's Lady's Book*, XXXI (Sept., 1845), 121.

wiser, and more refined,—still America could not originate or support a literature of her own, so long as English productions can be imported free of cost, and circulated through the Union at a cheaper rate than the best productions of the country. The remedy for this is obvious—a law for the protection of international copyright.[36]

Given this situation, it is hardly surprising that the professional author, the author who lived exclusively on the income from his writings (and I am excluding here, of course, magazine and newspaper editors, as well as writers of theology, law, medicine, etc.), was a rarity in the United States. According to one authority, the first American who attempted to live on the earnings from his books failed—the novelist Charles Brockden Brown (1771–1810).[37] In almost every case, an American author had to have another source of income in order to survive as a writer. Only when he was outstandingly successful and sure of the reception of his work was he able to live by his pen. Then he could go to England and get his work protected by British copyright or he could engage, either in person or through an agent, in negotiations with British publishers for that privilege. For the British copyright law, far more liberal than its American counterpart, provided for the protection of foreign works if they were first published in Great Britain or if their authors were residents of Great Britain at the time their books were published there. Typical of such arrangements was that made by Prescott with Richard Bentley, the London publisher. In negotiating for the British copyright to his *History of the Reign of Ferdinand and Isabella the Catholic* (1837), his first significant publication, Prescott wrote to Bentley on May 5, 1837: "I have provided in the contract with the publishers who have purchased the edition here [the American Stationers' Company in Boston, which bought the right to publish 1,250 copies of the book for $1,000, with the profits to be shared equally], that its publication shall not take place till some time in November [the book actually appeared in December], in order not to interfere with securing a copy-

36. *Foreign Quarterly Review,* XLIV (Jan., 1844), 324.
37. Robert E. Spiller (with passages by Alexander Cowie), "The Making of the Man of Letters" in *Literary History of the United States* (New York, 1948), I, 125.

right in England."[38] Irving and Cooper had also learned this trick of securing their literary property in Great Britain and thereby enlarging their incomes—a fact that accounts in large part for their spending so much time abroad.[39] But such men were conspicuous exceptions. They were sure that their books would sell and certain that publishers on both sides of the Atlantic would profit from publishing them, even if they insisted upon high royalties or outright purchase of the copyright.

British publishers, of course, were not more scrupulous than their American brethren. They republished unprotected literary property from America whenever it seemed profitable to do so, although their choice of plunderable material was more limited. When Longfellow, for example, in 1835 asked a British publisher for £100 for the British rights to his *Outre-Mer,* the publisher retorted: "Why, in three weeks I can get it for nothing." And in 1876 Longfellow wryly wrote a correspondent that he had a total of twenty-two publishers in England and Scotland, a number he underestimated according to his own record.[40] Some of Poe's stories, to adduce other instances of British piracy, appeared in *Bentley's Miscellany* with even his name omitted, and at least one of his books was pirated in England during his lifetime, *The Narrative of Arthur Gordon Pym* (London, 1841), not to mention other editions of that work that appeared there posthumously, or "The Gold-Bug" and similar stories that, brought out in paper wrappers, sold for a few pence.[41] And in 1848 Thoreau asked Emerson: "The newspapers say that they have printed a pirated edition of your Essays in England. Is it as bad as they say—an undisguised unmitigated piracy?"[42]

38. Wolcott, *Prescott's Correspondence,* p. 19.

39. Stanley T. Williams, *The Life of Washington Irving* (New York, 1935), I, 424 n. 149, and Grossman, *Cooper,* p. 49.

40. Clarence Gohdes, "Longfellow and His Authorized British Publishers," *Publications of the Modern Language Association,* LV (Dec., 1940), 1165–1166.

41. Charles F. Heartman and James R. Canny, *A Bibliography of First Printings of the Writings of Edgar Allan Poe* (Hattiesburg, Miss., 1943), pp. 40, 114–115, 154–155.

42. Letter dated Feb. 23, 1848 (Harding and Bode, *Thoreau's Correspondence,* p. 209).

Moreover, as a retaliatory measure and one designed to put British publishers on an equal footing with American publishers, Parliament in 1838 revised the copyright law to prevent the works of a foreign author from being copyrighted in Great Britain unless the country to which he belonged gave copyright to British authors.[43] Needless to say, the occasional American author who had been able to support himself by virtue of the British book market began to suffer financial difficulties at this time. According to a contemporary report, the works of such writers as Irving and Cooper, who earlier had been able to protect their property, were now pirated by British publishers.[44] American authors could still try to make arrangements with British publishers to bring out authorized editions, but once their works were issued, they could be reprinted by any British publisher. Cooper's arrangement with Richard Bentley, then his English publisher, became so unsatisfactory by 1850 that he decided to give up the writing of novels, a form that, however famous it had made him, had become unprofitable.[45]

This is not to suggest that in 1838 the relations between British publishers and American authors were settled once and for all until the International Copyright Act of 1891 and the Copyright Code of 1909. Except for brief flurries of piracy in 1838–1839 and 1850,[46] American authors, when they could make arrangements with British publishers, received payment, in royalties or for the copyright, more or less in proportion to the commercial value of their work, in spite of their now un-

43. Thomas R. Lounsbury, *James Fenimore Cooper* (Boston, 1886), p. 261, and Henry A. Beers, *Nathaniel Parker Willis* (Boston, 1885), p. 241.
44. *New York Mirror*, XVII (Oct. 12, 1839), 127.
45. Grossman, *Cooper*, p. 244.
46. The *Mirror* article referred to in note 44 above states that "No American writer can hereafter hope to derive any emolument from the sale of his works in England. . . . This is all fair in the way of retaliation." The New York *Home Journal* of Jan. 12, 1850, observed: "—Our friend Herman Melville is one of the first and most signal realizers of the recent [British] repudiation of copyright. As our readers probably know, it has been a rule among publishers abroad that an agreement of prior publication, between one of their number and an American author, should be as valid as the legal copyright of an English author. To punish us for our wholesale thieving of English books, they have broken up this protection, by mutual consent, and, now, an American author can no more sell a book in England than Dickens can sell one here—justly enough!"

clear legal right to such payment, provided, of course, that their works were published in Great Britain prior to their American publication. About 1850, however, British publishers began to test the right of American authors even to such payment, and the question was finally settled against the Americans by the House of Lords in 1854. Charles Richard Weld, an English lawyer and celebrity-hunter, reported that during an evening spent with Prescott, the "conversation took a literary turn, principally in relation to the vexed question of copyright; and it so happened, while we were deep in argument, Mr. Prescott received letters from England, informing him that the decision of the House of Lords being adverse to a foreigner possessing copyright in England, his bargain with a London publisher for a new historical work, for which he was to have been paid 6000£, ... had become void."[47] At all events, it can be said that generalizations based on British copyright law usually do not hold up. Statements must be based on particular and actual instances of American authors' relations with British publishers.[48]

Against the economic-literary background that has been sketched here, one can begin to see a clear relationship between the national copyright law and the urge for American literary nationalism. Cooper, whose concern made him as vociferous as Poe on the subject of professional authorship, explained in his *Notions of the Americans*: "The literature of the United States has, indeed, too [*sic*] powerful obstacles to conquer before ... it can ever enter into the markets of its own country on terms of perfect equality with that of England." The first obstacle, according to Cooper, was lack of pecuniary support of American authors. "The fact that an American publisher can get an English work without money, must ... have a tendency to repress a national literature. No man will pay a

---

47. *Traveller to America* (London, 1855), p. 46.
48. According to the researches of Mr. Charles A. Toase, my London informant, and those of the librarian of the Board of Trade (the British government department concerned with copyright), any fluctuations at different dates can be attributed to court decisions as points of law were contested. Mr. Toase adds: "It is amazing how difficult this makes it to determine the legal position at any given time in respect to American works."

writer for an epic, a tragedy, a sonnet, a history, or a romance, when he can get a work of equal merit for nothing."[49] The second obstacle to American literature which Cooper pointed out—and this statement was echoed and re-echoed by American authors from Irving to Hawthorne to Henry James[50]—was "poverty of materials":

There is scarcely an ore which contributes to the wealth of the author, that is found here, in veins as rich as in Europe. There are no annals for the historian; no follies (beyond the most vulgar and commonplace) for the satirist; no manners for the dramatist; no obscure fictions for the writer of romance; no gross and hardy offences against decorum for the moralist; nor any of the rich artificial auxiliaries of poetry. The weakest hand can extract a spark from the flint, but it would baffle the strength of a giant to attempt kindling a flame with a pudding-stone.

These two obstacles to fair competition between American and foreign authors were really two mutually inclusive problems, for if American writers were able to discover and exploit native materials instead of using materials common to English works, they would be able to offer their countrymen books the like of which could not be pirated from abroad and which would, as a consequence, make their works fare better on the open market. It certainly seems far from coincidence that in 1837 both Cooper (in *Gleanings in Europe: England*) and Emerson (in "The American Scholar") should call for an intellectual declaration of independence, though both, of course, were anticipated by many others during the period, notably by William Ellery Channing in *The Importance and Means of a National Literature* (1830). Nor does it appear as mere accident that during the relatively short span usually labeled the American Romantic Period or, less usually, the American Renaissance (a term far more expressive of the American effort toward and ultimate achievement of a national literature and surely less suggestive of American imitation of foreign writers), Cooper—to cite a few of multitudinous instances—introduced

49. II, 108.
50. Irving's explanation for the evident superiority of European literature over American literature is to be found in "The Author's Account of Himself" in *The Sketch-Book;* Hawthorne's explanation in his Preface to *The Marble Faun;* and James's explanation in his essay *Hawthorne.*

into American fiction the Revolutionary War, the American Indian, the American prairie, and the American frontiersman; that Irving capitalized on frontier and Western materials; that Hawthorne exploited Puritan history, not to mention the Brook Farm experiment and the American consciousness in Europe; and that Whitman sought to sing America in what he regarded as a distinctly American idiom. Nor, again, can it be accounted mere happenstance that Cooper and Irving, once they showed the richness of American ore, should become the models for untold numbers of American imitators.[51]

Moreover, charges of imitation and plagiarism, the nastiest epithets that could be leveled against an American work, became the commonplace of American criticism. American magazine critics opposed American imitations of "effete and bygone English schools," which they came to regard as symptomatic of "ignominious vassalage in literature." They insisted, to quote again from this typical American critical dictum, "on nationality and true Americanism in the book this country furnishes to itself and to the world . . . . It need not (though it may) speak of the Revolution—nor Washington—nor the declaration of independence—nor Plymouth Rock—nor Bunker Hill . . . . And yet it may be instinct with the life of the country . . . ."[52] And booksellers-publishers were also urging authors to treat American themes, according to various contemporary sources, including Poe. Poe argued for an originality stemming from vision rather than from materials, and therefore condemned the condition that made the weight of a foreign subject "more than enough to drag down into the very depths of critical damnation the finest writers owing nativity in the States . . . ."[53]

51. For one study of the numerous imitations of Irving's trans-Mississippi materials, see Ruth Hudson, "A Literary 'Area of Freedom' Between Irving and Twain," *Western Humanities Review*, XIII (Winter, 1959), 46–60. For a report on how one magazine became more and more partial to American themes, see Darwin Shrell, "Nationalism and Aesthetics in the *North American Review: 1815–1850*," *Studies in American Literature*, No. 8 (1960), 11–21. According to a contemporary appraisal, a significant condition governing the success of an American work was a subject "thoroughly American" (*Broadway Journal*, II, Aug. 23, 1845, 109).

52. *Broadway Journal*, II (July 19, 1845), 27.

53. *Graham's Magazine*, XX (Jan., 1842), 68.

Be this as it may (and one should recognize here the Hegelian contradiction that the very legal and economic forces that were stifling American literature were, at the same time, spasmodically becoming the forces that produced the American Renaissance), American publishing, exploiting both native and foreign writers, was emerging as Big Business by 1836.[54] In that year the number of American publications (reprinted and original) was about half the number issued in Great Britain, but the total number of copies printed was nearly equal in both countries—and this at a time when the population in America (some 17 million in 1840) was considerably less than the population in Great Britain (26 million in 1841). Whatever the cause of such production—most likely a combination of more diffused literacy, cheaper book prices, and greater buying power—this increasing output and circulation of books, not to mention magazines and newspapers, caused men to be appalled at their numbers and to wonder how they could all be read.

Yet, whether read or not, books were sold. Publishers, unlike modern ones, relied hardly at all upon advertisements for the sale of American works (and it is with the works of American authors that we are now concerned rather than with the reprinted works of British authors), even though they occasionally placed brief and matter-of-fact announcements of forthcoming titles in magazines and newspapers. Instead of depending upon such "advertising," American publishers exploited a method that, evolving rather haphazardly, developed into a smooth-working system. This system depended upon the

54. Statistics show that in 1798 "persons and firms engaged in employing printers, publishers, and booksellers" had the following distribution in the three major publishing centers of the United States: Boston: 41; New York: 56; Philadelphia: 88. During the period 1820–52, the publishing business emerged as a distinct and formidable enterprise, and something of the tremendous increase in publishing establishments may be gauged by comparing the following figures with the foregoing ones: Boston: 147; New York: 345; Philadelphia: 198. And these figures exclude bookbinders, retail booksellers, and printers who were not also publishers. In dollars, book production leaped from $2,500,000 in 1820 to $12,500,000 in 1850. See Helmut Lehmann-Haupt, Lawrence C. Wroth, and Rollo G. Silver, *The Book in America: A History of the Making and Selling of Books in the United States* (New York, 1931), pp. 120–129. The statistics that follow in the text regarding number of titles and copies are drawn from Stone's remarks at the booksellers' dinner (see n. 1 above).

cliques that Poe, among others, continually denounced—a system that had become common in England since the eighteenth century and that was frequently condemned in British journals. The chief feature of this system was puffing, a process of publishing highly laudatory, essentially uncritical reviews in magazines and newspapers which favored books coming from the proper presses and written by the proper authors, generally those authors who contributed to the journals that publicized their works. Sometimes these reviews were written by friends, whether the editor, or an acquaintance of the author, or the author himself. On occasion these people—editors, friends, or the author—would wield concerted pressure to insure favorable press notices throughout the country.[55] Charles Frederick Briggs, a successful magazinist and novelist and at one time Poe's colleague on the *Broadway Journal,* knew whereof he spoke when he wrote in *Holden's Dollar Magazine*: "The art of puffing is the art of all arts at the present day, when nothing will sell which is not first puffed into notice."[56] With this statement in mind, one can appreciate Cooper's boast that "without advertisement, puffing, or any of the ordinary movements of the trade," *The Prairie* (1827) was successful.[57]

It is germane to an explanation of the other "movements of the trade" to point out what was clearly recognized at the time, that without ready access to American publishers, American authors were forced to write for the magazines—a fact that accounts in some measure for the great burgeoning of periodicals during the period,[58] as well as for the popularity of such literary forms—call them magazine forms—as the *short* essay, the *short* story, and the *short* poem. Furthermore, it needs to be pointed out, American magazine editors treated American authors even more outrageously than did American publishers. Not

---

55. For a detailed study of one author's methods of promoting his books into the ranks of best-sellers, see Gardiner, *Prescott,* pp. 167–201.

56. II (July, 1848), 446. Briggs suggested, however, that a bad review was better than none at all.

57. Quoted by Robert E. Spiller and Philip C. Blackburn, *James Fenimore Cooper: A Descriptive Bibliography* (New York, 1934), pp. 222–223.

58. De Tocqueville, for instance, was impressed by the almost incredibly large number of magazines in the United States (*Democracy in America,* I, 199).

only did these editors pirate material from foreign periodicals for republication in their own magazines, but they pilfered articles from American journals as well. Such piracy finally led George Rex Graham of *Graham's Magazine* and Louis A. Godey of *Godey's Lady's Book* in 1845 to copyright each number of their magazines—an act that incited editors and owners of newspapers and magazines, not to mention the publishers of "gift books," almanacs, annuals, and other scissors-and-paste collections, to violent protest. The remark printed in the *Baltimore Saturday Visiter* on the occasion of Godey's taking out a copyright on the contents of his magazine—that it was a "narrowly selfish course" and that Godey "would rue it bitterly"—has been cited as typical of the general reaction.[59] A few editors, however, approved such a course, among them Poe. As owner and editor of the *Broadway Journal,* he commented in the columns of his magazine:

It is really very difficult to see how any one can, in conscience, object to such a course on the part of Mess. Godey and Graham. To our apprehension, a mere statement of the facts of the case should stand in lieu of all argument. It has been long the custom among the newspapers—the weeklies especially—to copy Magazine articles in full, and circulate them all over the country—sometimes in advance of the magazines themselves.[60] In other words Godey and Graham have been at all the cost, while the papers have enjoyed, if not the advantage—at least the most important item of it—the *origination* of the articles. To such an extent has this piracy been carried, that many magazine subscribers ceased to be such, because they could procure all that was valuable in those works from the newspapers very little later and often at less cost, than from the magazines themselves.[61]

Later in that year, to indicate the license with which editors pirated from American magazines, Poe publicly charged the *Chambersburg Times* with making up the "whole of its first page from a single number of 'The Broadway Journal.' This," Poe commented, "would be all very well, had it not forgotten

59. Ruth E. Finney, *The Lady of Godey's: Sarah Josepha Hale* (Philadelphia, 1937), p. 48.
60. This was a consequence of editors' sending out advance sheets of their magazines to other editors in order to obtain free press notices of their forthcoming issues, and explains, for instance, why Poe's "The Raven" appeared in the *Mirror* prior to its appearance in the *Democratic Review,* though the *Democratic Review* was the magazine that had accepted and paid for the poem.
61. I (April 26, 1845), 268.

to give us credit for our articles, contributed and editorial—
and had it not forgotten *not* to make certain improvements in
our compositions to suit its own fancy."[62]

With foreign and native materials available to them, magazine editors felt slight compunction in paying little or nothing
for original contributions, unless, of course, the author was a
sure drawing card. For, as Nathaniel Willis, the most successful magazinist of his time and successive editor of the *American
Monthly Magazine,* the *New York Mirror,* the *Corsair* (the
very name indicative of its piratical policy) and the New York
Home Journal, remarked in a letter, he would "take advantage
. . . of the privilege assured us by our piratical law of copyright. . . . As to original American productions, we shall, as the
publishers do, take what we can get for nothing, . . . holding, as
the publishers do, that while we can get Boz and Bulwer for a
thank-ye or less, it is not pocket-wise to pay much for Halleck
and Irving."[63] And Poe, who as former editor of *Graham's
Magazine* was in a position to know, observed that writers
"whose articles are certainly equal to any thing of Cooper's that
we have seen in Graham" were paid nothing by "that munifi-
cent publisher."[64] As late as 1844 Poe wrote "A Chapter of
Suggestions" for *Godey's Lady's Book* at the rate of fifty cents
a page for ten pages, a recompense he regarded as quite satisfactory,[65] and indeed it was compared with the experience of
less well-known writers such as Mary Nichols.[66]

It is, of course, incautious to generalize on authors' pay

62. *Broadway Journal,* II (Sept. 13, 1845), 158.
63. Letter dated Dec. 24, 1838 (Beers, *Willis,* p. 240).
64. *Broadway Journal,* I (Feb. 22, 1845), 127.
65. See his letter to Sarah J. Hale dated May 31, 1844 (Ostrom, *Poe's Letters,*
I, 255).
66. In her book *Mary Lyndon, or Revelations of a Life: An Autobiography*
(New York, 1855), pp. 287–288, she wrote: ". . . I was hoping to receive some
money for three stories which I had written for *Godey's Lady's Book.* . . . The
stories had been accepted, and in about a year after their acceptance had been
published. I had written to Mr. Godey asking him to give me what he thought
my stories were worth. He referred me to Mrs. Hale. I wrote to her, and told her
that I needed the money, and asked her to give as much as the work was worth
to one who needed all she earned. Mrs. Hale answered that the worth of matter
for their 'Book' depended entirely on the fame of the writers. I had made no
fame, and she therefore inclosed me fifteen dollars, which she assured me was
the best they could do. But days elapsed before this money came. . . ."

from magazines. Even in dealing with particular authors one must be careful, for few magazines had a fixed rate (the dollar-a-page rate offered by the *North American Review* from 1825 to 1850 was quite exceptional), not to mention that the size of the page and type used varied from magazine to magazine. Moreover, some editors boasted about their liberal rates but were either dilatory in paying, or paid less than they advertised, or failed to pay at all. Finally, the reputation of a writer at given points in his career had much to do with the payment he could command from the magazines. Thus, an obscure writer might consider himself quite fortunate to be published at all, whereas Longfellow received $50 for a poem from *Graham's* and Cooper $1,000 (or $10 a page) for a biographical series.[67] But it must be noted that it was not until 1842 that Graham decided to pay such "high" rates—a policy that was instrumental in boosting magazine pay in America in that it forced competing magazines to follow suit. It is hardly digressive to point out here that Poe was responsible for Graham's action. With financial backing promised him by Graham, and himself as co-owner and editor, Poe had contemplated launching a magazine for which such distinguished writers as Bryant, Cooper, Irving, and Longfellow would be induced to write exclusively for an entire year by the offer of unprecedentedly liberal rates. Although Poe actually sent letters soliciting their contributions under such terms, the magazine, at least as Poe envisaged it, never materialized.[68] Graham, however, whose magazine Poe edited during this period (April, 1841—May, 1842), applied Poe's principle to his own journal. This act not only gained Graham probably the largest magazine circulation of that time, but, as has been said, skyrocketed magazine pay in America, at least for those writers with reputation. The

---

67. See Frank Luther Mott, *A History of American Magazines, 1741–1850* (New York, 1930), I, 504–512. According to a writer in the *Weekly Mirror,* I (Oct. 19, 1844), 28, Graham and Godey paid $2 to $12 a page for prose and $5 to $50 per poem, which the writer regarded as "noble liberality" compared with the pay offered by other journals.

68. See Poe's letters to John P. Kennedy and Irving, both dated June 1, 1841, as well as his letters to Longfellow (June 22, 1841) and Fitz-Greene Halleck (June 24, 1841), in Ostrom, *Poe's Letters,* I, 161–170.

irony is that Poe could never command such pay for his own prose, not even from Graham (he was usually paid about $4 a page), and only rarely could he obtain $50 for a poem.

Poe in 1845 described the economic-literary situation as it affected magazines and magazine contributors. "The want of an International Copy-Right Law, by rendering it nearly impossible to obtain anything from the booksellers[-publishers] in the way of remuneration for literary labor, has had the effect of forcing many of our very best writers into the service of the Magazines and Reviews...." Magazines, in turn, Poe continued, suffer severe competition, not only from one another, but from piratical publishers who "furnish for eight dollars any four of the British periodicals for a year.... It would not do," Poe went on wryly, "to let our poor devil authors absolutely starve, while we grow fat ... on the good things of which we unblushingly pick the pocket of all Europe ... and hence we have Magazine publishers ... who, under certain conditions of good conduct, occasional puffs, and decent subserviency at all times, make it a point of conscience to encourage the poor devil author with a dollar or two, more or less as he behaves himself properly." Poe added that such paltry payment is generally made only six months after publication.[69]

Despite the general pecuniary difficulties that beset magazines and magazine contributors prior to 1842 and that, as Poe's statement suggests, were hardly settled immediately by the Poe-Graham innovations, authors derived two distinct benefits from publication in magazines. First, they earned a popularity that helped them to get their books published and sold. Secondly, once their books were published, magazine editors, willing to maintain their good will, puffed their books and thus helped them to even greater sales than would otherwise have been possible. Publishers, editors, and authors, finding this system mutually advantageous, if not necessarily ideal, worked hand in hand to keep it functioning smoothly.

A single pertinent instance of how this system worked in practice will illustrate the point graphically. Harper and

69. *Broadway Journal*, I (Feb. 15, 1845), 103.

Brothers was one of the publishing houses that, as a contemporary charged, attempted to monopolize the most profitable part of the book business in America by laboring "with their coadjutors, the newspaper hirelings, to convince authors and the public in general that no book can be sold or can be worth buying unless it comes out under [its] auspices...."[70] For reasons best known to themselves, Harpers agreed to publish the entire three numbers of Longfellow's *Outre-Mer*, and not only to publish them in two volumes without demanding a guarantee against loss, but also to pay the author an advance on royalties.[71] Considering that the work was imitative of Irving's *Sketch-Book* and that two of the three numbers had only recently been presented to the public (in 1833 and 1834 respectively), this agreement was indeed strange, unless, of course, Harpers had assurance that the book would sell. They could derive some assurance from the fact that the first number issued by Hilliard, Gray and Co. (the publishers who acted as booksellers; the work was originally printed at Longfellow's own expense by Joseph Griffin) had elicited favorable press notices, but they could derive none from the fate of the second number. Published by Lilly, Wait & Company, that book had failed because the publishers had become so entangled in financial difficulties that their credit seriously impeded the distribution of the work.[72] But assurance enough could be had from Lewis Gaylord Clark, friend of Longfellow and editor of the *Knickerbocker Magazine*. Even while *Outre-Mer* was in production, he often consulted with Harpers about that work, as his letters to Longfellow testify.[73] And just before Harpers issued *Outre-Mer* in 1835, he and his friends, many of them fellow editors, began beating their editorial drums for it. Lewis Clark wrote Longfellow on May 9,

---

70. L. A. Wilmer, *The Quacks of Helicon: A Satire* (Philadelphia, 1841), pp. 52–53.

71. Livingston, *Longfellow Bibliography*, p. 21.

72. Lawrance Thompson, *Young Longfellow, 1807–1843* (New York, 1938), pp. 187–188, 382–383 n. 15.

73. See Clark's letters to Longfellow dated Sept. 2, 1834, and March 2 and May 9, 1835, in Leslie Dunlap, ed., *The Letters of Willis Gaylord Clark and Lewis Gaylord Clark* (New York, 1940), pp. 80, 86, 88.

1835: "It will be signally popular, mark my words. I send you
...the Knickerbocker, containing a notice of it, and the
American Monthly.... The Courier, and American, and
Commercial, and Evening Star will do you full and ample
justice, as will the Penn[a] Inquirer, Phil[a] Gazette, &c in Phila.
On this subject, I 'speak the things which I do know.' "[74] The
advantage that accrued to Clark from such favors was that he
secured Longfellow's contributions for a period of almost five
years without feeling the need to recompense him for them.[75]
Longfellow, for his part, did not seem unhappy with this arrangement, however often he dunned Clark for payment and
however often Clark evaded the issue by reassuring him that
he would pay him for the contributions when times became
better[76]—even in 1839 when Clark was paying Irving a flat
$2,000 a year for monthly contributions to the *Knicker-
bocker*.[77] Longfellow certainly did not stop sending contributions to Clark; and for 1834 at least there are extant letters
which indicate that Longfellow took pains to puff the *Knickerbocker* at Clark's requests.[78] If no direct recompense could be
had, there was sufficient recompense of an indirect and finally
more lucrative kind.

74. *Ibid.*, p. 88.
75. Thompson (*Longfellow*, pp. 308, 416 n. 7) states that Longfellow never
received a cent from the *Knickerbocker* for his poems until Nov., 1840—almost
five years after *Outre-Mer* appeared—when he received $15 for "The Village
Blacksmith."
76. See Dunlap, *The Clark Letters, passim.*
77. Williams, *Irving*, II, 95. Pierre M. Irving, a nephew of the author, tells us
in his *Life and Letters of Washington Irving* (New York, 1867), III, 148, that
Irving, like Longfellow, had trouble collecting what was due him ("returns were
less prompt than he had anticipated"). Richard Henry Stoddard, a contributor
to the *Knickerbocker*, reports rather exaggeratedly in his *Recollections, Personal
and Literary* (New York, 1902) that there "was no money in the *Knickerbocker Magazine*,—certainly none for its contributors,—but its jaunty editor
managed to live out of it" (p. 49).
78. There are many such references in Clark's letters to Longfellow. One,
dated July 2, 1834, reads: "I thank you, heartily, for your kind intentions to say
good words for us in the paper." Another, dated Sept. 2, 1834, reads: "If you
think it [the *Knickerbocker* for Sept.] will bear some laudatory remarks in the
different Portland and Brunswick papers, it will do us much good, *just now.*" A
third, dated Nov. 2, 1834, reads: "You will receive . . . a few circulars by mail,
which I wish you would enclose to, and circulate among your friends" (Dunlap,
The Clark Letters, pp. 75, 80, 84).

If Clark had been a decisive factor in Harpers' decision to republish *Outre-Mer,* it was not the last time by any means that he was to involve himself in Longfellow's literary affairs, nor, by any means, the last time that Longfellow permitted him to do so. Some time in November, 1835, the *New Yorker* announced a story contest for a prize of $100. Lewis Clark, appointed to serve as one of three judges, wrote to Longfellow at once, asking that he submit one of the tales he had seen, "The Wondrous Tale of a Little Man in Gosling Green." Longfellow complied, submitting the story under the pseudonym of Charles F. Brown. The story was not awarded the full prize because, apparently, the other two judges disagreed with Clark's decision and preferred the story submitted by Eliza Leslie, a Philadelphia author and editor. The issue was resolved by dividing the hundred dollars—no trivial sum considering that Longfellow, with extra duties, was earning only $900 that year at Bowdoin College—between Leslie and Longfellow.[79]

Even as late as July 25, 1838 (1839?), Clark's twin brother, who was co-editor of the *Knickerbocker* as well as editor of the *Philadelphia Gazette,* extended Longfellow the services of the publicity review: "When you have a scrap . . . let me know *how* to make it public—once out it wins its illustrious way. I wish to do you all the good I humbly can thus. . . ."[80] And periodically we have evidence in the *Knickerbocker* itself of Clark's puffing of Longfellow's books, as well as of his poems and articles appearing in other magazines.

This system, as the crusaders against it noted, was not only immoral but actually militated against a national literature.

79. For details of this collusion, see James Taft Hatfield, "An Unknown Prose Tale by Longfellow," *American Literature,* III (May, 1931), 136–148; Clark's letters to Longfellow dated Aug. 29, Nov. 2, and Dec. 10, 1834 (in Dunlap, *The Clark Letters,* pp. 79, 82, 85) ; and Thompson, *Longfellow,* p. 201. None of these investigators interpret the event as I have, although Thompson says there was collusion but calls it harmless. He also suggests that Longfellow contributed often to the *Knickerbocker* in appreciation of Clark's assistance in this affair. For further details concerning Longfellow and the Clark brothers, see chaps. iv and v of the present study.

80. Dunlap, *The Clark Letters,* p. 52.

For once a clique had established itself, it became more and more clannish and powerful, discriminating in favor of belongers and working against outsiders, in a kind of mutual protection league. This was bound to happen, however haphazardly, so long as writers, living in the same city and having similar literary interests and publishers, met, as they often did, socially and professionally at one another's homes and offices, and were concerned, if only for the sake of their livelihood, with maintaining close relations for purposes of magazine publication, entrées to publishers, and the vitally needed puffs for their works. And since outsiders represented added competition in an already severely competitive market, it was economic folly to welcome them. For this reason a geographical bias developed that can properly be called sectional—a bias that was most pronounced in Boston and New York and against which Southern and Western magazines inveighed continually.

As a consequence of this sectionalism, magazine criticism was being vitiated by the predilections of the coteries. Earlier, literary works were judged by standards that, however rigid and objectionable they may appear today, at least tended to be impartial and resist revision by opportunistic groups.[81] Now, the reviews published by editors engaged in this traffic were, for the most part, superficial and, far worse, misleading, acclaiming or denouncing the work of an author in unqualified terms, depending upon whether the author was in favor with the clique. To entertain the notion of success, writers had first to come into the good graces of editors—a process that involved toadying and quackery, the current words of contempt for the truckling and charlatanry on the part of contributor to editor and editor to the public. Authors and editors who preferred to remain independent and self-respecting were, by and large, marked for failure. The occasional writer or editor who clashed with the cliques was practically doomed.

Another injustice of the system that literary reformers pointed out affected the unsuspecting public. Editors, in pre-

---

81. William Charvat in *The Origins of American Critical Thought, 1810–1835* (Philadelphia, 1936), pp. 27–58, 164–205, discusses these critical standards.

paring for the reception of certain works, were degrading public taste by recommending, not the best works, but only the ones they favored, and almost always in immoderate and uncritical terms. The works of authors not so favored were either treated to what Poe called the "dreadful damnation of silent contempt" or were reviewed abusively, so that the reading public either did not know of the existence of such works or were introduced to them in the worst way. Thus, the most publicized book became, in effect, the book most worth reading—a trick still being turned by modern publishers.

Aware of the power of this system to make or break literary reputations, Poe became a scourge of cliques, cliquish practices, and clique-sponsored writers, though he himself at times played favorites. In reviewing the enlarged second edition of the *Twice-Told Tales,* for instance, Poe confessed that he had withheld praise from Hawthorne because he had mistakenly believed him to have "been thrust into his present position by one of the impudent *cliques* which beset our literature."[82] Recognizing too that literary opinions were manufactured wholesale by the cliques, he argued that the popularity of a book was by no means the measure of its worth, else Newton's *Principia*—to use his example—would be inferior to Hoyle's *Games.*[83] The popularity of a book, he said in another article, is questionable in any case, since public opinion is manipulated by editors. "That the opinion of the press is not an honest opinion . . . is never denied [privately] by the members of the press themselves. Individual presses, of course, are now and then honest, but I speak of the combined effect." Favorable press notices, he explained, can be achieved by "influence, experience, or . . . effrontery," and are usually written by the author or "interested parties" and published by editors who have been courted by these quacks. "Now, men of genius will not resort to these manoeuvres, because genius involves in its very essence a scorn of chicanery; and thus for a time quacks always get the advantage of them, both in

82. *Graham's Magazine,* XX (May, 1842), 299.
83. *Ibid.* (Feb., 1842), p. 124.

respect to pecuniary profit and what appears to be public esteem."[84] In still another article, Poe pointed out the duty of the critic, to which, however, he was not unwaveringly faithful, despite his avowal: "It is ... the duty of all whom circumstances have led into criticism—it is, at least, a duty from which *we* individually shall never shrink—to uphold the true dignity of genius, to combat its degradation, to plead for the exercise of its power...."[85]

Though sometimes guilty of the practice himself, Poe also opposed the custom of anonymous reviewing, whether the reviewer lauded or lambasted a book, for, on the one hand, he argued, anonymity is a blind for easy adulation or, on the other, a concealment for attacks "most unfair—most despicable and cowardly."[86] Moreover, Poe objected to the vague generalities of critics as well as to their ignorance of critical principles, though on occasion, hard-pressed for time or merely impatient, he would satisfy himself with an exhibition of the "blemishes" and "beauties" of a work in what was the standard critical manner. He not only urged a responsible analysis of text, but he himself became the first American critic to use it as a characteristic technique. In summing up one review, he said with justifiable pride: "In our account of all this matter we have had reference to the book—and to the book alone."[87] Furthermore, and something that still takes courage, he refused to be awed by a reputation, whether Cooper's, Irving's, or Longfellow's. At his best he considered novels, poems, and stories, not novelists, poets, and story-writers. Poe also called for critical integrity, an integrity that could be achieved, he felt, only by independence from "home-dictation of the bookseller[-book publisher] *coteries*."[88] For this reason he praised the so-called independent critics. He acclaimed such men as

---

84. See Poe's critique on Bryant, *Godey's Lady's Book*, XXXII (April, 1846), 182–186, and its sequel, "Author's Introduction" to the "Literati of New York City," *ibid*. (May, 1846), pp. 194–195.

85. *Graham's Magazine*, XX (March, 1842), 186–187.

86. *Ibid*. (Jan., 1842), pp. 68–69, and *Southern Literary Messenger*, XV (May, 1849), 294.

87. *Southern Literary Messenger*, II (April, 1836), 336.

88. *Graham's Magazine*, XX (Jan., 1842), 68.

Park Benjamin who, he said, had "ability, activity, causticity, fearlessness, and independence," although, he added, he was "too frequently biassed by personal feelings—feelings now of friendship and again of vindictiveness," and Lambert A. Wilmer who, "as Editor of the Philadelphia Saturday Evening Post . . . has boldly and skilfully asserted the rights of independent criticism, speaking, in all instances—the truth."[89] As for himself, though aware of the fate of those critics who clashed with the cliques, he was in his published criticism, with obvious lapses, as honest and plain-spoken as he could be. Moreover, as one would expect, he opposed sectionalism, even to the point of becoming sectional in his opposition, arguing that such writers as William Wallace of Kentucky, Edward C. Pinkney of Maryland, and William Gilmore Simms of South Carolina were *"born too far South"* to receive the recognition due them.[90] In a more aggressive statement he said: "The manner in which the cabal of the [Boston] 'North American Review' first write all our books and then review them, puts me in mind of the fable about the Lion and the Painter. It is high time that the literary South took its own interests into its own charge."[91]

Poe himself on many occasions summed up the points that have here been drawn from a variety of his critical articles. Perhaps the most forceful of these summations appears in his review of Wilmer's *Quacks of Helicon*,[92] which, because of its cogency, is quoted here at length. Poe wrote that "we are glad to see this book . . . because, in the universal corruption and rigmarole amid which we gasp for breath, it is really a pleasant thing to get even one accidental whiff of the unadulterated air of *truth*." *The Quacks of Helicon*, he went on, "has many defects . . . but it has also many remarkable merits—merits which it will be quite useless for those aggrieved by the satire —quite useless for any *clique*, or set of *cliques*, to attempt to frown down. . . ." Poe then pointed out the faults of the poem, "although Mr. Wilmer is a personal friend of our own. . . ."

89. *Southern Literary Messenger*, II (Feb., 1836), 192.
90. *Ibid.*, XV (April and Sept., 1849), 220, 690.
91. *Ibid.*, XV (April, 1849), 220.
92. *Graham's Magazine*, XIX (Aug., 1841), 90–93.

But there remains to be mentioned the far loftier merit of speaking fearlessly the truth, at an epoch when truth is out of fashion, and under circumstances ... which would have deterred almost any man ... from a similar Quixotism. For the publication of the ... poem which brings under review, by name, most of our prominent *literati,* and treats them, generally, as they deserve (what treatment could be more bitter?)—for the publication of this attack, Mr. Wilmer, whose subsistence lies in his pen, has little to look for—apart from the silent respect of those at once honest and timid, but the most malignant open or covert persecution. ...

We repeat it: *it is* the truth which he has spoken; and who shall contradict us? He has said unscrupulously what every reasonable man among us has long known to be "as true as the Pentateuch"— that, as a literary people, we are one vast perambulating humbug. He has asserted that we are *clique*-ridden; and who does not smile at the obvious truism of that assertion? He maintains that chicanery is, with us, a far surer road than talent to distinction in letters. Who gainsays this? The corrupt nature of our ordinary criticism has become notorious. ... The intercourse between critic and publisher, as it now almost universally stands, is comprised either in the paying and pocketing of black mail, as the price of a simple forbearance, or in a direct system of petty and contemptible bribery, properly so called. ... We laugh at the idea of any denial of our assertions upon this topic; they are infamously true. In the charge of general corruption, there are undoubtedly many noble exceptions to be made. There are, indeed, some very few editors, who, maintaining an entire independence, will receive no books from publishers at all, or who receive them with a perfect understanding, on the part of these latter, that an unbiassed *critique* will be given. But these cases are insufficient to have much effect on the popular mistrust; a mistrust heightened by late exposure of the machinations of *coteries* in New York—*coteries* which, at the bidding of leading booksellers, manufacture, as required from time to time, a pseudo-public opinion by wholesale, for the benefit of any little hanger on of the party, or pettifogging protector of the firm.

We speak of these things in the bitterness of scorn. It is unnecessary to cite instances, where one is found in almost every issue of a book. ... We say it is supererogatory to dwell upon ... by-gone follies, when we have, before our eyes, hourly instances of the machinations in question. ...

It has become ... the plain duty of each individual connected with our periodicals heartily to give whatever influence he possesses to the good cause of integrity and the truth. ... We shall thus frown down all conspiracies to foist inanity upon the public consideration at the obvious expense of every man of talent who is not a member of a *clique* in power. We may even arrive, in time, at that desirable point from which a distinct view of our men of letters may be obtained, and their respective pretensions adjusted, by the standard of a rigorous and self-sustaining criticism alone....

Who writes [reviews]?—Who causes [them] to be written? Who but an ass will put faith in tirades which *may* be the result of personal hostility, or in panegyrics which nine times out of ten may be laid, directly or indirectly, to the charge of the author himself? ...A veteran reviewer loves the safety of generalities, and is therefore rarely particular....

The prevalence of the spirit of puffery is a subject ... for disgust. Its truckling yet dogmatical character, its bold, unsustained, yet self-sufficient and wholesale laudation, is becoming, more and more, an insult to the common sense of the community. Trivial as it essentially is, it has, yet, been made the instrument of the grossest abuse in the elevation of imbecility, to the manifest injury, to the utter ruin, of true merit....

And if, in one, or perhaps two, insulated cases, the spirit of severe truth, sustained by an unconquerable will, was not to be ... put down, then, forthwith, were private chicaneries set in motion; then was had resort, on the part of those who considered themselves injured by the severity of the criticism ... to arts of the most virulent indignity, to untraceable slanders, to ruthless assassination in the dark. We say these things were done, while the press in general looked on, and, with a full understanding of the wrong perpetrated, spoke not against the wrong. The idea had absolutely gone abroad ... that attacks however just, upon a literary reputation however obtained, however untenable, were well retaliated by the basest and most unfounded traduction of personal fame....

But the talent, the fearlessness, and especially the *design* of this book will suffice to save it from that dreadful damnation of "silent contempt," to which editors throughout the country, if we are not much mistaken, will endeavour one and all to consign it.

Poe, of course, was not alone in this crusade. If anything distinguished him in this respect, it was not the originality of his allegations but his forcefulness, courage, and steadfastness in asserting them. Only a month after Poe first attacked the New York clique—a battle detailed in the next chapter—Edward Sherman Gould (1805–1885), a free-lance New York writer and critic, delivered a lecture on "American Criticism on American Literature" in New York City, the points and even many of the phrases of which were strikingly like Poe's. In general, Gould observed that literary reviews were neither intelligent, discriminating, nor disinterested, and that public opinion in regard to the merit of authors was originated and controlled by the magazines rather than formed by impartial or aesthetic criteria. In particular, Gould inveighed against the practice of authors rather than publishers presenting copies of their books "with their compliments" to critics "as a sort of practical bribery" to elicit favorable reviews. He denounced reviews that were testimonials of friendship rather than evidences of critical acumen or even honesty. And he complained against authors and publishers who hired literary friends to prepare an assortment of articles about their books which they could submit to editors who, for reasons of laziness, indifference, or friendship, would publish them in their magazines. (Gould neglected to mention the even sharper practice engaged in by such writers as Whitman—that of anonymously inserting reviews of their own works in the periodicals.)[93]

What was needed to correct this state of affairs, Gould advised, was a sound and independent criticism—sound and independent in the sense that a critic would be competent in his craft and concerned with the book and not with the author or his affiliations.[94]

This, then, is the background of the literary battles which Poe fought, a familiarity with which, to paraphrase Poe, may induce in us some sympathy with the circumstances that impelled him in his criticism and thus with the objects for which he wrote, so that we shall not be too far misled in our judgment.[95] Awareness of this background—of the editorial and publishing practices that in Poe's time were finding a congenial atmosphere for growth and that could and still often do make an author successful out of all relation to his talents— will enable us to see Poe's critical career for what it essentially was—a fourteen-year attempt to extirpate practices injurious

93. Whitman owned to having inserted three puffing reviews of his *Leaves of Grass* in three periodicals. See Gay Wilson Allen, *The Solitary Singer: A Critical Biography of Walt Whitman* (New York, 1945), pp. 147, 171.

94. This lecture, delivered on Dec. 29, 1835, was published in the *New York Mirror* in two instalments, XIII (April 9 and 16, 1836), 321–322, 329–330. It was also published (together with a lecture by John H. Gourlie) by the Mercantile Library Association under the title *Lectures Delivered before the Mercantile Association* (New York, 1836), pp. 2–26.

95. The exact quotation appears as an epigraph to this chapter and was originally published in the *Broadway Journal*, II (Sept. 27, 1845), 177.

to American letters; a prolonged endeavor to get literary works judged by the canons of an honest and principled criticism; and a continual effort to develop and promulgate such canons.[96]

This is not to suggest that Poe is presented here as a literary hero hewn of a single honorable piece. Heroic and honorable he may have been at times, but in 1845–1846 he suffered a breakdown, and during that time and at subsequent intervals he was certainly not of a piece and surely not honorable, and no attempt is made to whitewash his character and make him appear at all times the crusader that for the greater part of his career he was. The shots, in short, are called as they are seen; and if Poe, in the periods mentioned, wielded his critical pen for personal retaliation, the damage he did, more to himself and his cause than to his enemies, is not ignored.[97]

96. Poe felt he had good grounds for his critical harshness and even his sarcasm. In *Biographia Literaria* (London, 1817), p. 203, his mentor had written: "Every censure, every sarcasm respecting a publication which the critic, with the criticized work before him, can make good, is the critic's right. The writer is authorized to reply, but not to complain."

97. In this study I ignore the political antagonism between the Locofocos (the radical Jacksonian Democrats such as Evert A. Duyckinck, Cornelius Mathews, and John Lewis O'Sullivan) and the conservative Democrats and Whigs (such as Rufus Wilmot Griswold, Lewis Gaylord Clark, and Edwin Percy Whipple)— first, because the subject has been sufficiently discussed by John Stafford in *The Literary Criticism of "Young America": A Study in the Relationship of Politics and Literature, 1837–1850* (University of California English Studies 3, 1952) and, more recently, by Perry Miller, *The Raven and the Whale: The War of Words and Wits in the Era of Poe and Melville* (New York, 1956); second, and more important, because political considerations did not enter into Poe's critical judgments.

2

COMMENCEMENT OF
A CAMPAIGN

Poe and the Norman
Leslie *Incident*

We shall ... frown down all conspiracies to foist
inanity upon the public consideration at the obvious
expense of every man of talent who is not a member
of a *clique* in power.—*Edgar A. Poe*

Poe, assuming the "generalship" of the *Southern Literary
Messenger* in December, 1835,[1] fired in that issue the first shot
in what was to become one of the major battles of American
periodicals—a battle that Poe was to wage single-handedly for
almost an entire year against four Northern journals, and in
the course of which he was even to make enemies of three
neutral Southern ones. More significantly, this battle was his
first campaign in a career-long war against the New York
clique.

It all began quite innocuously on July 11, 1835. The *New
York Mirror,* at that time the best literary weekly in the
United States, on whose staff the favorite of the New York

---

1. See "Publisher's Notice" in the *Messenger,* II (Dec., 1835), 1. Poe's connection with the *Messenger* began, of course, at an earlier date, but the relations
between him and Thomas Willis White, proprietor of the *Messenger,* were uncertain and unsatisfactory both before and after Dec., 1835. See Ostrom, *Poe's
Letters,* I, 53–107 *passim,* and White's letters reproduced by David E. Jackson
in *Poe and the Southern Literary Messenger* (Richmond, Va., 1934), pp. 96–115
passim.

littérateurs—Theodore Sedgwick Fay (1807–1898)—was an associate editor (together with George P. Morris and Nathaniel P. Willis), published by way of prepublication puffing a two-column extract from Fay's forthcoming novel. The extract was headed, "MR. FAY'S NOVEL—NORMAN LESLIE," and was prefaced as follows: "We this week present our readers with two detached passages from Mr. Fay's forthcoming novel —the first as a specimen of his powers of descriptive pathos, and his facility of touching the feelings, and the other as an example of his style of narrative."[2] The next month the *Mirror* again published a passage from *Norman Leslie,* this time devoting an entire page to it and introducing it in this manner: "The last extract we gave from Mr. Fay's forthcoming novel having been extensively copied, and spoken of in high terms by our brethren of the press, we are induced to present them with another selection from these beautiful volumes, which we shall continue from time to time until their publication."[3]

Again, at the end of that month, the *Mirror* presented another two-page "sample" of the forthcoming *Norman Leslie,* heralding the novel with this statement: "In our present number we continue our extracts from this beautiful performance, which will make its appearance in this city and in London simultaneously."[4] Nor was the *Mirror* satisfied with this spread alone. Noting that fine weather had come to New York, the *Mirror* felt that it could be adequately described only by another quotation from *Norman Leslie.*[5] Once more, in October, the *Mirror* felt obliged to charm its readers by printing another passage from Fay's book.[6]

In November, 1835, the long-trumpeted, widely puffed two-volume novel—*Norman Leslie: A Tale of the Present Times*—appeared anonymously under the banner of Harper and Brothers. The *Knickerbocker,* which was destined to become one of

2. *New York Mirror,* XIII (July 11, 1835), 10–11.
3. *Ibid.,* XIII (Aug. 8, 1835), 47.
4. *Ibid.,* XIII (Aug. 29, 1835), 66–67. The "simultaneous" appearance of *Norman Leslie* in America and England was designed, of course, to secure the English copyright to that work.
5. *Ibid.,* XIII (Aug. 29, 1835), 72.
6. *Ibid.,* XIII (Oct. 10, 1835), 114.

the leading monthly magazines of the next decade and with whose editor, Lewis Gaylord Clark, Poe was to carry on a sustained literary feud, reviewed *Norman Leslie* in this way:

With some faults, incident to a first attempt, this work of Mr. Fay is said by those critics who have perused it,—(a pleasure in which, owing to absence from town, we have been unable to participate,) to possess scenes of great power, and to be often characterized by that quiet ease of style and purity of diction for which the author is distinguished, and of which we have heretofore spoken in this Magazine. It may be taken as a conclusive evidence of the power of the novel to awaken interest, that in two weeks after the publication of the first large edition, not a copy remained in the hands of the publishers.[7]

Inadvertently or otherwise, this review was misleading, for although it is true that *Norman Leslie* represented Fay's first attempt at a novel, it was his third published work, *Dreams and Reveries of a Quiet Man* and *The Minute-Book* having appeared in 1832 and 1833 respectively. The sell-out of the first large edition, moreover, is not to be taken, as is urged, "as a conclusive evidence of the power of the novel,"[8] but rather of the power of the press to create a best-seller by puffing. Furthermore, the fact that the writer of this review, no doubt Lewis Clark himself, could praise a book which he blithely confessed he had not even read, shows, in addition to the general irresponsibility of both the magazines and the critics of the period, the favoritism accorded Fay.

The "anonymous" *Norman Leslie* formally came to Poe's attention in November, 1835. In reviewing it for the *Messenger* of December, 1835,[9] Poe devoted almost as much space to it (some four thousand words) as the *Mirror* had, periodically, in all its notices and extracts, and showed that he had read the novel with perhaps more thoroughness than its author had written it. Modeling his critical style on Jeffrey's of the

7. *Knickerbocker*, VI (Nov., 1835), 483.
8. "Affected and melodramatic" as the novel is, Mott (*American Magazines*, I, 635) thinks that it succeeded because "it used a notorious murder of the day as the center of the plot, and because its author was one of the editors of the popular *New York Mirror*. . . ."
9. *Southern Literary Messenger*, II, 54–57. Poe had actually written the *Norman Leslie* review sometime before Nov. 23, 1835. See T. W. White's letter to Lucian Minor of that date (Jackson, *Poe and the Messenger*, p. 105) in which he comments on "the Leslie critique."

Edinburgh Review, Wilson's of *Blackwood's Edinburgh Maga-zine,* and Gifford's of the *Quarterly Review,* which he had obviously studied, he went to work on *Norman Leslie:*

> Well!—here we have it! This is *the* book—*the* book *par excellence*—the book bepuffed, beplastered, and be-*Mirrored:* the book "attributed to" Mr. Blank, and "said to be from the pen" of Mr. Asterisk: the book which has been "about to appear"—"in press"— "in progress"—"in preparation"—and "forthcoming:" the book "graphic" in anticipation—"talented" *a priori*—and God knows what *in prospectu.* For the sake of every thing puffed, puffing and puffable, let us take a peep at its contents!
>
> Norman Leslie, gentle reader, a Tale of the Present Times, is, after all, written by nobody in the world but Theodore S. Fay, and Theodore S. Fay is nobody in the world but "one of the Editors of the New York Mirror."

Poe proceeded to deride the Preface, particularly Fay's plea for the "indulgence of the solemn and sapient critics," declaring that since he himself was neither solemn nor sapient, he was not bound to show Fay a shadow of mercy. Then Poe provided his readers with a detailed summary of the plot, after which he remarked: "Thus ends the Tale of the Present Times, and thus ends the most inestimable piece of balderdash with which the common sense of the good people of America was ever so openly or so villainously insulted.

"We do not mean to say," Poe continued, "that there is positively *nothing* in Mr. Fay's novel to commend—but there is indeed very little." That little Poe pointed out briefly, "for we can positively think of nothing farther worth even a qualified commendation. The plot, as will appear from the running outline we have given of it, is a monstrous piece of absurdity and incongruity. The characters *have no character,*" for reasons which he proceeded to explain. "As regards Mr. Fay's *style,* it is unworthy of a school-boy. The 'Editor of the New York Mirror' has either never seen an edition of Murray's Grammar, or he has been a-Willising so long as to have forgotten his vernacular language. Let us examine one or two of his sentences at random." This he did and found many faults in diction and syntax. He concluded: "Here we have a *blistering* detail, a *blistering* truth, a *blistering* story, and a *blistering* brand, to say nothing of innumerable blisters interspersed throughout the book. But we have done with Norman Leslie,— if ever we saw as silly a thing, may we be—blistered."

This critique differed from Poe's other harsh reviews in the *Messenger* in that it was directed against the work of a member of "one of the most powerful literary cliques in America,"[10] but *apparently* it was a dud, for it elicited no immediate comment from that coterie. But reactions from other journals were so instantaneous and numerous that White, no doubt at Poe's suggestion, added a Supplement to the next number of his magazine consisting entirely of notices of the *Messenger,* and calling attention to "the *source,* especially" of many of the notices—a gratifying matter considering the sectionalism of the times.[11]

The New York papers, however cordial they were to the *Messenger* (and the *Messenger* under Poe's editorship was uniformly praised for being the "neatest in typographical execution—in whiteness of paper and elegance of type, of any American publication of the kind"—a real novelty for the period), were, on the whole and as might be expected, less hospitable to the *Norman Leslie* review than the Southern journals. The New York *Courier and Enquirer* observed that the criticism in the *Messenger* was "the boldest, the most independent, and unflinching, of all that appears in the periodical world," but expressed certain reservations about the *Norman Leslie* review. For, "though we cannot deny the truth of the greater portion of it, [the review] is paralyzed by the strong symptoms of *personal* hostility not to Fay only, but to all who may be supposed to favor or admire him." The New York *Spirit of the Times* remarked of Poe's reviews that "in one instance undue severity is shown towards a clever young author; yet they are, in the main, clever and just." The *New Yorker,* the warmest of the metropolitan journals in its praise, noted that the "Editor examines with impartiality,

---

10. Quinn, *Poe,* p. 244.
11. The quotations that follow in the text appeared in the Supplement to the *Southern Literary Messenger,* II (Jan., 1836), 133–140.

judges with fairness, commends with evident pleasure, and condemns with moderation. May he live a thousand years!"

The Southern journals cited in the Supplement were in almost total accord in praising the *Messenger* in general and Poe's criticisms in particular. For example, the *Petersburg Constellation* said: "We have rarely read a review more caustic or more called for than the *flaying* which the new editor of the Messenger has so judiciously given Mr. Fay's 'bepuffed, beplastered and be-*Mirrored*' novel of 'Norman Leslie.' " The *Lynchburg Virginian* remarked: "Such reviews as that of Mr. Fay's 'Norman Leslie' will be read. Men—and Women alike—will always be attracted in crowds to behold an infliction of the Russian knout or to see a fellow-creature flayed alive. And Mr. Fay—who, by the way, is a great favorite with us—fully deserves a '*blistering*' for putting forth such a novel as Norman Leslie." And Major Mordecai M. Noah of distinguished reputation, whose loyalty to America can scarcely be described as sectional, remarked that "we are glad to see the censures so unsparingly, but judiciously directed against the mawkish style and matter of those ephemeral productions with which, under the name of *chef-d'oeuvres* in novel writing, the poor humbugged public are so unmercifully gagged and bamboozled."

So encouraged and by now no doubt aware of the journalistic value of "kicking up a bobbery," Poe in February, 1836, again peppered *Norman Leslie*, for that novel, despite Poe's review, had passed into a second printing within a few months,[12] and, made into a stage play, had drawn large audiences into the American Theatre in New York for almost a whole month.[13] In reviewing *Paul Ulric, or The Adventures of an Enthusiast*,[14] Poe began by saying: "These two volumes are by Morris Mattson, Esq. of Philadelphia, and we presume that Mr.

12. Rufus Wilmot Griswold, ed., *The Prose Writers of America* (Philadelphia, 1847), p. 447.

13. "The American Theatre, Bowery.—'Norman Leslie,' dramatised from Mr. Fay's well-known novel of that name, has for nearly a month drawn crowded auditories at this theatre"—*Knickerbocker*, VII (Feb., 1836), 215. See also the notices of the play *Norman Leslie* in the *Knickerbocker* (pp. 311 and 437), which show that from January through April the play crowded the American Theatre "with eager and admiring audiences."

14. *Southern Literary Messenger*, II (Feb., 1836), 173–180.

Mattson is a very young man. Be this as it may, when we called Norman Leslie the silliest book in the world we had certainly never seen Paul Ulric." In speaking of Mattson's style, he said, "all fine writers have pet words and phrases," that, for example, "Mr. Fay had his *'blisters'* . . . and Mr. M. must be allowed his *'suches'* and *'so muches.'* Such is genius. . . ."

Meanwhile, Poe, who had submitted a collection of short stories to Harper and Brothers, the publishers of the very novels whose worthlessness he had so savagely exposed, had his manuscript rejected. Paulding, writing to T. W. White on March 3, 1836, explained Harpers' refusal to publish: "The stories had so recently appeared in the *Messenger* that 'they would be no novelty.' "[15] But Harpers commented in a letter to Poe that they were generally pleased with Poe's criticisms and took pleasure in sending him all their books, at least such of them as they felt were worthy of his notice.[16]

The *Mirror,* hearing in a conjecturable way that Poe's manuscript was rejected, found ammunition for an offensive against Poe, an offensive designed to avenge their editor Fay, at whom Poe was still taking potshots. On April 9, 1836, the *Mirror* published an article called "THE SUCCESSFUL NOVEL!!"[17] which, introducing Poe under the sobriquet of Bulldog, sought to explain *ex post facto* his hostile criticism of popular literary successes in terms of his own personal failure. Typical of the satirical statements in that article is this: ". . . the Harpers, you know, have so little principle, that they publish only works which they think will sell." Lest readers of the *Mirror* should overlook this article or fail to detect its target, despite such obvious allusions as the *Southern Literary Passenger*, a squib, interspersed with pointing fingers, appeared on another page: "Those who have read the notices of American books in a certain 'southern' monthly, which is striving to gain notoriety by the loudness of its abuse, may find amuse-

<hr>

15. Quoted by Una Pope-Hennessy, *Edgar Allan Poe, 1809–1849: A Critical Biography* (London, 1934), p. 177 n. 1.
16. For the entire letter, dated June, 1836, see Quinn, *Poe,* pp. 250–251.
17. *New York Mirror,* XIII (April 9, 1836), 324–325.

ment in the sketch, in another page, entitled 'The Successful Novel!' The 'Southern Literary Messenger' knows, by experience! what it is to write a success*less* novel."[18]

Encouraged perhaps by Poe's failure to reply to the personal attack of the *Mirror*, or, as seems more likely, in league with the *Mirror*, the big guns began firing on Poe, the big guns being Willis Gaylord Clark of the *Philadelphia Gazette* and *Knickerbocker* and Colonel William L. Stone of the *New York Commercial Advertiser*. The attack that W. G. Clark made on Poe and printed in his newspaper,[19] W. L. Stone reprinted in his;[20] and not satisfied with this alone, Stone added his own strictures.

Clark's attack read:

The last number of the Southern Literary Messenger is very readable and respectable. Professor Dew's address is the best article in it, and was worth delaying the number for its insertion. The contributions to the Messenger are much better than the original matter. The critical department of this work,—much as it would seem to boast itself of impartiality and discernment,—is in our opinion, decidedly *quacky*. There is in it a great assumption of acumen, which is completely unsustained. Many a work has been slashingly condemned therein, of which the critic himself could not write a page, were he to die for it. This affectation of eccentric sternness in criticism, without the power to back one's suit withal, so far from deserving praise, as some suppose, merits the strongest reprehension.

While these remarks were personal and only suggested again that Poe's manuscript had been rejected, Stone's comments were more direct:

We are entirely of opinion with the Philadelphia Gazette in relation to the Southern Literary Messenger, and take this occasion to

18. *Ibid.*, XIII (April 9, 1836), 327. The last sentence of this squib was another misrepresentation, since Poe had submitted, not a novel, but a collection of tales—a fact that Poe duly noted in the *Messenger*, II (April, 1836), 327 n.: "The Editor of the Messenger never in his life wrote or published, or attempted to publish, a novel either successful or *successless*." As has been pointed out, Poe submitted the stories to Harpers after, not before, the *Norman Leslie* review, so that rejection of his stories cannot be adduced, as was adduced by the *Mirror*, as motivation for a hostile review. The simple truth is that *Norman Leslie* is an exceptionally inferior novel and, as such, received an exceptionally unfavorable review.

19. *Philadelphia Gazette, and Commercial Intelligencer*, April 8, 1836, p. 2. Also reprinted by Poe in the *Messenger*, II (April, 1836), 327, with the sentence beginning, "Professor Dew's address . . ." omitted.

20. *New York Commercial Advertiser*, April 12, 1836, p. 1.

express our total dissent from the numerous and lavish encomiums we have seen bestowed upon its critical notices. Some few of them have been judicious, fair and candid; bestowing praise and censure with judgment and impartiality; but by far the greatest number, of those we have read, have been flippant, unjust, untenable and uncritical. The duty of the critic is to act as judge, not as enemy, of the writer whom he reviews; a distinction of which the Zoilus of the Messenger seems not to be aware. It is possible to review a book, severely, without bestowing opprobrious epithets upon the writer: to condemn with courtesy, if not with kindness. The critic of the Messenger has been eulogized for his scorching and scarifying abilities, and he thinks it incumbent upon him to keep up his reputation in that line, by sneers, sarcasm, and downright abuse; by straining his vision with microscopic intensity in search of faults, and shutting his eyes, with all his might, to beauties. Moreover, we have detected him, more than once, in blunders quite as gross as those on which it was his pleasure to descant.

Poe, his critical integrity impugned, decided to level his charges against the cliquish practice of puffing works into reputation, however undeserving such books might be, and to rationalize, both by statement and demonstration, his principles of critical judgment to indicate that he was not malicious, but simply just. These were charges and principles that were central to the entire body of his criticism and were not formulated merely to stave off immediate difficulties. This he did in his Drake-Halleck review.[21] He asserted that American criticism, with "some noble exceptions," had willed itself into decline in consequence of adopting the wrong means of encouraging a native literature, the means being "indiscriminate puffing of good, bad, and indifferent...." Such uncritical and meaningless laudation, far from producing a native literature of which we can be proud, is, he said, injurious to it, for it encourages the bad and indifferent as indiscriminately as it encourages the good. But critics, "far from being ashamed of the many disgraceful literary failures to which our own inordinate vanities and misapplied patriotism have lately given birth, and so far from deeply lamenting that these daily puerilities are of home manufacture,... adhere pertinaciously to ... the gross paradox of liking a stupid book the better, be-

21. *Southern Literary Messenger,* II (April, 1836), 326–336.

cause, sure enough, its stupidity is American." Admittedly, once we were too subservient to British critical dicta, he went on, but, however servile that subservience was, those dicta at least forced us to discriminate between what was good and bad in our own literature. Now, "boisterous and arrogant in the pride of a too speedily assumed literary freedom," we give up all effort at such discrimination in favor of wholesale laudation.

Deeply lamenting this unjustifiable state of public feeling, it has been our constant endeavor, since assuming the Editorial duties of this Journal, to stem, with what little abilities we possess, a current so disastrously undermining the health and prosperity of our literature. We have seen our efforts applauded by men whose applauses we value. From all quarters we have received abundant private as well as public testimonials in favor of our *Critical Notices,* and, until very lately, have heard from no respectable source one word impugning their integrity or candor.

Having made these statements, Poe proceeded to deal with Clark and Stone, alluding in a footnote to the attack ("THE SUCCESSFUL NOVEL!!") that had recently been made upon him in the *Mirror*. Clark's charge he chose to treat summarily, since it was personal. But Stone's charges he answered in detail, since they questioned his critical practice:

But there is something equivocal, to say the least, in the remarks of Col. Stone. He acknowledges that *"some* of our notices have been judicious, fair, and candid, bestowing praise and censure with judgment and impartiality." This being the case, how can he reconcile his *total* dissent from the public verdict in our favor, with the dictates of justice? We are accused too of bestowing "opprobrious epithets" upon writers whom we review, and in the paragraph so accusing us we are called nothing less than "flippant, unjust, and uncritical."

But there is another point of which we disapprove. While in our reviews we have at all times been particularly careful *not* to deal in generalities, and have never, if we remember aright, advanced in any single instance an unsupported assertion, our accuser has forgotten to give us any better evidence of our flippancy, injustice, personality, and gross blundering, than the solitary *dictum* of Col. Stone. We call upon the Colonel for assistance in this dilemma. We wish to be shown our blunders that we may correct them—to be made aware of our flippancy, that we may avoid it hereafter—and above all to have our personalities pointed out that we may proceed forthwith with a repentant spirit, to make the *amende honorable.* In default of this aid from the Editor of the Commercial we shall take it for granted that we are neither blunderers, flippant, personal, nor unjust.

When he had finished with Clark and Stone, Poe proceeded to accuse the majority of American critics of having no critical standards and to formulate his own in regard to poetry, since the poems of Drake and Halleck were the subject of his critique:

Who will deny that in regard to individual poems no definitive opinions can exist, so long as to Poetry in the abstract we attach no definitive idea? Yet it is a common thing to hear our critics, day after day, pronounce, with a positive air, laudatory or condemnatory sentences, *en masse,* upon metrical works of whose merits and de-merits they have, in the first place, virtually confessed an utter ig-norance, in confessing ignorance of all determinate principles by which to regulate a decision.

Then, conceding that poetry as a term was troublesome, if not impossible, to define, he felt that he could describe its nature in such a way that it would be "sufficiently distinct for all the purposes of practical analysis"—a description that he pro-ceeded to give and was to give in critique after critique until, after much modification, it reached its final form in "The Poetic Principle." Unlike his eighteenth-century predecessors who had striven to formulate a body of objective rules by which to test the merits of a poem, Poe, in common with all Romantic critics, relied upon a species of impressionism—upon an innate faculty—to recognize a work of art. Thus, he said that poetry is not primarily concerned with human passions, however magnificent, or scenes of nature, however august, or moral lessons, however practicable. Instead, poetry is concerned with Beauty, which Poe called its only legitimate province. All else, whether passion, nature, or truth, is subsidiary to this concern. As Poe put the principle in its definitive form:

An immortal instinct [Imagination], deep within the spirit of man, is thus, plainly, a sense of the Beautiful. . . . He who shall simply sing, with however glowing enthusiasm, or with however vivid a truth of description, of the sights, and sounds, and odours, and colours, and sentiments, which greet *him* in common with all man-kind—he, I say, has yet failed to prove his divine title [of poet]. There is still a something in the distance which he has been unable to attain. . . . It is no mere appreciation of the Beauty before us—

but a wild effort to reach the Beauty above . . . to attain a portion of that Loveliness whose very elements, perhaps, appertain to eternity alone. And thus when by Poetry—or when by Music, the most entrancing of the Poetic moods—we find ourselves melted into tears— we weep then—not . . . through excess of pleasure, but through . . . sorrow at our inability to grasp *now,* wholly, here on earth, at once and for ever, those divine and rapturous joys, of which *through* the poem, or *through* the music, we attain to but brief and indeterminate glimpses.

The struggle to apprehend the supernal Loveliness—this struggle, on the part of souls fittingly constituted—has given to the world all *that* which it (the world) has never been enabled at once to understand and *to feel* as poetic.[22]

In passing, we may notice, however perfunctorily, that this in essence is Poe's statement as to what constitutes poetry and, by implication, the means by which one may recognize poetry. Poets and critics must be transcendent and catch these apocalyptic glimpses of supernal beauty, however briefly and indeterminately. The only significant difference between the true poet and the true critic is that one renders the vision and the other understands and feels its genuineness. For Poe, it followed from these statements that critical principles could be fixed once and for all, since that which the poem adumbrated was eternal.

Poe then passed to an analysis of books by two then renowned American poets, *The Culprit Fay and Other Poems,* a posthumous work by Joseph Rodman Drake (1795–1820), and *Alnwick Castle with Other Poems* by Fitz-Greene Halleck (1790–1867), to demonstrate how his theoretical remarks could be applied to poetry. The conclusion he reached after a close reading of Drake's volume had equal validity for Halleck's: "Yet such are the puerilities we daily find ourselves called upon to admire, as among the loftiest efforts of the human mind, and which not to assign a rank with the proud

22. "The Poetic Principle," *Sartain's Union Magazine,* VII (Oct., 1850), 233, and also in the *Home Journal* of Aug. 31, 1850, where it appeared earlier in consequence of being copied from advance sheets of Griswold's forthcoming edition of Poe's *The Literati.* If Poe differs in this respect from other Romantics of his time—and one must remember that Romantics are pathetically few, even in a period so labeled—it is largely in the degree of his insistence upon this principle and in the nature of his vision.

trophies of the matured and vigorous genius of England, is to prove ourselves at once a fool, a maligner, and no patriot."

Though Poe had acknowledged that Clark had "a right to think us *quacky* if he pleases," and that he had not assumed for a moment, despite Clark's charges, "that we could write a single line of the works we have reviewed," Clark was not content to leave the matter there. On May 10, he published the following in his newspaper:

The last number of the Southern Literary Messenger evinces that its editor has had the chalice of criticism commended back to his own lips, and that there is an unpleasant potency in the draught. We have been among the last to speak disparagingly of the literary merits of a part of the Messenger; on the contrary, we have spoken of many of the contributions in terms of commendation. But we say, that in the critical portion of the Messenger, there has been such a palpable conflict between *precept* and *practice,* that we wonder any one with half an eye could have failed to discover the same. We said lately that there was an affectation of sternness in this department of the work, without the power to support it. Let any one look at the butcher-like manner in which Fay's Norman Leslie was there treated. We grant that there is a lack of the *unities* of fiction in those volumes, but they abound in scenes and passages of superior power, such as stamp their author a man of keen and observant genius. Moreover, while the Messenger has *pretended* objections to the puffing of the day, its editor has clipped with indefatigable scissors, and copies into the pages of the Messenger, every syllable of praise that could be gleaned from the four corners of the Union, respecting his periodical,—and not content with thus trumpeting itself, has quoted dispraise of other works, towards which it has either fears or envyings. There is a spirit of unfairness about such a course, which ought to be chastised; and we intend, should it continue hereafter, to have a hand in the infliction.[23]

23. *Philadelphia Gazette,* p. 2. Poe remarked in a preface to the Supplement he added to the July, 1836, number of the *Messenger* (p. 517) carrying the extracts that he had "duly weighed the propriety and impropriety of this course" before he decided to comply "with the suggestion of many of our friends, and . . . a majority of our contributors"; and lest some readers might suspect that the extracts were culled so that only favorable ones were published, he would "now publish *every* late criticism received." One obvious, if tacit, objection that Clark had to such an imposing array of decidedly favorable notices was that it provided impressive testimony that the *Messenger* was becoming a serious rival of the *Knickerbocker.* As the *National Intelligencer* remarked in an earlier notice of the *Messenger* (Jan., 1836, p. 135): "This journal has, very unexpectedly, left its Northern competitors behind in the race for fame, and assumed all at once a pre-eminent rank among American periodicals."

As for Stone, he did not take up the gauntlet that Poe had thrown, for not only did he fail to answer Poe's request to be shown his blunders, his flippancy, and, above all, his personalities, but he ignored him entirely. Opportunely enough, however, Colonel Stone's novel, *Ups and Downs in the Life of a Distressed Gentleman,* came "anonymously" to Poe's attention some two months later. Already a past master of the "hanged, drawn, and *Quarterly*" method, Poe analyzed the *Ups and Downs* in about the same way that he had analyzed *Norman Leslie.* The introduction to the novel he found to be "much the best portion of the work—so much so, indeed, that we fancy it written by some kind, good-natured friend of the author." He then labored through most of the sixteen chapters of the work, chapter by chapter, giving an extract of one of the best passages in the book, to let the book condemn itself by an objective presentation of its own ludicrousness. He concluded: "We have given the entire pith and marrow of the book. The term *flat,* is the only general expression which would apply to it. It is written, we believe, by Col. Stone of the New York Commercial Advertiser, and should have been printed among the quack advertisements, in a spare corner of his paper."[24] The use of the word *quack* must have amused Poe, since he had managed to turn the point of that word—first used by Clark to describe Poe's criticism and then reprinted by Stone— against Stone. Moreover, in heralding the *Sketches by Boz* in the same number of the *Messenger,*[25] Poe took occasion to observe: "We should like very much to copy the whole of the article entitled *Pawnbrokers' Shops* [from the *Sketches*], with a view of contrasting its matter and manner with the insipidity of the passage we have just quoted [in the Stone review] on the same subject from the '*Ups and Downs*' of Colonel Stone, and by way of illustrating our remarks on the

24. *Southern Literary Messenger,* II (June, 1836), 455–457.
25. *Ibid.,* II, 457–460. The *Knickerbocker,* VII (May, 1836), 550, reviewed *Ups and Downs* enthusiastically: "Having read it entirely through . . . and at a single agreeably-protracted sitting, we are enabled to pronounce it entertaining in the extreme."

unity of effect. . . . So perfect, and never-to-be-forgotten a picture cannot be brought about by any such trumpery exertion, or still more trumpery talent, as we find employed in the ineffective daubing of Colonel Stone."

Single-handed and under fire, yet still blasting away at the Northern periodicals, Poe at this time received successive attacks from the most unexpected quarters, which must have made him lose heart momentarily. The *Southern Literary Journal* of Charleston, South Carolina, which had hitherto been, if not an active ally, at least a sympathetic neutral, printed an article called "The Puffing System"[26] in which the editor denounced American journals which filled up columns with puffs and which, anonymously and under the pretext of criticism, vented their "private spleen or malignity . . . against worthy persons . . . whose literary reputation . . . may be sacrificed to gratify the revenge of the cowardly critic. . . ." The anonymous writer then puffed "The Uses and Abuses of Criticism" in a recent number of the *Knickerbocker,* as well as an article by Paulding in the current *Knickerbocker.*

Poe felt that he was the party so broadly alluded to by the *Southern Literary Journal,* and he had good reason to feel sensitive. He had republished puffs of the *Messenger* and had anonymously criticized the works of "worthy persons" with a causticity hardly precedented in American journals, not to mention the fact that, at the same time, he had eulogized the novels of friends—namely, Nathaniel Beverley Tucker's *George Balcombe* and John Pendleton Kennedy's *Horse-Shoe Robinson.* Thus, with a tone of regret, conspicuous for its singularity and not to be sounded again, he replied:

We are sorry to perceive that our friends of the *"Southern Literary Journal"* are disposed to unite with the *"Knickerbocker"* and *"New York Mirror"* in covert, and therefore unmanly, thrusts at the *"Messenger."* It is natural that these two Journals (who refused to exchange with us from the first) should feel themselves aggrieved at our success, and we own that, bearing them no very good will, we care little what injury they do themselves in the public estimation by suffering their mortification to become apparent. But we are embarked in the cause of *Southern* Literature, and (with perfect amity

26. II (June, 1836), 312–315.

to all sections) wish to claim especially as a friend and co-operator, every *Southern* Journal. We repeat, therefore, that we are grieved to see a disposition of hostility, entirely unprovoked, manifested on the part of Mr. Whittaker [*sic*]. He should reflect, that while we ourselves cannot for a moment believe him otherwise than perfectly upright and sincere in his animadversions upon our Magazine, still there is hardly one individual in ninety-nine who will not attribute every ill word he says of us to the instigations of jealousy.[27]

Whitaker, of course, could not allow Poe's innuendoes to pass unchallenged. After puffing the *Knickerbocker* again, he proceeded to "praise" the *Southern Literary Messenger,* adding ambiguously, among other left-handed compliments: "Its criticisms betray, in most cases, but little of the spirit of puffing—on the contrary, the editor seems resolute to avoid any such charge, and knows no better way than to rush into an opposite extreme. . . . So far from universally puffing, he does not often praise; and he discriminates more justly, where he does so, than all the rest of our periodicals." He added that he was happy to see that the *Messenger* had abandoned the "practice of reprinting in its own pages the voluminous newspaper encomiums that are every month so generously and so justly paid to it." Coming to the point at last, Whitaker said:

Its respected editor . . . thinks we intended to make a special application of our hints to the pages of the Messenger. . . . The practice inveighed against was, and is, a *common one,* and our remarks were *general.* . . . While the editor of the Messenger, however, justly acquits us of any thing like want of "sincerity or uprightness" in our remarks, he is inclined to think that the public will form a different estimate of our motives, and will attribute that for which he is disposed to indicate so worthy a cause, "to the instigation of jealousy." We know not whether or not the Southern Literary Messenger has a more extended circulation than the magazine with which we are connected, so that we cannot entertain towards it any feelings of jealousy. . . . When it intimates, however, that we are "disposed to unite with the 'Knickerbocker' and the 'New-York Mirror,' in covert and therefore unmanly thrusts at the Messenger," we confess, that we are quite unable to understand the meaning of such language. We exchange with the "Knickerbocker," but there is no sort of concert between us . . . except that which results from our being engaged in the promotion of similar literary aims. . . . We have uniformly

27. *Southern Literary Messenger,* II (June, 1836), 460.

sent our Magazine to the "New-York Mirror," but have never had a reciprocation of the favor. There certainly is no concert between us and the "Mirror" to injure the Messenger, either by manly or "unmanly thrusts."

Then, as if to justify his disavowal of "concert" with the *Knickerbocker,* Whitaker remarked: "The 'Knickerbocker' continues to reprint compliments paid to itself. . . . The editors of that magazine may have their reasons for this policy which are unknown to us, and which we cannot surmise. All that we have a right to say . . . is that we disapprove the practice altogether. . . ."[28]

In addition to the attack by the *Southern Literary Journal,* the *Newbern Spectator* of North Carolina also took issue with Poe's unrelenting critical tactics:

With the talent available in any particular spot in the southern country, it is out of the question, truly ridiculous, to assume the tone of a Walsh, a Blackwood or a Jeffries; and to attempt it, without the means to support the pretension, tends to accelerate the downfall of so indiscreet an attempt. . . . Without these advantages, however, the Messenger has boldly put itself forth as an arbiter whose dicta are supreme; and with a severity and an indiscreetness of criticism,— especially on American works,—which few, if any, of the able and well established Reviews have ventured to exercise, has been not only unmerciful, but savage.[29]

Poe was braced and ready for all comers. Adding a Supplement to the July number of the *Messenger,* he quoted the *Newbern Spectator* in full and responded: "We are at a loss to know who is the editor of the Spectator, but have a shrewd suspicion that he is the identical gentleman who once sent us from Newbern an unfortunate copy of verses. It seems to us that he wishes to be taken notice of, and we will, for the once, oblige him with a few words—with the positive understanding, however, that it will be inconvenient to trouble ourselves hereafter with his opinions." Poe went on, quite contemptuously, to ridicule the remarks of the *Spectator* editor, and, to humiliate him further, to quote various celebrities such as Paulding who said that the *Messenger* "is decidedly superior to any

28. *Southern Literary Journal,* II (July, 1836), 396–403.
29. Reprinted by Poe in Supplement, *Southern Literary Messenger,* II (July, 1836), 517.

Periodical in the United States, and Mr. Poe is decidedly the best of all our young writers; I dont [sic] know but I might add all our old ones, with one or two exceptions, among which I assure you I dont include myself." Poe concluded:

We wish only to add that the poet's assertion in regard to the Messenger "putting itself forth as an arbiter whose dicta are supreme," is a slight deviation from the truth. The Messenger merely expresses its particular opinions in its own particular manner. These opinions no person is bound to adopt. They are open to the comments and censures of even the most diminutive things in creation—of the very Newbern Spectators of the land. If the Editor of this paper does not behave himself we will positively publish his verses.

Poe could afford to be proud, though the contempt he evinced here was quite unwarranted. The editor of the New York *Courier and Enquirer,* as well as an impressive number of other newspapers and magazine editors both in the North and the South, had hailed the *Messenger* as being "at the very head of the periodical literature of its class, in the United States," and this in Virginia where, as the editor of the *Richmond Compiler* rightly remarked, such a venture was "looked upon as chimaerical in the last degree; and when . . . speedy downfall [for the *Messenger*] was universally predicted."[30] The editor of the *Courier and Enquirer* added, however, as might be expected from one who favored his renowned fellow New Yorker: "We do not agree by any means with some of its literary *conclusions.* For instance, it is very wide of our opinion on the merits of Halleck; but there is a vigor and manliness in most of the [editorial] papers that appear in the Messenger, which we are almost ready to admit, are found *no where* else in American periodicals." In the Supplement containing these remarks, there were many other quotations copied from various magazines and newspapers. Two excerpts appeared from the *New Yorker,* one of which found fault with Poe, who, like an Indian, "cannot realize that an enemy is conquered till he is scalped," but which praised him for his ability. The editor thought him "too severe, as in the case of 'Norman Leslie,' " but found the review of Drake and Halleck

30. All these quotations appeared in the Supplement, *ibid.,* II, 517–524.

done "faithfully, fairly, and with discrimination." The second excerpt from the *New Yorker* found the criticisms "spirited but just," and observed that "Col. Stone's unfortunate 'Ups and Downs...' [had been] most unsparingly shown up."

Similarly, a Philadelphia journal, the *Weekly Messenger,* judged the *Southern Literary Messenger* to be "as good as any, if not the very best [magazine], in these United States," but objected to the *Norman Leslie* review on the grounds that it was "burlesque, or caricature, not criticism...." From the Southern journals, however, there was almost universal acclaim. The *Petersburg Constellation,* alluding to the *Mirror's* satire of Poe, said: "Let the New York Mirror snarl if it will; there are papers in each Messenger which will outlive all the Norman Leslie['s, Willis's] 'Pencillings by the Way,' and [Morris's] 'Wearies my Love of my Letters?' of its erudite editors. Kennel a stag-hound with a cur, and the latter will yelp in very fear."

Typical of many of the other Southern notices was that of the *Baltimore American,* which praised Poe for his "spirited and just remarks on the puffing system" and for the "vindication of his course": "He is on the strong side, whatever ... influences may be arrayed against him, and will do much good even though he run occasionally into the extreme of severity. ... Let the editor of the Messenger and others, go on ... assuming a high standard of literary merit, require substantial qualifications in candidates for fame, and condemn unsparingly all who do not unite genius with cultivation, a union indispensable for the production of works of permanent value."

The last and most timid assault came from the South again; this time from the Richmond *Courier and Daily Compiler—* in Poe's own city. Though allowing that the *Messenger* was well received by most editors; that the commendations of the editorial corps "may be valued, because they emanate from sources beyond influence of private friendship"; and adding his own testimony that the criticisms in the *Messenger* "are pithy and often highly judicious," the editor nevertheless remarked that "the editors must remember that it is almost as injudicious to obtain a character for regular cutting and slashing as for indiscriminate laudation."[31]

Poe responded to this "attack" in the columns of the *Daily Compiler* itself: "Your notice of the Messenger would generally be regarded as complimentary—especially so to myself. I would, however, prefer justice to a compliment, and the good name of the Magazine to any personal consideration." He said there was but one editor of the *Messenger:* "It is not right that others should be saddled with demerits belonging only to myself." The point to which he took special objection, however, was that the *Messenger* had obtained a reputation for regular cutting and slashing. Were this statement just, Poe commented, "I would be silent, and set immediately about amending my editorial course. You are not sufficiently decided, I think, in saying that a career of 'regular cutting and slashing is *almost* as bad as one of indiscriminate laudation.' It is infinitely worse—it is horrible. The laudation may proceed from—philanthropy, if you please; but the 'indiscriminate cutting and slashing' only from the vilest passions of our nature." Poe then inventoried his reviews for the period to show that he had not regularly cut and slashed:

Since the commencement of my editorship in December last, 94 books have been reviewed. In 79 of these cases, the commendation has so largely predominated over the few sentences of censure, that every reader would pronounce the notices highly laudatory. In 7 instances [specified] ... praise slightly prevails. In 5 [specified] ... censure is greatly predominant; while the only reviews decidedly and harshly condemnatory are those of Norman Leslie, Paul Ulric, and the Ups and Downs.—The "Ups and Downs" alone is *unexceptionably* condemned. Of these facts you may satisfy yourself at any moment by reference.

Poe continued:

But this charge of indiscriminate "cutting and slashing" has *never been adduced*—except in 4 instances, while the rigid justice and impartiality of our Journal has been lauded even *ad nauseam* in more than four times four hundred. ... The 4 instances to which I allude, are the *Newbern Spectator*, to which thing I replied in July—

31. Aug. 31, 1836, p. 1. For a review of the *Messenger* so favorable that the editor of the *Courier and Daily Compiler* felt called upon in advance to exonerate himself from the charge of puffing, see the July Supplement to the *Messenger*, p. 518.

the *Commercial Advertiser* of Colonel Stone, whose Ups and Downs I had occasion (pardon me) to "use *up*"—the *N. Y. Mirror*, whose Editor's Norman Leslie did not please me—and the *Philadelphia Gazette*, which, being conducted by one of the sub-editors of the Knickerbocker, thinks it his duty to abuse all rival Magazines.

The *Daily Compiler,* hitherto quite sympathetic with the *Messenger,* beat a hasty and rather apologetic retreat: "... we did not mean to assume that the *editor* had *already* obtained 'a character for regular cutting and slashing.' We only *warned* him *against* that unenviable sort of reputation. ... It is not probable we shall ever again disturb the current of laudation, even by a hint. ..."[32] Even Colonel Stone was far from aggressive when, in the *Commercial Advertiser* of September 8, he replied to Poe's remarks in the *Daily Compiler.* Citing the substance of Poe's statement given above, he demurred by saying:

The natural and necessary inference is, that the charge [of cutting and slashing] was brought in the Commercial Advertiser because the editor of the Messenger had had occasion to *"use up"* a volume entitled "Ups and Downs"; this inference involving a charge of personal and interested feelings against one of the editors of the Commercial. The gentleman of the Messenger would have shown more candor if he had stated, as was the fact, that the "charge" was adduced in the Commercial Advertiser, long before "Ups and Downs" was either published or printed. So that if personal feelings had any influence in the matter, it must have been the editor of the Messenger who was governed by them, in his review of "Ups and Downs."

Poe answered neither of these editors, though, if he had been really sincere in setting the record straight, he would have acknowledged the truth of Colonel Stone's statements. Nevertheless, his attitude shows that he was becoming quite sure of himself and of the journalistic value of his critical pen. Alone, he had harried and defied the powerful literary clique of New York and had defended himself against the editorial powers of the South, to emerge triumphant and with reputation. Subscriptions to the *Messenger* were mounting impressively; money was pouring into White's coffers; Poe had made the new Southern monthly a leading national magazine; and accolades

32. Poe's defense and the apology of the editor of the *Daily Compiler* both appeared in the *Courier and Daily Compiler,* Sept. 2, 1836.

from established authors were being showered upon him.[33] Meantime, Poe seems to have assumed an ambivalent attitude toward Fay, mindful that it was his novel that had been the impetus for his editorial success and the stimulus for the hostility against him. This attitude became evident in August, 1836, when Poe, introducing a unique column called "Autography," printed as a last entry the signature of T. S. Fay and commented:

Mr. Fay writes a passable hand. There is a good deal of spirit—and some force. His paper has a clean appearance, and he is scrupulously attentive to his margin. The MS. however, has an air of *swagger* about it. There are too many dashes—and the tails of the long letters are too long. [Mr. Messenger thinks I am right—that Mr. F. shouldn't try to cut a dash—and that *all* his tales are too long. The swagger he says is respectable, and indicates a superfluity of thought.][34]

Hardly by chance, Colonel Stone's autograph immediately preceded Fay's, about which Poe remarked in part: "From the chirography no precise opinion can be had of Mr. Stone's literary style. [Mr. Messenger says no opinion can be had of it in any way.]"

At this time the controversy, marked by such clamorous, if sporadic, violence, came lamely to a halt, if only for want of an adversary. Having defended himself against the *New York Mirror,* the *New York Commercial Advertiser,* the *Knickerbocker* and the *Philadelphia Gazette* (which Poe lumped together, since Willis Clark was co-editor of the *Knickerbocker*), the *Southern Literary Journal,* the *Newbern Spectator,* and the Richmond *Courier and Daily Compiler,* Poe in the September number of the *Messenger* pleaded that "illness of both Pub-

---

33. According to Poe, he began the editorship of the *Messenger* with 700 subscribers, and "the general outcry was that because a Magazine had never succeeded south of the Potomac, therefore a Magazine never could succeed. Yet, in despite of this, and in despite of the wretched taste of its proprietor, which hampered and controlled me at all points, I increased the circulation in fifteen months to 5,500 subscribers paying an annual profit of $10,000 when I left it. This number was never exceeded by the journal, which rapidly went down and may now be said to be extinct" (letter to Charles Anthon written in Oct., 1844). See James A. Harrison, ed., *The Complete Works of Edgar Allan Poe* (New York, 1902), XVII, 177–178, and Ostrom, *Poe's Letters,* I, 269. Killis Campbell in "Contemporary Opinion of Poe," *Publications of the Modern Language Association,* XXXVI (June, 1921), 160–161, states that Poe's boast was valid.

34. *Southern Literary Messenger,* II, 604.

lisher and Editor will, we hope, prove a sufficient apology for the delay in the issue of the present number, and for the omission of many promised notices of new books."[35] October saw no renewal of the quarrel; and in November Poe again wrote that a "press of business ... has prevented us from paying, in this Messenger, the usual attention to our Critical Department."[36] In December the *Messenger* did not appear at all,[37] and the January number contained Poe's brief valedictory: "Mr. Poe's attention being called in another direction, he will decline, with the present number, the Editorial duties of the Messenger. ... With the best wishes to the Magazine, and to its few foes as well as many friends, he is now desirous of bidding all parties a peaceable farewell."[38]

In the atmosphere of such editorial practices as these, Poe's criticisms were written, criticisms sometimes so forthright and often so caustic that he provoked hostility, particularly, as might be expected, in those who were partial to the authors reviewed. Accused of undue severity, Poe was impelled to explain that if he was unkind, it was to perform a great good for American literature. Charged with being dictatorial in his judgments, he was forced to expound the principles on which his judgments rested—statements that became part and parcel of his reviews. Poe himself, standing off in time and space and resurveying that old campaign, tells us the issues for which he fought, even while fighting the same battle on new fields. The occasion was his review of Wilmer's *Quacks of Helicon,* the essence of which has already been quoted:[39]

It is needless to call to mind the desperate case of Fay—a case where the pertinacity to gull, where the obviousness of the attempt at forestalling a judgment, where the wofully over-done be-Mirrorment of that man-of-straw, together with the pitiable platitude of his production, proved a dose somewhat too potent for even the well-prepared stomach of the mob. We say it is supererogatory to dwell upon "Nor-

35. *Ibid.,* II, 668.
36. *Ibid.,* II, 788.
37. White was ill; a printers' strike was on; and White complained of lack of funds (Quinn, *Poe,* 259).
38. III, 72.
39. See chap. i, n. 92.

man Leslie," or other by-gone follies, when we have, before our eyes, hourly instances of the machinations in question. . . .

Whether, when Poe went to New York a month after he left the *Messenger* (February, 1837), the New York clique managed a more insidious revenge upon him for his treatment of *Norman Leslie* (not to mention his other attacks upon books by favored Knickerbocker writers) by preventing his employment on a periodical is still uncertain, however likely. It is known that Poe bore Fay no personal animosity, if it counts for evidence that when he edited *Graham's Magazine* (April, 1841—May, 1842) Fay was represented by a series of papers on Shakespeare. It is also known that he bore no grudge toward Willis or Morris, two of the editors of the *Mirror,* nor they to him, inasmuch as he joined their staff sometime in October, 1844, having previously contributed to it under its new name, the *Evening Mirror* (a daily except Sunday) and to its Saturday supplement, the *Weekly Mirror.*[40] But Poe was to wage continual war with Lewis Gaylord Clark, the editor of the *Knickerbocker* and was to show only contempt for Colonel Stone. In renewing his "Chapter on Autography" for *Graham's Magazine,*[41] Poe recalled that in the *Messenger* days there was "one instance only" that his *jeu d'esprit* was resented: "Colonel Stone and the Messenger had not been on the best of terms. Some one of the Colonel's little brochures had been severely treated by that journal, which declared that the work would have been far more properly published among the quack advertisements in a corner of the Commercial." He added with gross exaggeration, "The colonel had retaliated by wholesale

40. An article that appeared in *Alexander's Weekly Messenger,* with which Poe was connected from Dec., 1839, to May, 1840, and that Clarence S. Brigham in his *Edgar Allan Poe's Contributions to Alexander's Weekly Messenger* (Worcester, Mass., 1943), pp. 19–20, cites and ascribes to Poe, reviewed a number of the *Mirror* in which a "well written critical notice commends, in the highest terms, Mr. Poe's 'Tales of the Grotesque and Arabesque.' " The writer of the article attributed this review "to the pen of General Morris; and it certainly has a double weight in coming from him; for, if we are not mistaken, Mr. Poe evinced much hostility to the 'Mirror' during his editorship of the Southern Literary Messenger. Or, perhaps, his thrusts were aimed only at the author of Norman Leslie?"
41. XIX (Nov., 1841), 224–234.

vituperation of the Messenger." Again in December, 1841, Poe expressed his opinion of Stone, this time more fully:

Colonel Stone, editor of the New York Commercial Advertiser, is remarkable for the great difference which exists between the apparent public opinion respecting his abilities, and the real estimation in which he is privately held. Through his paper, and a bustling activity always prone to thrust itself forward, he has attained an unusual degree of influence in New York, and, not only this, but what appears to be a reputation for talent. But this talent we do not remember ever to have heard assigned him by any honest man's private opinion.... His MS. is heavy and sprawling, resembling his mental character in a species of utter unmeaningness, which lies, like the nightmare, upon his autograph.[42]

Years later, in response to an anonymous writer in the *Mirror,* Poe uttered his last sentiments about *Norman Leslie.* Mr. or Mrs. Asterisk, as Poe called the nameless writer, had argued that Poe "seems to have quite an original and peculiar standard of judging of the merits of men and books. *Success,*" the writer asserted, "is the common measure of talent," whether in literature or business. "We doubt if the copy-right of all Mr. Simms' collected works would bring as good a price in America or England, as the 'Norman Leslie' of Fay, or the 'Sketch Book' of Irving." Poe, after pulverizing the article, concluded: "Putting the author of 'Norman Leslie' by the side of the author of the 'Sketch-Book,' is like speaking of . . . a Mastodon and a mouse. If we were asked which was the most ridiculous book ever written upon the face of the earth— we should answer at once, 'Norman Leslie.' "[43]

It was the *Norman Leslie* incident, then, and the editorial corruption that Poe exposed that led Poe into his fight with the New York coterie and eventually with the Boston clique—a fight that was to be fought openly and in ambush, that was to draw other combatants, and that, finally, was to engage Poe during most of his critical career.

42. *Graham's,* XIX, 274–275. In the same number of *Graham's* (p. 277), Poe again printed the autograph of Fay and referred to *Norman Leslie* as "The Great Used Up."

43. *Broadway Journal,* II (Oct. 11, 1845), 216. *Norman Leslie* made its final appearance in 1869 in a one-volume edition published by G. P. Putnam and Son and re-subtitled, "A New York Story."

3

BEHIND THE
BATTLELINES

The New York Clique

The fact is, some person should write . . . a . . . paper
exposing—*ruthlessly* exposing, the *dessous de cartes*
of our literary affairs. He should show how and why
it is that the ubiquitous quack in letters can always
"succeed," while genius (which implies self-respect,
with a scorn of creeping and crawling,) must inevitably succumb. He should point out the "easy arts" by
which any one base enough to do it, can get himself
placed at the very head of American letters . . .—
Edgar A. Poe

Poe's conduct in the *Norman Leslie* incident was high-
principled and courageous, however arrogant and acidulous he
was on occasion and whatever bid he was making for notoriety.
He recognized the dangers of attacking men who, individually
powerful, were made even more powerful by belonging to
coteries. He certainly knew that Theodore S. Fay—a power
in his own right—was a figurehead of the most formidable
literary clique in America, and that to attack him was to con-
front the phalanx of a group that could destroy his burgeoning
reputation in a matter of months. Not that the coterie was
tightly organized. The membership was a shifting one; there
were too many personal rivalries and affronts, real or imagined,
for any group of writers to maintain perfect solidarity at all

times. Despite this, however, the power a clique could and did wield when it banded together to defend an issue was enormous, as such men as James Fenimore Cooper and James Gordon Bennett discovered.[1]

If Poe had any doubt on this score, he had simply to recall the well-known case of James McHenry, which parallels the *Norman Leslie* affair at every turn and which even involved many of the men who attacked him.

James McHenry (1785–1845) was born in Ireland and came to the United States in 1817. Besides being a practicing physician, he wrote poetry, plays, and novels. He settled at length in Philadelphia, where in 1827 he served as critic for the *American Quarterly Review,* a magazine that came to thrive on provocative criticism, even as the *Southern Literary Messenger* thrived under Poe's editorship. In 1828 McHenry became a naturalized citizen, and in 1842 was appointed to the consulate in Londonderry, Ireland.

Like Poe, McHenry had clashed with the New York clique. In an article called "American Lake Poetry" published anonymously in the *American Quarterly Review* in 1832,[2] McHenry called attention to the fact that American poets were imitating (imitation was a nasty accusation long before Poe took up the charge) the Lake poets, whose influence he considered baneful. Far from being condemned for such imitation, however, McHenry declared, these poets were receiving injudicious praise from "pretended friends and sciolous editors"—an

1. For a detailed and thoroughly documented account of how the coteries operated in the case of Cooper, see Dorothy Waples, *The Whig Myth of James Fenimore Cooper* (New Haven, Conn., 1938). For the so-called Moral War in which the New York papers sought to smash the invincible Bennett and his *New York Herald,* see Don C. Seitz, *James Gordon Bennetts, Father and Son: Proprietors of the New York Herald* (New York, 1928).

2. XI (March, 1832), 154–174. Three of Poe's critical tenets coincide with McHenry's in this article—the first, that the voice of the public is often in direct opposition to critics because of the falsification involved in puffing (p. 156); the second, that a long poem is a contradiction in terms ("In all long poems, there are necessarily occasionally passages which partake in some degree of that abstruse dulness which is characteristic of the Lake poetry. . . . Nor is Paradise Lost, itself, totally exempt from the blemish") (p. 161)—the very example that Poe often used to make the identical point; and the third, an opposition to Wordsworth in particular, a hostility most flagrantly expressed in Poe's "Letter to B—."

"editorial trumpeting" that not only confirmed them in their imitativeness but induced other American poets to follow suit. He criticized these "good-natured editors" for lending their periodicals to this "immoderate trumpeting" from motives of "courtesy" either to the poets themselves or to their publishers. In addition to these "seducers of young poets," McHenry asserted, "there are the hireling puffers, whose business is, for pay, to write commendatory notices and reviews of new books" for the publishers—"easy-conscienced critics" whose purpose is to dupe the public into buying works of the "merest trash."

Having pointed out his objections to the cliques and their tactics, McHenry criticized Nathaniel P. Willis and William Cullen Bryant—the first with savage dispraise and the other with faint praise, incidentally peppering James Gates Percival, another New York favorite, in the process.

This article, like Poe's review of *Norman Leslie,* precipitated violent editorial reaction, with such periodicals as the *Baltimore Gazette,* the *National Gazette,* the *United States Gazette,* the *New York American,* the *Album,* the *New York Mirror,* the *New York Commercial Advertiser,* the *New England Review,* the *New England Magazine,* and the New England *American Monthly Review* becoming embroiled. As with the *Norman Leslie* review, editors seemed to resent both the exposure of their system and the apparent high-handedness of the reviewer. The *New York Commercial Advertiser,* edited by Colonel Stone, observed that the *American Quarterly Review* "might have to cease publication because of the controversy."[3]

McHenry became not only the target of magazine and newspaper editors who attempted to destroy him as a critic, even as Poe became during the *Norman Leslie* incident; he also became the subject of an anonymous satire, just as did Poe. In the same year that McHenry's article appeared, Harpers —the publishers of *Norman Leslie* and the rejecters of Poe's

---

3. Quoted by Robert E. Blanc, *James McHenry (1785–1845): Playwright and Novelist* (Philadelphia, 1939), pp. 94–95. I am indebted to this study for many details concerning Dr. McHenry.

tales—published a two-volume collection of stories by writers who were members of the Knickerbocker group—Catharine M. Sedgwick, James Kirke Paulding, William Cullen Bryant, William Leggett, and Robert C. Sands—called *Tales of Glauber-Spa*. One of the stories written by Sands, a native New Yorker and a member of the staff of Colonel Stone's *Commercial Advertiser*,[4] satirized Dr. McHenry under the sobriquet of Green-Bice, quite like the way Poe was satirized in the *Mirror* article under the name of Bulldog. Lest the reader fail to identify the original of Green-Bice, who is portrayed as a pretentious humbug, McHenry's own words, lifted from his "American Lake Poetry," are echoed.[5] In similar fashion, the original for Bulldog was identified in the *Mirror*.

McHenry's controversy with the New York coterie continues to have its parallels with the *Norman Leslie* incident. The twin brothers Lewis and Willis Gaylord Clark, the latter of whom Poe engaged when defending himself from attack, had hitherto not joined the fray against McHenry, however much they wanted to exterminate him as a critic. Willis Clark, for his part, did not intend to waste his powder in sniping. Rather, he was carefully enlisting his allies so that he could blast McHenry once and for all out of the critical ranks.[6] Once Clark was ready, his brother Lewis identified the character of Green-Bice as McHenry and published in the same number of the *Knickerbocker* Willis Clark's anonymous fourteen-page

4. Identification of Sands as author of the satire appears in the *Knickerbocker*, VII (Jan., 1836), 101: "Poor departed Sands, in the fine portrait which he drew of the author of 'The Antediluvians' [the book-length poem by McHenry], under the similitude of 'Mr. Green Bice' " etc. Sands's affiliation with the *Commercial Advertiser* began in 1827 and ended with his death in Dec., 1832.

5. "But, believe me, Mr. Green," says one of the characters to Green-Bice, "that the injudicious praise which some poets have received from pretended friends and sciolous editors of newspapers have been their great misfortune." To which the silly Mr. Green replies, burlesque-style, "Sci-what?" If this did not serve to identify Green-Bice, Sands noted ironically, "But he is a great writer in one of the leading Reviews . . ." (*Tales of Glauber-Spa* by Several American Authors, New York, 1832, II, 136–138).

6. See Dunlap, *The Clark Letters*, pp. 64–66, 70, for evidence of how Willis Clark proceeded in this effort.

blast at McHenry.[7] In that article, "American Poets and Their Critics," Clark systematically reviled McHenry for his intermittent criticisms of such New York favorites as Washington Irving, Fitz-Greene Halleck, James Gates Percival, and William Cullen Bryant, and asserted that McHenry's own volume of poetry, which had recently been published, contained "more palpable *plagiarisms* [McHenry had charged Bryant and Willis only with imitation] than can be found in any book of its size in Christendom." Despite Willis Clark's disclaiming in that article "every sentiment of unkindness and sinister partiality," his attack was so effective that years later Lewis Clark claimed that "literarily and literally speaking, this paper ["American Poets and Their Critics"] killed the *Quarterly* critic 'very dead' indeed."[8]

All that needs to be added here is that, according to McHenry's biographer, this "killing" article was, with a single exception, a tissue of misrepresentations and lies.[9]

With the difference that Poe survived attack and gave back better than he received, the resemblance of this affair to the *Norman Leslie* incident continues to be noteworthy. Clark's article, although of prohibitive length for republication, was nevertheless reproduced almost *in toto* in the *New York Mirror,* with which, of course, Nathaniel Willis—one of the men whom McHenry had assailed—was associated, and was, in addition, given front-page prominence.[10] With pious satisfaction, the editorial comment subjoined to the reprinted article read: "We believe our readers will coincide in our opinion,

7. The identification of Green-Bice as McHenry appeared in the "Editor's Table" of the *Knickerbocker,* IV (July, 1834), 76–77—a series of disconnected comments which Clark insisted he alone wrote. The blast at McHenry appeared in that same number (pp. 11–24). Lewis Clark years later in the *Knickerbocker,* LIII (April, 1859), 422–423, proudly announced that his brother wrote the attack.

8. *Knickerbocker,* LIII (April, 1859), 422–423. Mott, *American Magazines,* I, 274, corroborates Clark's statement. Willis Clark's article, Mott comments, "pretty effectually finished him [McHenry] as a critic with an audience."

9. Blanc, *McHenry,* pp. 98–99.

10. XII (July 19, 1834), 17–19. The pages of the *Mirror* were numbered serially, beginning with number one in January and July; thus, page 17 of this issue was the front page.

that there is *very little left* of this second McGrawler—this contemporary editor of a contemporary Asinaeum."

McHenry's biographer notes what has been detailed here in earlier chapters, that the storm which McHenry loosed with his attack on a few favorites of the New York clique reflects the temper of literary criticism of the time—the violent sectional antagonisms, the personal malice which vitiated impartiality of criticism, the cavalier resort to invective and lies, and the not at all infrequent use of an ostensibly critical article to assault a critic of an opposing camp.[11]

Familiar as he was with the American literary scene, Poe, at the time at least that he assumed the editorship of the *Southern Literary Messenger,* could scarcely have been unaware of the McHenry incident and of the men who had joined to destroy him as a critic—something that may account in part for his oversensitivity and caustic defensive tactics in the *Norman Leslie* incident. In *Graham's Magazine,* of which he was then editor, Poe had this to say: "Dr. James McHenry, of Philadelphia, is well known to the literary world as the writer of numerous articles in our Reviews and lighter journals, but, more especially, as the author of The Antediluvians, an epic poem which has been the victim of a most shameful cabal in this country...."[12] Poe's allusion to a "most shameful cabal" was directed, of course, at the New York group whose members were continually deriding McHenry through such publications as the *Knickerbocker,* which had recently called *The Antediluvians, or the World Destroyed* a "tuneless abortion."[13] And again in the *Broadway Journal,* of which he was then co-editor, Poe noted on the death of McHenry that he "fell a victim to the arts of a *clique* which proceeded, in the most

11. Blanc, *McHenry,* p. 102.
12. *Graham's Magazine,* XX (Jan., 1842), 48. Earlier, in the same magazine, XVIII (Feb., 1841), 92–93, Poe, in reviewing *The Antediluvians,* had come to the same conclusion regarding that poem as that which appeared in the *Knickerbocker,* XVII (June, 1841), 524–525. Apparently he regretted his remarks concerning that poem because, concurring as they did with the consensus of the New York group, he found himself reinforcing their fire with his own.
13. *Knickerbocker,* XVII, 524.

systematic manner, to write him down—not scrupling, either, to avow the detestable purpose."[14]

Despite his presumed awareness of the McHenry case and his certain knowledge of the retributive power that the New York clique could wield against those who threatened its interests, Poe did not stop with criticizing only one New York favorite. Once he had published his review of *Norman Leslie,* and even while answering his attackers, Poe proceeded to criticize others of that group, notably Fitz-Greene Halleck, a favorite of the New York coterie in general and of the Clark brothers in particular. That Halleck was favored by the Clark brothers is clearly shown by Willis Clark's letter to Halleck dated January, 1836, in which the following passage occurs: "By the way, your work will be handsomely reviewed in the next number of the *American Quarterly,* and the part relating particularly to you will be from my pen, dove-tailed into the rest of the article. . . . I tell you this as a *profound secret,* to be repeated to no one. . . ."[15] Yet, in April, 1836, Poe had asserted in the Drake-Halleck review cited earlier: "Halleck's poetical powers appear to us essentially inferior, upon the whole, to those of his friend Drake. He has written nothing at all comparable to [Drake's] *Bronx.* By the hackneyed phrase, *sportive elegance,* we might possibly designate at once the general character of his writings and the very loftiest praise to which he is justly entitled."[16]

Although Poe's review was well-mannered enough, not to mention brilliant in its analysis of individual poems, it created a disturbance sufficiently great to put Poe on the defensive. The Supplement to the July, 1836, number of the *Messenger* contained Poe's remarks on the "disputed matter of Drake and Halleck," and two quotations, one from a correspondent who rightly thought Poe's "article on Drake and Halleck one of the

14. II (Aug. 23, 1845), 110.
15. Dunlap, *The Clark Letters,* pp. 35–36. Clark took the opportunity in this letter to solicit a poem from Halleck for the *Knickerbocker.*
16. *Southern Literary Messenger,* II (April, 1836), 334, 336. Compare this review with Willis Clark's fulsome review of Halleck's *Alnwick Castle with Other Poems* in the *Knickerbocker,* VII (Jan., 1836), 87.

finest pieces of criticism ever published in this country," the other from Halleck himself who, Poe commented, "since our *abuse* of his book, writes us thus: 'There is no place where I shall be more desirous of seeing my humble writings than in the publication you so ably support and conduct. It is full of ... frank, open, independent manliness of spirit. ...' "[17]

Another member of the New York coterie whom Poe attacked on more than one occasion during and after the *Norman Leslie* affair was the redoubtable Colonel Stone of the *New York Commercial Advertiser*.[18] Stone had antagonized a number of literary figures before he and Poe clashed, among them Bryant, who, in 1831, struck Stone over the head with a whip,[19] and Cooper, who twice sued Stone for libel.[20] How dangerous it was to attack Stone, or any member of the Knickerbocker clique for that matter, and with what alacrity that group went to work to protect its members, is exemplified by the following episode. When the eccentric Laughton Osborn (1809–1878) wrote his *Vision of Rubeta* (1838), a *Dunciad*-like satire of the two leading New York newspaper editors, Stone of the *Commercial Advertiser* and Charles King of the *New York American,* he had to publish his poem anonymously and in Boston, for apparently no New York publisher would accept it. Moreover, in his preface, he defied anyone to discover his identity. When the book appeared, the *New York Mirror* wrote:

"Vision of Rubeta."—What a waste of good paper, ink and type have we here! Four hundred large octavo pages of imbecile, idiotick, and most incomprehensible trash. ... And all this with the sole object apparently of satirizing our friends, Stone of the Commercial Adver-

17. II, 517.
18. "Although Colonel Stone's influence was widely extended throughout the country, yet in New York city was it more particularly felt." William L. Stone, Jr., "The Life and Writings of William Leete Stone" in his edition of *The Life and Times of Sa-Go-Yo-Wat-Ma, or Red Jacket by the Late William L. Stone* (New York, 1866), p. 83. Laughton Osborn, a contemporary of Stone, wrote: "It will hardly be believed, out of New York, that half of the mass of ordinary readers are in the city governed in their literary tastes by such a man of Rubeta [Col. Stone]." *A Vision of Rubeta: An Epic Story of the Island of Manhattan* (Boston, 1838), p. 289.
19. For an eyewitness account, see Bayard Tuckerman, ed., *The Diary of Philip Hone* (New York, 1889), I, 30.
20. William Stone, Jr., "Stone," pp. 77–78.

tiser, and King of the American! The author defies discovery and advises no one to attempt to find him out. The warning is quite supererogatory; for the work will not be remembered a week. ... We advise the author, however, to be careful to preserve his incognito, for if he were known, it would be the duty of the police to provide him with a strait-jacket immediately.[21]

A short time later the *Mirror* carried this item under the heading, *"An injurious rumour contradicted"*: "We are assured that there is no truth whatever in the malicious report that the 'Gingerbreadman' is the author of the 'Vision of Rubeta.' That gentleman disclaims the authorship with becoming indignation."[22]

The person, however, who became the hub of the New York group was Lewis Gaylord Clark, a man with whom Poe contended almost his entire critical career and who had much to do with shaping Poe's reputation. When Clark arrived in New York City in 1833 or 1834, Charles Fenno Hoffman, founder of the *Knickerbocker Magazine* and intimate friend of Colonel Stone and Rufus Wilmot Griswold (destined to become Poe's first "official" biographer and literary executor), introduced him to the literati of the city.[23] Shortly afterward, Clark contributed a story to the *Knickerbocker,* which was immediately accepted,[24] and which, when published, was widely copied.[25] Though copying from magazines, including American ones, was perfectly legitimate at this time and continued to be so until magazine proprietors learned to copyright each number of their periodicals, not infrequently such copying, far from being piracy, was planned in order to give wider circulation to an attack (as, for instance, in the *Mirror's* wholesale copying of Willis Clark's attack on McHenry), or, as seems true

21. XVI (Oct. 27, 1838), 142. Poe had mixed views regarding *A Vision of Rubeta,* to which he frequently alluded. One of his strongest objections was to its "vulgarity and gross personality," which he found inexcusable in a work that called for amused detachment. See *Godey's Lady's Book,* XXXII (June, 1846), 272.

22. XVI (Nov. 13, 1838), 151.

23. Charles Hemstreet, *Literary New York: Its Landmarks and Associations* (New York, 1903), pp. 175–176.

24. "A Contrasted Picture," III (April, 1834), 281–289.

25. Herman E. Spivey, "The Knickerbocker Magazine, 1833–1865: A Study of Its Contents, History, and Significance," unpublished Ph.D. dissertation (University of North Carolina, 1936), p. 21.

in the case of Lewis Clark's story, to create a reputation. The incident is noteworthy because Samuel D. Langtree had replaced Hoffman as editor of the *Knickerbocker* when he resigned that post, and Langtree was the literary editor of Stone's *Commercial Advertiser.*[26]

In May, 1834, a month after his story appeared, Clark and his friend, Clement M. Edson, bought the *Knickerbocker,* and Clark assumed the position of editor. A sure sign of Clark's persistent co-operativeness with the New York literati is the fact that his editorship of the magazine (1834–1861) was one of the longest in periodical history—in fact, almost commensurate with the existence of the *Knickerbocker* itself. It may be supererogatory to add that the *Knickerbocker* in his hands soon became notorious as the "specially appointed guardian of New York reputations."[27] The *New York Mirror,* like many another metropolitan journal, recognized a cohort by praising Clark's first number and continuing to puff succeeding numbers *ad nauseam.*[28]

Once Clark had established himself in New York, he began to make alliances in Boston and Philadelphia, the only other vital spheres of literary influence.[29] He enlisted the services of his twin brother, Willis Clark, who owned and edited the *Philadelphia Gazette,* and those of Longfellow, some of whose relations with Clark were discussed earlier. Willis Clark contributed only poems to the May and June, 1834, numbers of the *Knickerbocker,* but in October of that year his official con-

26. Mott, *American Magazines,* I, 606.
27. *Ibid.,* p. 407. Mott elsewhere notes (p. 610) the conspicuous exceptions Clark made of Cornelius Mathews and his friend, Evert A. Duyckinck, whom Clark consistently attacked.
28. See, for example, the *Mirror,* XI (May 10, 1834), 359; XIII (Aug. 15, 1835), 55; (Aug. 22, 1835), 63; (Dec. 19, 1835), 199; (March 26, 1836), 311; XIV (April 15, 1837), 335. Clark's tastes may be gauged by a contributor to the *Knickerbocker,* one who defended Clark at the same time that he condemned Poe. Mine, he said, "was obvious verse, but it suited Mr. Clark, who was an obvious man, not remarkable, perhaps, for his literary attainments, but knowing what he wanted and what his readers wanted." Stoddard, *Recollections,* pp. 49–50.
29. Poe, in heralding Longstreet's *Georgia Scenes* in the *Southern Literary Messenger,* II (March, 1836), 287, acknowledged that "Thanks to the long indulged literary supineness of the South, her presses are not as apt in putting forth a *saleable* book as her sons are in concocting a wise one."

nection with the magazine was announced.[30] In March, 1835, Willis Clark began a series of monthly articles called "Olla-pondina"—a play on his pen name, Ollapod—that helped to popularize "Old Knick," as it was beginning to be called with punning affection. Needless to say, the magazine under such management consistently puffed members of the coterie, Fay and Stone being only two upon whom such puffs were lavished.[31]

At the time Poe attacked *Norman Leslie*, Lewis Clark had become strongly intrenched among the New York literati, and the *Knickerbocker* was a bulwark probably second only to the Boston *North American Review*, another magazine that inter-mittently became Poe's target in his struggles with the cliques. In combination with the *New York Mirror*, the *Knickerbocker* "refused to exchange" issues of magazines with the *Southern Literary Messenger* "from the first," though such exchange was common practice and expected courtesy among magazine editors, and united as we have seen, "in covert, and therefore unmanly, thrusts at the '*Messenger*' "[32] in retaliation for Poe's attack on Fay.

Lewis Clark could afford to be covert in his attacks on Poe and thereby retain his reputation for good-naturedness, for he had sufficient allies to do his hatchet work for him. Two of his allies, for instance, Willis Clark and Stone, were ap-parently in the habit of combining their forces and their

30. *Knickerbocker,* IV (Oct., 1834), 327.
31. For some mentions of Fay, see *ibid.,* VI (Sept., 1835), 284; (Nov., 1835), 483; VII (March, 1836), 311; etc. For some mentions of Stone, see VI (Aug., 1835), 159–160; VII (May, 1836), 550; X (Nov., 1837), 455; XI (April, 1838), 390; etc. It may be gratuitous to add that the *Mirror* also puffed Stone. See, for example, its review of his *Ups and Downs,* XIII (May 28, 1836), 383. What really provides an index to Stone's influence with the press is the announcement in the *Mirror,* XIII (July 25, 1835), 31, that a two-thousand-copy edition of Stone's *Matthias and His Impostures* had sold out in forty-eight hours and that another printing, this time of ten thousand copies, was being prepared.
32. Poe's charges in the *Southern Literary Messenger,* II (June, 1836), 460. Poe no doubt meant from the first of his acknowledged editorship, which was marked by the publication of the *Norman Leslie* review; for earlier, on July 4, 1835, the *Mirror* (XIII, 6) had written: "We have derived no little gratification from the perusal of the 'Southern Literary Messenger,' published at Richmond, Virginia—and we utter no unmeaning compliment, or mere words, of course, when we say that the present number entitles it to take its stand in the very foremost ranks of our periodical literature."

newspapers to attack an enemy. In the same month that Clark and Stone united to attack Poe, they had, curiously enough, adopted similar tactics to slur the reputation of Willis, one of the editors of the *Mirror*. The *Mirror* retorted in a paragraph titled, *"Slanders of the publick press"*: "Our attention has been called to the following paragraph in a late *Commercial Advertiser* [Stone's journal], copied from the Philadelphia Gazette [Clark's journal]. Its appearance in a respectable paper . . . induces us to take that notice of it, which, from its origin, it would not have merited." The writer then reproduced the original squib which stated that Fay, who had recently been appointed as Secretary of the American Legation in Berlin, could be trusted not to abuse his office as "some of his immediate contemporaries" had done. The writer in the *Mirror* noted that the "allusion which cannot be mistaken" was to Mr. Willis, the only immediate contemporary of Mr. Fay who had filled a similar office abroad, and he proceeded to attack Willis Clark, the originator of the squib, in order "to pluck forth," as he put it, "this reptile to the light."[33]

But there is even more damaging extant evidence of collusion between Clark and Stone. In 1837 Willis Clark wrote the following letter to Stone, from which it may be legitimately inferred that such a combination as instanced both in regard to Willis and Poe was neither their first nor their last:

> Rest assured, in the matter of [C. F.] Durant, and all the others, *I will do the right thing,* and to *your liking.* You must however, give me a little time, and my own way. You shall see, and be pleased. [Willis Clark then asked for a favor in return, which was to have Stone publish in his newspaper a stricture on the *Philadelphia Public Ledger,* a rival of his own newspaper, the *Philadelphia Gazette,* which had been clipped from the *Daily Focus* and to which Clark had written a preface.] I enclose the article . . . and if you will publish it, you will do me a favor I will take all occasions to requite. . . .
>
> I wish you to send me the work on Brandt, and I shall do the Review you speak of, with *pleasure.* . . .

33. XIV (Sept. 24, 1836), 103. This, of course, was precisely the tactic used against Poe after he had reviewed *Norman Leslie.* See the *Commercial Advertiser,* April 12, 1836, p. 1, in which Stone copied Clark's strictures on Poe from his *Gazette* (April 8, 1836) and added his own. By Feb. 25, 1837, Willis Clark wrote Longfellow that Nathaniel "Willis and me have made up. . . ." Dunlap, *The Clark Letters,* p. 38.

By the way, if you have read my art. on Lockhart's Scott in the Q. [*American Quarterly Review*] or on Halleck, and think them worthy, perhaps you can allude to them favorably in the notice which I suppose is yet to be made in the Commercial [Advertiser] of my Ollapod in November's Knickerbocker, or mayhap of my poem in the Rel. Keepsake.

I salute you with my very best regards. If you wish me to give a blow on the head of any one whom you despise and contemn ... my arm and club are *yours.*[34]

The machinations of the New York group inspired several verse satires, two of which have already been mentioned, Osborn's *Vision of Rubeta* and Wilmer's *Quacks of Helicon*. Though both these satires blasted away at essentially the same powers that Poe had bombarded, Poe, when he considered them as poetry, reviewed them harshly. His severest statement labels the *Vision of Rubeta* a "vast gilded swill-trough over-flowing with Dunciad and water,"[35] and, though he confessed that "Mr. Wilmer is a personal friend of our own," he never-theless condemned his poem for "gross obscenity."[36] Yet as contemporary comment these works are revealing, whatever epithets they deserve as poems. Osborn, in the copious notes to his satire, pointed out such collusions as the following:

A long puff of the periodical pamphlet [the *Knickerbocker*] ... was inserted in ... the N. Y. American, (June 30th, 1838) as a com-munication. Nay, the editor of this journal went so far as to preface the matter in these words:—"The Knickerbocker has full *justice* done to all its merits in a *communication* to be found in another place." Now this very communication had appeared a few days be-fore in the *Commercial Advertiser* [of Col. Stone], and, for aught I know to the contrary, in other journals. ... The reader shall judge of the style of this article, which is passed off upon the public ... as a simple literary notice, and one of a fair kind.[37]

Wilmer, a fiery editor who, like Poe, despised cliques and cliquish practices, wrote:

> Say, ye concoctors of diurnal news,
> Ye greater far, the Quarterly Reviews;
> Ye Monthlies, high on the tribunals raised;—
> Say, on what system are your bards beprais'd?
> . . . .

34. Dunlap, *The Clark Letters*, pp. 68–69.
35. *Southern Literary Messenger*, XV (March, 1849), 189.
36. *Graham's Magazine*, XIX (Aug., 1841), 90.
37. *Vision of Rubeta* (Boston, 1838), p. 373.

Some of your bright fraternity are found
With ivy wreaths ridiculously crown'd,
And joined in cliques, reciprocally give
The lying praise in which your glories live.
M-rr-s, delivered of a song, shall get
A puff grandiloquent in C—k's Gazette.

. . . .
And, not ungrateful, M-rr-s shall maintain
That C—k displays the true Pindaric vein.

. . . .
Woe to you scribes! who make the veriest clod,
The most insensate thing of earth,—a god!

. . . .
And still unblushing adoration pay
To puling W-ll-s and inebriate F-y! [38]

It is clear, then, that Poe was aware that he was facing a powerful clique when he criticized, among other works, Fay's *Norman Leslie,* Stone's *Ups and Downs,* and Halleck's *Alnwick Castle* during his brief career on the *Messenger.*

Poe, of course, did not spend all his editorial time on the *Messenger* bombarding the New York clique. Nevertheless, in his analyses of books stemming from whatever quarter of America, he made it a point to articulate the principles he indorsed and to censure practices antagonistic to the emergence of a genuine American literature. Months before he had attacked *Norman Leslie* and even before he had definitely established himself as editor of the *Messenger,* he derided puffing: "If half the praise be due, which is lavished on the works that daily issue from the press, we may live to see the writings which instructed and delighted our youth, laid on the same shelf with Thomas Aquinas and Duns Scotus." As

38. Those referred to in this poem are, of course, George Pope Morris (1802–1864), then principal editor of the *New York Mirror,* whom Poe praised as "our best writer of songs" in *Burton's Gentleman's Magazine,* V (Dec., 1839), 332–333, and whose popularity was not "altogether attributable to his editorial influence," whatever "his enemies would fain make us believe," he added in *Graham's Magazine,* XIX (Dec., 1841), 277; Willis Gaylord Clark (1808–1841), then editor of the *Philadelphia Gazette* and co-editor of the *Knickerbocker,* whom Poe described as "the first of our Philadelphia poets" in *ibid.,* p. 274, despite earlier editorial clashes with him and his brother; Nathaniel Parker Willis (1806–1867), the most successful magazinist of his time and then an editor of the *Mirror,* whom Poe consistently praised as a tale writer; and Theodore Sedgwick Fay (1807–1898), whom we have already discussed sufficiently. It was such "personalities" (to use the contemporary word) as *inebriate* Fay that caused Poe to brand the poem as gross obscenity.

for himself, "we never expect to travel as caterers for a public journal."[39] He objected, as we have seen, to any form of chicanery in gaining a reputation. In reviewing, for instance, the prolific Lydia Huntley Sigourney, he said: "It would be an easy, although perhaps a somewhat disagreeable task, to point out several of the most popular writers in America ... who have manufactured for themselves a celebrity by ... very questionable means"; that though Mrs. Sigourney "does not *owe* her reputation to ... chicanery ... it cannot be denied that it has been thereby greatly assisted"; and that inquiry into her real merits shows that she had acquired the title of the "American Hemans" "*solely by imitation*" of that English poet.[40] He rebuked publishers not only for tolerating poor typography, miserable paper, and slipshod misprints (at the same time lauding those publishers who did respectable print jobs), but also for publishing worthless manuscripts. Of the novel *Paul Ulric,* he said: "In itself, the book before us is too purely imbecile to merit an extended critique—but as a portion of our daily literary food—as an American work published by the Harpers—as one of a class of absurdities with an inundation of which our country is grievously threatened—we shall have no hesitation, and shall spare no pains, in exposing fully before the public eye its four hundred and forty-three pages of utter folly, bombast, and inanity." His elaborate examination of the novel revealed unquestionable plagiarism from Isaac Disraeli's *Curiosities of Literature* (five series, 1791–1834). Clearly, Poe remarked ironically, Disraeli was "one of the most scoundrelly plagiarists in Christendom. He had not scrupled to steal entire passages verbatim from Paul Ulric!" The author of *Paul Ulric,* Poe continued, had even transcribed typographical errors from his source. He concluded: "In summing up an opinion of Paul Ulric, it is by no means our intention to mince the matter at all. The book is despicable in every

39. *Southern Literary Messenger,* I (May, 1835), 521. This and the quotations or summaries that follow are merely offered as specimens; such statements permeate his criticism, whether that written for the *Messenger* or for other magazines.
40. *Ibid.,* II (Jan., 1836), 112.

respect. Such are the works which bring daily discredit upon
our national literature. We have no right to complain of being laughed at abroad when so villainous a compound ... of
incongruous folly, plagiarism, immorality, inanity, and bombast, can command at any moment both a puff and a publisher." [41]

In another review he urged that authors who possess talent
should "either think it necessary to bestow a somewhat greater
degree of labor and attention upon the composition of their
novels, or otherwise ... *not* think it necessary to compose
them at all."[42] In still another review, he asked: "When
shall the artist assume his proper situation in society ... ?
How long shall the veriest vermin of the Earth, who crawl
around the altar of Mammon, be more esteemed of men than
they, the gifted ministers to those exalted emotions which link
us with the mysteries of Heaven? To our own query we may
venture a reply. Not long." He added, with what may be an
allusion to his own crusading activities: "A spirit is already
abroad at war with it."[43] He decried American imitations of
the "Ratcliffe [*sic*] dynasty, the Edgeworth dynasty, and [par-
ticularly of] the Scott dynasty" and those who "study, as at
a glass, to make themselves like him, as if ambitious to display their thefts."[44] And, in a subsequent review, he said of
Robert M. Bird's *Hawks of Hawk-Hollow* that, had the novel
reached him some years ago, and had the title page borne the
statement, *"A Romance by the author of Waverley,"* he would
have noted, "It is unnecessary to tell us that this novel is written by Sir Walter Scott; and we are really glad that he has at
length ventured to turn his attention to American incidents,
scenery, and manners." And then, in a mock sigh: "But alas!
for our critical independency ... Robert M. Bird is an
American."[45] In similar blunt terms he said that for "unde-
filed, vigorous, and masculine prose," Robert Southey was

41. *Ibid.*, II (Feb., 1836), 173–180. *Paul Ulric* was favorably noticed in the
Knickerbocker, V (Dec., 1835), 569.
42. *Southern Literary Messenger,* II (Aug., 1836), 596.
43. *Ibid.*, II (Feb., 1836), 195.
44. *Ibid.*, I (May, 1835), 520.
45. *Ibid.*, II (Dec., 1835), 43–44.

Irving's superior, despite the views of Alexander Hill Everett, then editor of the *North American Review*. "In saying thus much we do not fear being accused of a deficiency in patriotic feeling. No true—we mean no sensible American will like a bad book the better for being American," nor dislike a good one because it is written by an alien.[46]

Aside from such statements, Poe presented models of criticism in his own critiques. Years later he asked, "What American ... thinks of making his critique a work of art in itself?"[47] Could he have violated editorial modesty, he might, of course, have less subtly suggested himself, for some of his criticisms written during the *Messenger* period, as many of his later ones, are models of literary analysis. Even his subjective criticism of Marvell's "Nymph Complaining for the Death of Her Fawn" is a classic of its kind.[48] Moreover, while he dutifully gibbeted literary charlatans and incompetents, he also did the far more agreeable work of heralding Augustus Baldwin Longstreet, Dickens, and Hawthorne on the threshold of their careers and paying homage to Keats, Shelley, and Coleridge at the end of theirs.

Much of Poe's criticism during his editorship of the *Messenger*, then, was written in opposition to the New York coterie or to the principles which it, in common with other groups, kept trumpeting, which made his remarks harsher than they might otherwise have been. Those principles sounded respectable, for they were designed to foster a national literature, which was the concern of every American writer. First, the group clamored in their editorials for an international copyright law which would prevent American publishers from reprinting foreign books and thereby inhibit them from discriminating against native works. Second, they opposed harsh criticism of American writers, and even argued for critical indulgence of their books as a kind of patriotic duty in encouraging an American literature. Yet, in practicing these basic

46. *Ibid.*, I (Sept., 1835), 780, and II (Dec., 1835), 64.
47. *Broadway Journal*, I (June 7, 1845), 354–357.
48. *Southern Literary Messenger*, II (Aug., 1836), 586.

principles, this clique, like others, became involved in serious contradictions. Though calling for an international copyright law, for instance, members of the clique often engaged in literary piracy themselves, the practice they loudly denounced. The profit to be gained from republishing foreign materials was simply too great a temptation to resist, whether one was a publisher, an editor, or a writer. Rufus Wilmot Griswold (1815–1857),[49] for example, passed himself off as an advocate of international copyright law, yet plundered literary works wholesale as co-editor of *Brother Jonathan* and as an anthologist.[50] Worse still, he seems to have stolen some books outright. As an avowed enemy of Griswold pointed out publicly,[51] Griswold, "who denounces ... our Congress for not protecting the works of authors, has himself taken D'Israeli's Curiosities of Literature, and tacking on a few 'American Curiosities,' so as to usurp the English edition in the American market, issued it with his name on the title page." Nor was this his only theft, his accuser asserted. He had seized a book entitled "Sacred Poetry of England" that was issued in England and "by a few additions ... publishes it as his own. He takes advan-

49. Griswold's alliance with the New York coterie was subsequent to the *Norman Leslie* episode. Throughout this study I shall indicate how Griswold's connection with the clique resulted in the kind of vindictive obituary he wrote two days following Poe's death (*New York Tribune*, Oct. 9, 1849) under the pseudonym of Ludwig and in the kind of defamatory memoir he prefixed to his edition of Poe's *Literati* (1850) under his own name, a part of both memoirs being lifted with only the slightest alterations from Bulwer's characterization of the reprobate Francis Vivian in *The Caxtons* (Part Eighth, chap. iii) that had been published in 1849. For the moment it will suffice to mention that Lewis Clark said of Griswold: ". . . we have known him . . . for nearly the entire period of our connection with the *Knickerbocker*" (*Knickerbocker*, XLVI, Oct., 1855, 398), and that Griswold's biographer notes that in Sept., 1841, he "tried to work out a scheme whereby he could do his work in New York, combining it with an associate editorship of the *Knickerbocker Magazine,* which Lewis Gaylord Clark led him to expect" (Joy Bayless, *Rufus Wilmot Griswold: Poe's Literary Executor,* Nashville, Tenn., 1943, p. 265 n. 84).

50. See Mott, *American Magazines,* I, 359, and Miller, *Raven and the Whale,* p. 169.

51. Joel T. Headley, "The Prose Writers of America," a review of Griswold's anthology of the same title, in *Miscellanies* (New York, 1850), p. 296. This article is republished from a magazine which I have not located. Poe's funniest, if one of his most atomizing reviews, written in the tradition of Macaulay's essay on Robert Montgomery and Mark Twain's "Fenimore Cooper's Literary Offenses," satirized Headley's *Sacred Mountains.* See the *Southern Literary Messenger,* XVI (Oct., 1850), 608–610, where it appeared posthumously. Clark, as might be expected, puffed Griswold's version of the *Curiosities* in the *Knickerbocker,* XXIII (May, 1844), 490–492, as he did all his works.

tage of a state of things which he declares to be 'immoral, unjust, and wicked,' and even while haranguing the loudest, is purloining the fastest." Griswold, moreover, had no hesitation in disgracing Cornelius Mathews, perhaps the warmest of all proponents of international copyright, largely because Mathews was cordially detested by the Knickerbocker group in general and by Lewis Clark in particular.[52]

Though the coterie in New York, not to mention those in Boston and Philadelphia, also called for a national literature, its members tended to be sectionalists and were continually accused of sectional bias by Southern and Western journals. Sectionalism was the inevitable tendency of the striving for fame and the struggle for sales of books and magazines in an extremely competitive market; and such accusations and counter-accusations only served to intensify sectional loyalties.

Again, since the coteries professed to favor native literary works, they felt bound to retaliate upon a critic such as Poe or McHenry or Simms who criticized an author of their set. Characteristically, retaliation took the form of an attack upon the critic's character or upon his books. These being American works, the cliques found themselves, not uncomfortably it would seem, in the paradoxical position of attacking American works in order to defend American works.

Finally, the mutual puffing by members of a clique on the principle that they were encouraging a native literature was bound to provoke reaction, if only because they tended to subject the works of outsiders to silence or abuse. When critics such as Poe exposed the more outrageous instances of this practice, as in the case of *Norman Leslie,* and urged that the practice be stopped entirely as inimical to an American literature, all that such exposés and exhortations accomplished was to make the clique more clannish, to confirm its members in their sectional loyalties and their hostility to outsiders, and to inspire them to even windier puffing to counteract the damage that might have been done.

52. One of Griswold's attacks was so bitter that Duyckinck, Mathews' friend, took Griswold to task for it in the *Literary World,* I (March 20, 1847), 150.

Once Poe recognized the enemy of a self-supporting, self-respecting authorship—an enemy whose banner was nationalism, whose power derived from cliques, and whose weapons were the adulatory review for those in favor and silence or the abusive review for those out of favor—Poe assailed it whenever he could, whether by exposing cliquism as a racket or by assaulting those who were implicated in the cliques. To this end he mustered all the methods of the critical art, from Wilson's tomahawk attack, to Macaulay's point-by-point bombardment that pulverizes a work, to Coleridge's examination of the philosophic bases upon which to ground his criticism.[53]

The publication of *Norman Leslie* concurrent with his first editorship provided Poe with his initial opportunity to engage the New York clique in a battle royal—to state his objections to cliquism, to gibbet a few members of the clique, and to test the strengths and weaknesses of his methods. From this battle he emerged victorious but with a reputation for caustic candor unique in America until Mencken appeared on the literary scene. This reputation was sufficient to make the Knickerbocker group chary—so much so, in fact, that when he mounted his second major attack upon that clique (represented by his review of Wilmer's blast at the New York coterie), the clique apparently felt that the best response was silence. But whatever the response, Poe continued to assail the New York group (peppering the Boston clique in the meanwhile) and the corruption it was encouraging in all areas of authorship, whether in publishing, merchandising, or reviewing. Again and again, however unsuccessful were his efforts, Poe struggled to reform

53. Though Poe admired John Wilson's "moral courage" which expressed itself in his criticism, according to Poe, as "sheer audacity," he charged him with making literary judgments without the benefit of analysis (". . . there has been no period at which he ever *demonstrated* anything beyond his own utter incapacity for demonstration"), something that Poe at his best avoided in his own critical articles, but of which he was sometimes guilty. (See the *Broadway Journal*, II, Sept. 6, 1845, 136.) For Macaulay as critic, Poe also had mixed admiration: he disliked his sophistry but warmly approved his manner. (See, for instance, *Graham's Magazine*, XXXVI, Jan., 1850, 49–51.) For Coleridge as literary theoretician and poet, though he caviled at times with his distinction between the Fancy and Imagination, had only the highest respect. (See among his other notices of Coleridge, *Southern Literary Messenger*, II, June, 1836, 451–453; *Burton's Gentleman's Magazine*, VI, Jan., 1840, 53–58; and *Graham's Magazine*, XXV, March, 1844, 137.)

a practice that, as it stood, militated in favor of certain authors and against others, not so much on the grounds of literary merit as on the adventitiousness of geographical location and editorial connections, not so much on the basis of creative ability as on the talent to truckle and conspire.

That in an age of underhanded publishing and journalistic tactics—of anonymous reviewing, critical collusion, and vicious gossip originated or at least exaggerated and disseminated by cliques—Poe was not silenced by the coteries as McHenry had been is astonishing. That he survived as a writer and for short periods even flourished as an editor is almost incredible. Besides planning several magazines that failed to materialize, he managed somehow to contribute to more than fifty known periodicals, annuals, and daily papers, and to help edit five journals in a space of little more than ten years (1835–1845), one of which (if we ignore the success of the *Southern Literary Messenger*) he brought to a position of leadership—namely, *Graham's Magazine*.[54]

The upshot of Poe's continual attacks upon the New York and, later, the Boston cliques was the formation of a loose alliance against him, an alliance that was to hound him during his life and even after his death, and that did much to create the Poe myth.

It was characteristic of the editorial hypocrisy that flourished during Poe's lifetime that the *New York Mirror*, guilty of every charge Gould had made, should print Gould's lecture ("American Criticism on American Literature") in two instalments and even feature it on its front pages. An even greater travesty was that the number of the *Mirror* containing the first instalment of Gould's lecture should also contain Fay's lampoon of Poe, "THE SUCCESSFUL NOVEL!!"[55]

One quotation should indicate the kind of reputation Poe was earning by his critical candor, and that any independent and even less plain-spoken critic of the period was bound to

54. See Heartman and Canny, *Poe Bibliography*, p. 139.
55. Kendall B. Taft (*Minor Knickerbockers: Representative Selections*, New York, 1947, p. 398) identifies Fay as the author of the lampoon.

earn. Park Benjamin, whom his biographer calls "one of the most feared of critics,"[56] had this to say in Greeley's *New Yorker*:

> Our critical journals are brought into contempt abroad by the superlative tone which they always assume in praise or condemnation. There seems to be no proper mean, no *juste milieu* to our criticism. A book is either the most magnificent production of the age, or it is the wretchedest stuff that ever proceeded from the brain of a miserable driveler.... Their object seems to be that of promoting the sale of a book.... They seem never to imagine that they are making themselves and the author supremely ridiculous....
>
> We could adduce several amusing instances of this species of criticism; but the truth of our observation is so apparent, that the corroboration of examples would be superfluous.... The system, if pursued, will be ruinous to our literature.
>
> Few critics have the temerity to express their real opinions, even if they are willing to be troubled with forming any. Should they do so, they are well aware that they will receive what, in vulgar parlance, is called 'more kicks than coppers.' All kinds of disingenuous feelings and motives are attributed to the man who dares to speak the truth. He is envious; he is malignant; he wishes to ruin another; he looks at objects through a distorted medium; he has become disgusted with the world, and seeks revenge in abuse; he has a sour, crabbid [*sic*] disposition; he breakfasts upon tomahawks and dines upon cross-cut saws. Such are the gentle observations, with which fairness and boldness in criticism are met.[57]

And such we know, with what justice is yet to be determined, were the observations made of Poe.

56. Merle M. Hoover, *Park Benjamin: Poet & Editor* (New York, 1948), p. 189. In *Graham's Magazine*, XIX (Nov., 1841), 226, Poe observed that Benjamin "exerted an influence scarcely second to that of any editor in this country."

57. VII (April 6, 1839), 45.

4

THE ANATOMY OF A CAMPAIGN

Poe and Lewis Gaylord Clark

One or two years, since elapsed, may have mellowed down the petulance, without interfering with the rigor of the critic. Most surely they have not yet taught him to read through the medium of a publisher's interest, nor convinced him of the impolicy of speaking the truth.——*Edgar A. Poe*

The battle between Poe and Lewis Gaylord Clark constitutes a campaign that can be isolated from the melee and studied almost clinically. Poe and Clark crossed swords time and time again in journals, in the form of defamatory and derisive articles. These articles, culled from those periodicals and arranged chronologically, serve to document the shifting fortunes of their quarrel. More important, they reveal for what reasons and under what circumstances Poe became one of the most maligned persons in literary history.

Not that some of the charges leveled against Poe were baseless. Poe in his letters, both private and public, stands self-confessed as an unstable person and an occasional drunkard. But Clark and his friends did not proclaim Poe's faults, nor exaggerate them, nor ascribe to him vices of which he was guiltless, nor hint at unmentionable acts of wickedness, until Poe singled them out for attack.

Clark, as will be seen, enjoyed a singular advantage over
Poe: he had his own magazine, the *Knickerbocker*, which was
widely circulated, whereas Poe had to take his stand wherever
opportunity afforded. And if Clark was not altogether a com-
batant worthy of Poe's mettle, he had more than enough allies
to make up the difference.

Even as Rufus Wilmot Griswold was Poe's posthumous
nemesis,[1] Clark was Poe's contemporary one. The reasons for
Clark's consistent baiting of and hostility toward Poe are not
obscure, as some writers believe; they are simply numerous.

First, as we have said, Clark was the self-appointed protector of New York reputations, and Poe's assaults upon the
works of members of his clique were enough to antagonize him.
Second, being the pivot of the New York group, Clark tended to
be a sectionalist and to favor only New York writers, although
he did not discriminate against such New Englanders as Longfellow when they proved serviceable to him. Clark's hostile
treatment of one Southerner, William Gilmore Simms, to cite
only one instance, became so notorious that one writer, signing
himself "S. T.," blasted the *Knickerbocker* on this score from
three separate journals.[2] And Simms's own letters are full of
such statements as: "Clarke [*sic*] is a creature to be kicked
or spit upon not argued with or spoken to," and, "Had I been
living in N. Y. I could not have refrained, long ago, to have
scourged him hip & thigh for the scoundrel & puppy that he
is."[3] On the grounds of such sectionalism, perhaps aggravated
by the fear of rivalry, can Poe's remark be explained, that the
Knickerbocker "refused to exchange with us [the *Southern
Literary Messenger*] from the first."[4]

1. See Killis Campbell, "The Poe-Griswold Controversy," in *The Mind of
Poe and Other Studies* (Cambridge, Mass., 1933), pp. 63–98.
2. The article first appeared in the *New York Evening Mirror*, III (Nov. 7,
1845), and was reprinted in the *New York Weekly Mirror*, III (Nov. 15, 1845),
96, as well as in part or in whole in *Godey's Lady's Book*, XXXII (May, 1846),
240, and in the New York *Morning News*, Nov. 8, 1845. The writer has been
identified as Evert A. Duyckinck, a friend of Simms, by Mary C. Simms
Oliphant *et al.*, eds., *The Letters of William Gilmore Simms* (Columbia, S. C.,
1953), II, 114 n. 338.
3. *Ibid.*, pp. 115, 117. Both letters are dated Nov. 13, 1845.
4. *Southern Literary Messenger*, II (June, 1836), 460.

Third, Clark's twin brother Willis, co-editor of the *Knicker-bocker*, had attacked Poe on more than one occasion, as we have seen, and it was only natural, perhaps, that Lewis Clark should bombard the same target.

A fourth, if less likely, reason for the mutual antagonism between Poe and Lewis Clark "may have been partly due to the latter's role in the 'Moon Hoax.' "[5] Poe had hoaxed the country with his "Hans Phaall—a Tale," which was published in the June, 1835, number of the *Southern Literary Messenger*. A similar hoax was perpetrated only a few weeks later in New York. As a contemporary reported the incident:

The chief perpetrator was a . . . young Englishman named Richard Adams Locke who . . . was then editor of the *Sun* newspaper, in the columns of which it appeared, credited to a supplement of the Edinburgh *Philosophical Journal*. . . .

It was a pretended account of wonderful discoveries on the surface of the earth's satellite made by Sir John F. W. Herschel at the Cape of Good Hope, by means of a newly-constructed telescope. . . .

The newspapers throughout the country copied the article and commented on it. Some dishonestly withheld credit to the *Sun*, leaving the inference that they had taken it from the famous "supplement." The more stately newspapers—the "respectable weeklies"—were thoroughly hoaxed. The New York *Daily Advertiser* . . . said that "Sir John had added a stock of knowledge to the present age that will immortalize his name and place it high on the page of science." The Albany *Daily Advertiser* read "with unspeakable emotions of pleasure and astonishment an article from the last Edinburgh *Philosophical Journal*. . . ." Some of the grave religious journals made the great discovery a subject for pointed homilies. . . .

In a few days the story was discovered to be a pure fiction. Locke had . . . engaged in preparing the "Moon Hoax" . . . for the purpose of testing the extent of public credulity. It was a successful experiment. . . .

What our contemporary narrator calls "the secret history" of the "Moon Hoax" has possible bearing on the antagonism between Poe and Lewis Clark:

Mr. Moses Y. Beach had recently become sole proprietor of the *Sun*, and Richard Adams Locke was the editor. It was desirable to have some new and startling features to increase its popularity, and Locke for a consideration proposed to prepare for it a work of fiction. To

5. T. O. Mabbott's suggestion in Dunlap, *The Clark Letters*, p. 16 n. 108.

this proposal Mr. Beach agreed. Locke consulted Lewis Gaylord Clark, the editor of the *Knickerbocker Magazine,* as to the subject. The Edinburgh *Scientific Journal* was then busied with Herschel's astronomical explorations at the Cape of Good Hope, and Clark proposed to make these the basis of the story. It was done. Clark was the real inventor of the incidents, the imaginative part, while to Locke was intrusted the ingenious task of unfolding the discoveries.[6]

In regard to this hoax, Poe wrote his friend, John P. Kennedy, on September 11, 1835:

Have you seen the "Discoveries in the Moon"? Do you not think it altogether suggested by *Hans Phaal?* It is very singular,—but when I first purposed writing a Tale concerning the Moon, the idea of *Telescopic* discoveries suggested itself to me—but I afterwards abandoned it. I had however spoken of it freely, & from many little incidents & apparently trivial remarks in those *Discoveries* I am convinced that the idea was stolen from myself.[7]

As late as 1846 Poe publicly repeated these charges and amplified them:

It was three weeks after the issue of "The Messenger" containing "Hans Phaall" that the first of the "Moon-Hoax" editorials made its appearance in "The Sun," and no sooner had I seen the paper than I understood the jest, which not for a moment could I doubt had been suggested by my own *jeu d'esprit.* Some of the New York journals ... saw the matter in the same light, and published the "Moon Story" side by side with "Hans Phaall," thinking that the author of the one had been detected in the author of the other.

Poe then stated that he was "bound to do Mr. Locke the justice to say that he denies having seen my article prior to the publication of his own; and I am bound to add, also, that I believe him." Unfortunately, however, "Having read the Moon story to an end and found it anticipative of all the main points of my 'Hans Phaall,' I suffered the latter to remain unfinished." [8] Clark and Poe may have become antagonistic on this account, the former because Poe suggested plagiarism in the "Moon Hoax," which Clark had had a hand in perpetrating; the latter because he had been despoiled of his idea.

Whatever the background of the animosity between Poe and Clark, it was Poe's repeated bombardment of the New

---

6. Benson J. Lossing (1813–1891), *History of New York City* (New York, 1884), pp. 360–362.

7. Ostrom, *Poe's Letters,* I, 74. Poe was not consistent in his spelling of "Phaall."

8. *Godey's Lady's Book,* XXXIII (Oct., 1846), 159–162.

York coterie that finally caused Clark to cease his sniping at Poe and to open fire at him with everything in his arsenal. Poe seemed to consider Clark and his antics contemptible and noticed him only occasionally. Nevertheless, Clark grew more and more vituperative, and it is not too much to say that the reverberations of his charges are still echoing.

Sniping began on August, 1838. The May, 1837, issue of the *Knickerbocker* had carried Harpers' announcement of the publication of Poe's *Narrative of Arthur Gordon Pym*,[9] and Lewis Clark's review of the novel duly appeared fifteen months later. Clark began by reprinting the long title, making certain to italicize the word *incredible* in the phrase, "together with the incredible adventures and discoveries ... to which that distressing calamity gave rise," then remarked:

There are a great many tough stories in this book, told in a loose and slip-shod style, seldom chequered by any of the more common graces of composition, beyond a Robinson Crusoe-ish sort of simplicity of narration. This work is one of much interest, with all its defects, not the least of which is, that it is too liberally stuffed with 'horrid circumstances of blood and battle.' We would not be so uncourteous as to insinuate a doubt of Mr. Pym's veracity, now that he *lies* 'under the sod;' but we should very much question that gentleman's word, who should affirm, after having thoroughly perused the volume before us, that he *believed* the various adventures and hairbreadth 'scapes therein recorded.[10]

That Clark, in dealing with an imaginative story, should dwell upon "Mr. Pym's veracity" is ironic. The same irony was involved in Clark's questioning the veracity of Herman Melville's *Typee* (1846), a novel that by and large was founded on fact.[11]

Despite Lewis Clark's boast to Longfellow at the time that *Outre-Mer* was in production, that Harpers "tell me, that they can lose on *no* book, now—even the *worst*,"[12] such reviews[13]

9. *Knickerbocker*, IX, 529.

10. *Ibid.*, XII (Aug., 1838), 167.

11. *Ibid.*, XXVII (May, 1846), 450.

12. In a letter dated Nov. 2, 1834 (Dunlap, *The Clark Letters*, p. 83). William Gowans, a man who became a distinguished bookseller, bears out Clark's statement. He wrote that *Pym* "was the most unsuccessful of all his writings, although published by the influential house of Harper & Brothers, who have the means of distributing a single edition of any book in one week" (quoted by Quinn, *Poe*, p. 267).

13. See the *New York Mirror*, XVI (Aug. 11, 1838), 55, for a curiously similar review.

made this Harpers' book sell "less than a thousand copies."[14] In England, however, where no clique militated against the book, the "authorized" edition of *Pym* appears to have been successful, if the fact that the work was pirated is indicative of success.[15]

In December, 1839, the *Knickerbocker* carried this announcement: "Notices of the following works, although in type, are unavoidably postponed till our next number: ... Tales [of the Grotesque and Arabesque] by E. A. Poe. ..."[16] But the promised notice, "although in type," never appeared. Instead, Clark, in reviewing a number of *Burton's Gentleman's Magazine,* made it a point to indicate that the "Journal of Julius Rodman," which had been appearing serially in that magazine since January, 1840, was another fabrication like *Pym.*[17]

In June, 1840, Poe began circulating his "Prospectus of the Penn Magazine, a Monthly Literary Journal, To Be Edited and Published in the City of Philadelphia, by Edgar A. Poe." In this prospectus he stated the critical principles he intended to observe in the projected magazine, a statement that reveals mature self-examination:

To those who remember the early years of The Messenger, it will be scarcely necessary to say that its main feature was a somewhat overdone causticity in the department of Critical Notices. The Penn Magazine will retain this trait of severity in so much only as the calmest and sternest sense of literary justice will permit. One or two years, since elapsed, may have mellowed down the petulance, without interfering with the rigor of the critic. Most surely they have not

14. William F. Gill, *The Life of Edgar Allan Poe* (New York, 1877), p. 86.
15. According to Heartman and Canny, *Poe Bibliography,* pp. 39–40, Wiley and Putnam issued the volume in London in 1838 and a third edition—this one pirated—appeared in London in 1841 (not to mention numerous pirated editions that appeared subsequent to Poe's death). Judging from the remarks of another zealous bibliographer of Poe, who published his *Edgar A. Poe: A Study* (San Francisco, 1921) privately and anonymously, the first London edition of *Pym,* a mutilated version, appears to have been authorized by Harpers (or else Harpers sold the right to Wiley and Putnam), since that edition appeared "simultaneously" with the Harpers' edition to protect the work under British copyright law. Contrast these statements with this of Griswold in his Memoir to Poe's *Literati,* p. xv: "The publishers sent one hundred copies to England, and being mistaken at first for a narrative of real experiences, it was advertised to be reprinted, but a discovery of its character, I believe, prevented such a result."
16. *Knickerbocker,* XIV, 564.
17. *Ibid.,* XV (April, 1840), 359.

yet taught him to read through the medium of a publisher's interest, nor convinced him of the impolicy of speaking the truth. It shall be the first and chief purpose of the Magazine now proposed, to become known as one where may be found, at all times, and upon all subjects, an honest and fearless opinion. This is a purpose of which no man need be ashamed. It is one, moreover, whose novelty at least will give it interest.[18]

Turning to another matter, Poe wrote: "To the mechanical execution of the work the greatest attention will be given. . . . In this respect, it is proposed to surpass, by very much, the ordinary Magazine style. The form will nearly resemble that of The Knickerbocker. The paper will be equal to that of The North American Review." Clearly, Poe intended to compete with the two magazines he contemned, magazines that represented the two most powerful literary cliques then operating in America and in whose pages he refused to compromise himself by appearing.[19] Another reason Poe had for singling out the *Knickerbocker* and the *North American Review* may be explained by his remarks in a subsequent prospectus issued August, 1840, in which, reiterating what he had said earlier, he added:

It shall be a leading object to assert precept, and to maintain in practice the rights, while in effect it demonstrates the advantages, of an absolutely independent criticism—a criticism self-sustained; guiding itself only by the purest rules of Art; analyzing and urging these rules as it applies them; holding itself aloof from all personal bias; acknowledging no fear save that of outraging the right; yielding no point either to the vanity of the author, or to the assumptions of antique prejudice, or of the involute and anonymous cant of the Quarterlies, or to the arrogance of those organized *cliques* which, hanging like nightmares upon American literature, manufacture at the nod of our principal booksellers, a pseudo-public opinion by wholesale.[20]

Clark, when news reached him that William E. Burton had put up his *Gentleman's Magazine* for sale, used his chance to

---

18. Heartman and Canny, *Poe Bibliography,* pp. 54–55.
19. In *Doings of Gotham,* ed. by Jacob E. Spannuth and Thomas Ollive Mabbott (Pottsville, Pa., 1929), p. 44, Mabbott remarks that Poe never contributed to either the *Knickerbocker* or the *North American Review,* "although at one time or another he succeeded in selling something to almost every other really important magazine of the time, and many unimportant ones."
20. Heartman and Canny, *Poe Bibliography,* pp. 58–59.

gloat at what he considered the failure of a rival enterprise, as well as to make a rather garbled gibe at Poe's prospectus:

The 'Gentleman's Magazine,' issued monthly at Philadelphia ... is offered for sale; 'the proprietor being about to engage in a more profitable business.' Mr. E. A. Poe, a spirited writer, and hitherto the principal editor of the miscellany in question, announces his retirement from its supervision. He has issued proposals for a new monthly magazine, 'to be executed in the neatest style, after the manner of the Knickerbocker,' to which he promises to bring great additions to the literary aid he has hitherto diverted into a different channel.[21]

The distortions in this brief paragraph are many. First, the initial quotation marks are sneers of disbelief, something that "S. T." called attention to when he wrote of Clark's inveterate use of inverted commas as "one of those small typographical tricks in which the Magazine delights." Second, the assertion that Poe was the principal editor, when actually he was only Burton's assistant, implies that Poe was responsible for the "downfall" of the "miscellany in question." And third, the misquotation of Poe's prospectus statement makes it appear that Poe intended to imitate, not rival, the *Knickerbocker*.

Despite all this sniping, Poe refrained from noticing Lewis Clark. Only in a private letter to a fellow editor, Joseph Evans Snodgrass, did he fleetingly express his contempt for Clark when he wrote that the *Knickerbocker* was "still edited by Clark the brother of W. Gaylord,"[22] an expression almost identical to the one he used five years later in his *Literati* paper on Clark: "*Mr. Clark* is known principally as the twin brother of the late *Willis* Gaylord Clark."[23]

The hostility that Clark felt toward Poe was not eased by the fact that Poe, who had become editor of *Graham's Magazine,* was proceeding to make that periodical the chief competitor of the *Knickerbocker.*[24] Nor was Clark pacified when Poe went on the literary warpath, hacking at the scalps of such men as

---

21. *Knickerbocker,* XVI (July, 1840), 88.
22. This letter is dated Sept. 19, 1841 (Ostrom, *Poe's Letters,* I, 183).
23. *Godey's Lady's Book,* XXXIII (Sept., 1846), 132.
24. Frank Luther Mott in *American Journalism: A History of Newspapers in the United States Through 250 Years, 1690–1940* (New York, 1941), p. 319, notes that the *"Knickerbocker's* chief rival after 1841 was the Philadelphia *Graham's Magazine."*

Thomas Ward, popularly known as Flaccus, who was a permanent contributor to the *Knickerbocker*.[25] The article called "Our Amateur Poets, No. 1—Flaccus"[26] was Poe's typical attack on the New York coterie. To this article he signed his name, an unusual procedure in a period of anonymous reviewing:

> The poet now comprehended in the *cognomen* Flaccus, is . . . merely a Mr. ———— Ward, of Gotham, once a contributor to the New York "American," and to the New York "Knickerbocker" Magazine.
> . . . The sum of his deserts has been footed up by a *clique* who are in the habit of reckoning units as tens . . . but with deference to the more matured opinions of the "Knickerbocker," we may be permitted to entertain a doubt whether he is either Jupiter Tonans, or Phoebus Apollo. . . .

Poe then "used him up" according to the familiar pattern:

> But we are fairly wearied with this absurd theme. *Who* calls Mr. Ward a poet? He is a second-rate, or a third-rate, or perhaps a ninety-ninth-rate poetaster. . . . But neither Mr. Ward nor "The Knickerbocker" would be convinced.

Poe ended the review by announcing that he was throwing Flaccus's book to the pigs.[27]

About the same time that this tomahawking took place, Poe reached for Lewis Clark's head, among others. The article, entitled "Our Magazine Literature," appeared with only an "L" as signature on March 11, 1843, in the *New World* and, despite the mixed views that Poe scholars have regarding its authorship,[28] the fact that Clark attributed it to Poe is sufficient to make it figure as a shot in the continuing war between them:

25. The announcement of "Flaccus" "as a permanent contributor of this Magazine" appeared in the *Knickerbocker*, XV (Jan., 1840), 88.

26. *Graham's Magazine*, XXII (March, 1843), 195–198.

27. Poe seemed to have a fondness for throwing books to pigs, the implication being that they would be more digestible to pigs than to human beings. He used the expression, for instance, to conclude his reviews of William Harrison Ainsworth's *Guy Fawkes* (*Graham's Magazine*, XIX, Nov., 1841, 249) and Henry B. Hirst's *The Coming of the Mammoth . . . and Other Poems* (*Broadway Journal*, II, July 12, 1845, 8).

28. Herman E. Spivey in his article "Poe and Lewis Gaylord Clark," *Publications of the Modern Language Association*, LIV (Dec., 1939), 1124–1132, discusses the various opinions respecting the authorship of this article and cites evidence to prove that it was written by Poe. In the light of the information I have assembled, I second Spivey's judgment. Such statements as the "only *redeeming* quality which *we* . . . can find in this gentleman, is in the fact that he is the brother of the late Willis G. Clark," the laudation of the "old" *Southern*

The glory of the Knickerbocker is for ever departed. Once, it was a thrice welcome messenger of intellectual entertainment to everybody, ladies, gentlemen and all. Nearly all our distinguished literary men have at times, made it the medium of their communication to the public. But, alas! the good names now connected with it are few and far between, and its subscription list is rapidly dwindling away. A secondary reason for this, we imagine, is in the bad management of its pecuniary affairs; it has been sold to a Boston publisher, and, being printed there, is a Boston magazine, and no more the *Knickerbocker*. But the principal cause of its melancholy decline, may be traced to the peculiar and unappreciated talent of its editor, Lewis G. Clark. The only *redeeming* quality which *we* (mind, we don't say the *public*) can find in this gentleman, is in the fact that he is the brother of the late Willis G. Clark, who was one of the most gifted of our poets, and an exceedingly pleasant prose-writer. Mr. Lewis Clark has made a considerable noise in the literary world, but *how* he has made it, would be difficult for his best friends to explain. ... The present condition of this periodical is that of a poorly-cooked-up concern, a huge handsome-looking body, but without a soul. The sooner it dies, the better will it be for the proprietors; but if they will secure an able and efficient editor, we doubt not but that it might be placed in the noble station which it once occupied.

Then praising Graham, whose magazine Poe had edited, for his liberal payment for articles and for "patronizing a large[r] number of eminent writers in prose and verse, than any other publisher in the country," the writer turned to Griswold, who had replaced Poe as editor of *Graham's*. "Neither do we like the nominal editor of Graham's Magazine. And why? Because ... he possesses too many of the peculiar characteristics of Lewis G. Clark. Mr. Rufus W. Griswold is wholly unfit, either by intellect or character, to occupy the editorial chair of Graham's Magazine."[29]

More than three years after this article appeared, Lewis Clark suggested that Poe had first submitted it to the *Knickerbocker*.[30] It is impossible to credit this suggestion, considering what their relations were at this time. What makes the sugges-

---

Literary Messenger, and the treatment of Griswold leave positive clues to the authorship of the article.

29. *New World,* VI (March 11, 1843), 302–303. Park Benjamin, himself a caustic critic "hated and feared by many of his contemporaries" (Taft, *Minor Knickerbockers,* p. 403), for reasons best known to himself, allowed the article to appear, although he had once shared the editorship of this selfsame paper with Griswold and Sargent (see *Knickerbocker,* XXXVI, Aug., 1850, 168).

30. *Knickerbocker,* XXVIII (Oct., 1846), 368 n.

tion equally incredible is that Clark did not mention the rejection at once when he could have capitalized on it, but waited for more than three years to publish the assertion—and then only when he was openly assailed by Poe in the *Literati* papers. Neither, as Clark suggested in his initial statement below, was the article submitted to Epes Sargent of *Sargent's New Monthly Magazine* before Park Benjamin, editor of the *New World,* accepted it.

Clark, more concerned for himself than for his friend and contributor, Thomas "Flaccus" Ward, responded to the *New World* article in the next issue of the *Knickerbocker*:

Our friend and old correspondent, Sargent . . . has thought it advisable to notice an attack in the *'New World,'* by some 'rejected contributor,' upon his publication.[31] This was unwise. Even the editor [Park Benjamin] was ashamed of his importunate correspondent, and disclaimed him. All that such a small-beer 'complainant' desires, is the notoriety of *any* notice whatsoever. If left to his native insignificance, he mourns with Meddle in the play, that he can 'get nobody to kick him.' Now to *our* mind, one of the most amusing spectacles in life, is a mortified but impotent littérateur of this sort; an ambitious 'authorling' perhaps of a small volume of effete and lamentable trash, full of little, ragged ideas, stolen and disguised among original inanities, which has fallen dead-born from the press, before the first fifty copies printed are exhausted in a *'third edition!'*[32] Disturb not, friend Sargent, the leaden repose of a 'critic' which is even more harmless than it is malignant. Something was said, we believe, in it's [*sic*] communication about the 'Old Knick's dwindling away,' and 'all that sort of thing and so forth;' but having received on that day an accession of thirty-eight new names to our list of subscribers, with what complacency did we consign the paragraph to the 'receptacle of things lost upon earth!'[33]

Clark's statement that Park Benjamin disclaimed the writer of "Our Magazine Literature" was a falsehood. Typical of Benjamin's caustic irony—a technique that Clark himself

---

31. Sargent's response to "Our Magazine Literature" appeared in *Sargent's New Monthly Magazine,* I (April, 1843), 192. Sargent took issue with what he called "two injurious untruths," but never so much as suggested, as Clark does by the words "rejected contributor," that the anonymous writer ever submitted that article to his magazine.

32. The allusion to "a small volume . . . in *'a third edition'* " appears aimed at Poe's *Poems* of 1831, which purported to be a second edition, either because Poe considered this volume a revision of *Al Aaraaf, Tamerlane, and Minor Poems* (1829) or because he wanted to encourage sales.

33. *Knickerbocker,* XXI (April, 1843), 380.

might have admired in other contexts—was the comment he subjoined to the article, a comment that, far from disclaiming, reinforced the remarks of his anonymous contributor:

Comments by the Editor.—We have consented to publish the foregoing, not because we agree with it, but because we do not. . . . Now the writer of the above is, of course, altogether in the wrong; the magazines of our country are the most admirable affairs imaginable —polished corners of the temple—carved cariatides [*sic*] on the portico of literature. The generous commendations in the newspapers which always herald their monthly appearance are perfectly disinterested and just, and if we are to believe them, nor heaven nor earth nor the waters under the earth ever contained anything so beautiful, so exquisite, so superb, so splendid, so entrancing and soul-subduing. What makes it very wonderful is, that though every number never can be surpassed, the next is better still, and thus "the agony of praise is piled up. . . ."[34]

It was not until July that Clark took Poe to task for his review of Flaccus, and then indirectly, through an unnamed correspondent:

Seeing the other day a number of 'Graham's Magazine,' I read in it an article by E. A. Poe, who comes down on your old correspondent 'Flaccus' like a mountain of lead! It is clear that 'Flaccus' has in many places exposed himself to the charge of unmelodious rhymes, incongruous figures, and occasionally faulty taste. But there is a difference between a Pope that sometimes nods, and a Cibber that *never wakes*! I am not easily moved, in the matter of poetry; I *think,* at least, that it must have merit to please me; and I well remember that Flaccus's metrical love-tale in your pages seemed to me very sweet and original, and strongly redolent of the early English odor. His 'Epistle from my Arm-chair' was in good hexameters, and his 'Address to the President of the New-England Temperance Society' had a Tom Moore-ish spice of elegant wit about it, and might have been written by Mr. Poe in about a century of leap-years.[35]

Clark, contrary to his own advice to Epes Sargent, did not leave the "critic" to his "native insignificance." Instead, he began gunning for Poe with a vengeance. Poe in August, 1843, had published another in his series "Our Amateur Poets" in *Graham's,*[36] this time dealing with William Ellery Channing, a nephew of the brilliant Unitarian minister. A rationalist in his criticism and one who liked to imagine himself rigorously so in

34. *New World*, VI (March 11, 1843), 303.
35. *Knickerbocker*, XXII (July, 1843), 89.
36. XXIII, 113–117.

the creation of his poems and stories (see "The Philosophy of Composition," for instance), Poe was inveterately opposed to Transcendentalism, especially to what he considered its lack of clarity and intellectual rigor. While lambasting this Transcendental poet whose poems, he demonstrated, were "full of all kinds of mistakes, of which the most important is that of their having been printed at all," Poe asserted that Channing had become infected with the Carlyle virus in that he seemed to have deduced from Carlyle "an opinion of the sublimity of everything odd, and of the profundity of everything meaningless. . . ."

Mr. Carlyle [Poe affirmed] . . . is obscure only. . . . Either a man intends to be understood, or he does not. If he write a book which he intends *not* to be understood, we shall be very happy indeed not to understand it; but if he write a book which he means to be understood, and, in this book, be at all possible pains to prevent us from understanding it, we can only say he is an ass—and this, to be brief, is our private opinion of Mr. Carlyle, which we now take the liberty of making public.

Using another person as a shield again, this time the editor of the *Louisville Daily Journal*, George Denison Prentice—a form of attack that was becoming characteristic of him—Clark wrote:

Mr. Prentice, the well-known Louisville Journalist, is 'down upon' a 'gentleman of some smartness who rejoices in the euphonious name of Poe,' (a correspondent of ours spells it 'Poh!') for terming Carlyle, in one of his thousand-and-one Mac-Grawler critiques, 'an ass.' The Kentucky poet and politician thus rejoins: 'We have no more doubt that Mr. Edgar A. Poe is a very good judge of an ass, than we have that he is a very poor judge of such a man as Thomas Carlyle. He has no sympathies with the great and wonderful operations of Carlyle's mind, and is therefore unable to appreciate him. A blind man can describe a rainbow as accurately as Mr. Poe can Carlyle's mind. What Mr. Poe lacks in Carlyleism he makes up in jackassism. It is very likely that Mr. Carlyle's disciples are as poor judges of an ass as Mr. Poe is of Carlyle. Let them not abuse each other, or strive to overcome obstacles which are utterly irremovable. That Mr. Poe has all the native tendencies necessary to qualify him to be a judge of asses, he has given repeated evidences to the public.'[37]

Though Poe did not reply to this attack, he remembered both Prentice and Clark for their abuse. In revising his sketch

37. *Knickerbocker,* XXII (Oct., 1843), 392.

"The Literary Life of Thingum Bob, Esq." (which first appeared in the *Southern Literary Messenger* in December, 1844) for the *Broadway Journal* (July 26, 1845), Poe wrote: "I bought auction copies (cheap) of ... 'Prentice's Billingsgate,' (folio edition,) and 'Lewis G. Clarke [*sic*] on Tongue.' "[38]

The quarrel lapsed for a while. In the meantime, Poe's criticism was of such a caliber that he was winning much prestige among some of the independent critics. James Russell Lowell, for example, observed in *Graham's* (at this time the most widely circulated magazine in the country) that Poe was

at once the most discriminating, philosophical, and fearless critic upon imaginative works who has written in America. It may be that we should qualify our remark a little, and say that he *might be*, rather than always *is*, for he seems sometimes to mistake his phial of prussic-acid for his inkstand. If we do not always agree with him in his premises, we are, at least, satisfied that his deductions are logical, and that we are reading the thoughts of a man who thinks for himself, and says what he thinks, and knows well what he is talking about. His analytic power would furnish forth bravely some score of ordinary critics. ... Had Mr. Poe had the control of a magazine of his own, in which to display his critical abilities, he would have been as autocratic, ere this, in America, as Professor Wilson has been in England; and his criticisms, we are sure, would have been far more profound and philosophical than those of the Scotsman. As it is, he has squared out blocks enough to build an enduring pyramid, but has left them lying carelessly and unclaimed in many quarries. ...[39]

In addition, Poe had sold "The Raven" to the *American Review,* where, appearing under the pseudonym of "Quarles" on February, 1845,[40] it proceeded to make an impression that in all likelihood has not been surpassed by any single piece of American poetry.

Apparently, and only apparently, veering with the critical wind, Clark published in the *Knickerbocker* a favorable report of Poe—a report conspicuous because unique:

The second number of '*The American Review and Whig Journal,*' ... has made its appearance. The very best thing in its pages is an

38. *Messenger*, X, 719–727; *Broadway Journal*, II, 33–39.
39. XXVII (Feb., 1845), 49–53.
40. I, 143–145.

unique, singularly imaginative, and most musical effusion, entitled
'*The Raven.*' We have never before, to our knowledge, met the author, Mr. Edgar A. Poe, as a poet [!]; but if the poem to which
we allude be a specimen of his powers in this kind, we shall always
be glad to welcome him in his new department.[41]

But Clark, by the time the next number of the *Knickerbocker*
appeared, had recovered from his ostensible surprise and revised his opinion of "The Raven":

We have already encountered one or two parodies upon Mr. Poe's
'*Raven,*' but have seen nothing so faithful to the original, nor so well
executed in all respects, as one which has been sent us, entitled,
'*The Black Cat.*' The lines purport to have 'slipped from the hat of a
wild-looking young man, as he rushed from the door of a respectable
house in one of our inland towns. It only serves to show the effect
upon country minds of so large an amount of 'pokerishness' as was
contained in the poem alluded to.'[42]

Clark then quoted a few stanzas of the parody.

This solitary favorable report of Poe in the *Knickerbocker*
may be explained most likely by the fact that George H. Colton,
then editor of the *American Review,* was Clark's relative,
and that Clark may only have been doing Colton a good turn
by noting the appearance of "The Raven" in its pages with
approbation.

In any event, the *Broadway Journal,* of which Poe officially
became a co-editor on March 8, 1845, treated the *Knickerbocker* and its editor—at least at the outset—quite flatteringly,
declaring in one instance that the *Knickerbocker* was one of the
few magazines that exhibited a "higher reach in the department of magazine literature than the country has ever offered
before," and, in another instance, favorably noticing the
Knickerbocker Sketch Book that had been edited by Lewis
Clark.[43] Clark, however, still nursing his grudge against
Poe for having written "Our Magazine Literature," and looking
for an opportunity to express his animosity, took issue with an
unsigned article by Poe—"Magazine-Writing—Peter Snook"
—that appeared in the *Broadway Journal* on June 7, 1845:[44]

41. *Knickerbocker*, XXV (March, 1845), 282.
42. *Ibid.*, XXV (April, 1845), 368.
43. *Broadway Journal*, I (May 10, 1845), 297, and I (June 7, 1845), 363.
44. *Ibid.*, I, 354–357.

Some sage correspondent of the 'Broadway Journal' has temporarily resuscitated from oblivion an article from an Old England magazine, entitled 'Mr. Peter Snook,' which it lauds without stint, but the very 'plums' of which we defy any person of taste to swallow with pleasure. . . . 'Chaçun [sic] à son goût,' however; and had it not been for an indiscriminate fling at American periodicals, we should not have quarrelled with the commentaries of the nil-admirari critic in question: he is simply one of a numerous class, who are 'nothing if not critical,' and even less than nothing at that.

Clark then called the "sage correspondent" a "literary Aristarchus," and contrasted his taste for literary works produced abroad with the bias of the *Knickerbocker* for those produced at home to imply that the "correspondent" was anti-American. Hardly by coincidence, Clark also contrasted Rufus Griswold's pro-American literary attitudes with those of the unnamed writer of the article, whom he alluded to as an "anonymous decrier of our own periodicals."[45]

The statement regarding the "indiscriminate fling at American periodicals" may be an allusion to "Our Magazine Literature" or to the "Peter Snook" article, or both. In the latter article (a revision of the original that appeared in the *Southern Literary Messenger* in October, 1836), Poe had said that American critics were deficient: "The best American review ever penned is miserably ineffective when compared with the notice of [Macaulay's] . . . Bacon—and yet this . . . is, in general, a piece of tawdry sophistry. . . ." Moreover, he added, American tale-writers, who supplied the very staple of the magazines, showed the "most remarkable deficiency in skill. If we except first Mr. Hawthorne—secondly, Mr. Simms— thirdly Mr. Willis—and fourthly, one or two others, . . . there is not even a respectably skilful tale-writer on this side the Atlantic."

Clark must have suspected that Poe had written the "Peter Snook" article, for, beginning with the March 8 number of the *Broadway Journal*, Poe's name appeared on the masthead as one of its editors. Furthermore, in five weekly numbers of the *Journal* (from March 8 to April 5) Poe had replied to

45. *Knickerbocker,* XXVI (July, 1845), 76.

"Outis" in the so-called Longfellow war that had created an uproar among the Boston and New York cliques, the details of which are recounted in the next chapter.

Poe, in his ironic way, responded to the veiled attack. In the *Broadway Journal* of July 12, he called the forty-two-line attack a three-line compliment, which he "sincerely" hoped it was not. In the process of correcting Clark's error in French— an unnecessary cedilla—he omitted a circumflex and insisted rather perversely that the preposition was a verb:

The *Knickerbocker* for July has ... some meritorious contributions—but neither man nor devil can dissuade its editor from a monthly *farrago* of type so small as to be nearly invisible, and so stupid as to make us wish it was quite so. In three lines devoted to the "Broadway Journal" intended to be complimentary, we believe, although we sincerely hope not, he makes use of what he supposes to be a French proverb, and writes it *Chaçun à son gout* [*sic*], taking great pains to place a grave accent on the verb, mistaking it for the preposition, and complimenting the hard c with a cedilla. Within the compass of the same three lines, he talks about a *nil admirari* critic; some person, we presume, having quizzed him with the information that the meaning of *nil admirari* is "to *admire* nothing." We certainly do not admire Mr. Clarke [*sic*]—nor his wig—but the true English of the Latin phrase is "to *wonder* at nothing," and we plead guilty to having wondered at nothing since we have found the *Knickerbocker* sinking day by day in the public opinion in despite of the brilliant abilities and thoroughly liberal education of Mr. Lewis Gaylord Clarke.[46]

These exchanges almost led to a street fight between Poe and Clark. Thomas Holly Chivers, a rather unreliable witness, who, after Poe had died, claimed that "The Raven" and "Ulalume" were plagiarized from two of his poems,[47] takes up the story. He met Poe in New York soon after the July number of the *Knickerbocker* had appeared, in which Clark had denounced the writer of the "Peter Snook" article. "Edgar A. Poe," wrote Chivers, was "as drunk as an Indian." He joined him nevertheless, and they

met Lewis Gaylord Clark, the editor of the *Knickerbocker Magazine*. The moment Poe saw him—maddened by the remembrance of some-

46. II, 11.
47. For the merits of Chivers' claim, see Joel Benton, *In the Poe Circle* (New York, 1899) and Foster Damon, *Thomas Holly Chivers: Friend of Poe* (New York, 1930).

thing that he had said in a recent Number of the Magazine touching
one of his own articles which had appeared in the *Broadway Journal*
—he swore, while attempting to rush away from my hold, that he
would attack him. . . . Clark was then talking with another man; but
as soon as this man saw the determined attitude of Poe, he immediately left him and went on his way—when Poe approached him, giving him his hand. As Clark responded to Poe's offer of his hand, he
exclaimed, "Why, Poe! is this you?" "Yes, by G-d! this is Poe?" answered he; "Here is my friend Dr C— from the South." "What!"
exclaimed Clark, giving me his hand—"Dr. C., the author of so
many beautiful poems?" "Yes, by G-d" said Poe—"Not only
the author of some of the beautifullest Poems ever written any
where, but my friend, too, by G-d!" I was very much pleased, said I,
with Willis Gaylord Clark's Poems. "Yes, he was a noble fellow,"
said Clark, "and I am his twin-brother!" "Good Lord!" said I, inter-
nally—while Poe looked Good Lord all over—exclaiming in a rather
belligerent tone, "What business had you to abuse me in the last
Number of your Magazine?" "Why, by G-d Poe!" exclaimed Clark,
siding off towards the curbstone of the pavement—"how did I know
the Article referred to, was yours? You had always attached your
name to all your articles before, and how, in H--l, did I know it was
yours?"

By this time Clark had completely bowed himself away from the
middle of Nassau Street, on his way to his office.

Poe, then, turning suddenly round to me, and locking his arm in
mine, and pulling me impetuously along, with him, in a self-
consciousness of his triumph, exclaimed in an indignant chuckle—
"A d--d coward! by G-d!" and went on his way rejoicing.[48]

When Poe, on August 23, in writing an obituary of Dr. James
McHenry, pointed out that, as a literary critic, McHenry had
fallen victim to the maliciousness of a clique, which had
systematically written him down and which afterward had no
scruples in publicly boasting of the triumph,[49] Clark preferred
to ignore the unmistakable allusion to himself and company,
apparently recognizing the truth of the charge and perhaps re-
membering his recent encounter with Poe. Clark, in fact, did
not spoil for an editorial fight with Poe again until November.
In the meantime, the *Broadway Journal* with due justice noticed that the September number of the *Knickerbocker* "has a
remarkably pleasant appearance and abounds in good things;
which no one can better supply than its editor—when he feels

48. Richard Beale Davis, ed., *Chivers' Life of Poe* (New York, 1952), pp. 57–
59.
    49. *Broadway Journal,* II, 110.

'in the vein.' "[50] And again in October—with Poe now in full editorial control—the *Journal* remarked that the *"Knicker-bocker* for October is unusually good...."[51]

The antagonism that Clark had withheld from venting on Poe for a few months he released on Cornelius Mathews in a review of his *Big Abel, and the Little Manhattan.*[52] In asserting that the volume contained mere commonplaces when it did not involve "ridiculous verbal imitations of Dickens and Carlyle," Clark committed the libel of remarking that one cannot help thinking that Mathews "has 'a screw loose' somewhere in his mental machinery...."

Poe, incensed at the imputation of insanity in an ostensibly literary review, made his comment in the *Broadway Journal*:

> *The Knickerbocker Magazine,* for November, is really beneath notice and beneath contempt. And yet this work was, at one time, *respectable.* We should regret, for the sake of New York literature, that a journal of this kind should perish, and through sheer imbecility on the part of its conductors. Its present circulation, we believe, is not more than 1400 at the most. Its friends should come to its rescue.[53]

But Duyckinck had far more at stake than Poe. That he was a very close friend of Mathews was as widely known as the fact that he was the editor of the *Library of American Books* in which series *Big Abel* had appeared. Duyckinck, signing himself "S. T.," wrote a furious denunciation of Clark and submitted the article broadcast to the journals, some of which were sufficiently in sympathy with his views to publish it— namely, the *New York Evening Mirror,* the New York *Weekly Mirror,* the New York *Morning News,* and *Godey's Lady's Book:*[54]

> During eight years the Knickerbocker Magazine has published various attacks upon Mr. Mathews and his writings, with a malignity

50. *Ibid.,* II (Sept. 6, 1845), 138.
51. *Ibid.,* II (Oct. 11, 1845), 213.
52. *Knickerbocker,* XXVI (Nov., 1845), 451–453.
53. II (Nov. 8, 1845), 276.
54. The passage is quoted from the *Weekly Mirror,* III (Nov. 15, 1845), 96, but see note 2 above for citation of other sources in which the article has been found.

and pertinacity which once induced the *Tribune* to call loudly for the private reasons which instigated such a course. It has misrepresented and traduced him in many ways by mistatements [*sic*], by partial quotations, by hints and inuendos [*sic*] and all the machinery which a little mind knows so well to employ for its ends; the titles of his books have been misquoted falsely; paltry insinuations of an injurious character, as to his private dealings with publishers have been made; his writings have been systematically depreciated; and according to a cheap and favorite argument with this journal, it has been suggested that he is out of his mind. So John Neal was called in the Knickerbocker "crazy Neal." It is time this should cease, or that the Knickerbocker should be put into Coventry by the respectable press.

Duyckinck added that the *Knickerbocker* selected high game and cited Simms and Poe as two of his examples.

After Duyckinck's article appeared, Poe published these remarks on the front page of the *Broadway Journal*:

The *Knickerbocker Magazine* has received a severe rebuke from the city press, during the last week, for some peculiarities in its general conduct, and especially for the spirit and letter of an article in the last number, upon Mr. Mathews. The inquiry has arisen in many quarters, what has Mr. Mathews done . . . that he should be pilloried in the small print and pelted with the pleasant missives of the "Editor's Table?" Better dine with Duke Humphrey than sit down to the scraps and cheese-parings of such a *table*.[55]

Clark had had formal opportunities for attacking Poe when two of his books appeared during the year: the *Tales* (June) and *The Raven and Other Poems* (November), but he failed to take advantage of either—for a time. Moreover, these books had appeared in the very series (*Library of American Books*) in which *Big Abel* had appeared, a series Poe felt called upon to defend by defending the works recently issued in that series— namely, Simms's and Mathews'. Poe's stake was more than personal. As he observed later, Duyckinck, as editor of Wiley and Putnam, "afforded unwonted encouragement to native authors by publishing their books, in good style and in good company, without trouble or risk to the authors themselves, and in the very teeth of the disadvantages arising from the want of an international copyright law."[56] Thus, on October 4, 1845, he

55. II (Nov. 15, 1845), 284.
56. *Godey's Lady's Book*, XXXIII (July, 1846), 15–16.

had called Simms's *Wigwam and the Cabin* "decidedly the most American of American books," declaring that all the stories in it had merit, and gave it as his "deliberate opinion" that, despite certain faults, Simms was, upon the whole, "the best novelist which this country has produced . . . ."[57] And again, in the January, 1846, number of *Godey's Lady's Book,* Poe observed:

Had he been a Yankee, his genius would have been rendered immediately manifest to his countrymen, but unhappily (*perhaps*) he was a southerner, and united the southern pride—the southern dislike of making bargains—with the southern supineness and general want of tact in all matters relating to the making of money. His book, therefore, depended entirely upon its own intrinsic value and resources, but with these it made its way in the end.[58]

Poe had also reviewed *Big Abel* in the November, 1845, number of *Godey's,* but unable to muster any enthusiasm for the work, he suspended his critical judgment and dutifully declared: "This is by all means an original book . . . a book especially well adapted to a series which is distinctly American." He allowed that its "chief defect is a very gross indefinitiveness, not of conception, but of execution. . . . Out of ten readers nine will be totally at a loss to comprehend the meaning of the author. Of course, nothing so written can hope to be popular;— but we presume that mere popularity is by no means Mr. Mathews' intention."[59]

Poe's critical indulgence provided Clark with the opportunity to satirize both his assailants in the December number of the *Knickerbocker*: "What a pudder our last number has created among two or three inferior members of the small 'Mutual Admiration Society,' who for 'mutual' ends swear just now by the author of . . . 'Great [*sic*] Abel,' but usually by each other recriprocally!" Clark amusedly observed that the writer in the *Mirror* ("S. T.") regrets the *Knickerbocker's* " 'attacks upon our *best* writers,' including especially the author of . . . 'Big Abel'. . . ." In the *Morning News,* Clark continued, "the same commentator complains of our notice of 'Big Abel' as 'a

57. *Broadway Journal,* II, 130–131.
58. XXXII, 41–42.
59. XXXI, 218–219.

departure from common decency, purporting to be a criticism'. . . ." Clark then speculated that Poe was the author of both the "S.T." articles he had alluded to: "Probably it is the same writer who adopts or dictates kindred 'reasoning' with the foregoing in a weekly journal [*Broadway Journal*] now living; a print which in one number deems the Knickerbocker 'utterly beneath notice and beneath contempt'. . . ." Irony aside, Clark went on, he wanted to "justify ourselves from the serious charge of uttering slanderous words," and to that purpose he would "waste a leaf or two of our Magazine. . . ." He said that no publisher ever twice made the mistake of publishing Mathews; that he had been given *Big Abel* to review and he had reviewed it honestly; that the press of the country had been even harsher than he in his condemnation of Mathews. He himself had a great regard for Mathews as a gentleman, but not, unfortunately, as a writer. Because Mathews was an American, patriotism would lead him "rather to exaggerate than lessen his merits; and if he were only half as good as Dickens, we should likely think him superior." He trusted that "our readers will not charge us with manifesting any thing like a disposition to decry our own authors. Our sins all lie in an opposite direction." He then called his remarks on *Big Abel* "candid and forbearing," and could scarcely understand why Mathews should talk about a libel suit, or why the "Forcible-Feeble of a weekly sheet" (Poe) should inform the publisher of the *Knickerbocker* that "our Magazine was doomed." Clark then cited the *London Spectator* to second his opinion that *Big Abel* was incomprehensible, after which he quoted Poe, "the personal friend and client of Mr. Matthews [*sic*], his admirer and reviewer, the Aristarchus of the Ladies' Magazines": " 'It's [*sic*] (Big Abel's) chief defect is a very gross indefinitiveness, not of conception, but of execution. (What chiefer defect could it have?) *Out of ten readers, nine will be totally at a loss to comprehend the meaning of the author!* Of course, nothing so written can hope to be popular.' " Of course not, Clark commented, for "in works of humor, popularity is an infallible test." In summarizing, he said that *Big*

Abel "is an utterly incomprehensible farrago, or rather, that the only comprehensible thing about it is a very palpable aim to copy the peculiarities of Boz." He then quoted an article from the *North American Review* of April, 1844, that had condemned Mathews, and wondered why his complainants did not pounce upon that magazine "for its bold heresy." Why didn't they "pretend that that grave Quarterly journal is influenced by 'personal malignity' toward Mr. Matthews, as it is that the Knickerbocker is thus actuated. It is, in fact, 'as easy as *lying*,' to assume that position, in relation to either publication." All that he liked about Mathews was his choice of American subjects and his advocacy of international copyright, but in the latter instance, he asserted, he does the cause infinite harm, since influential men refuse to play second fiddle to Mathews. As an author, the only way Mathews could pass without ridicule was to pass without observation.[60]

Clark, assuming that Poe was the writer of the "S. T." articles and resenting him now with rankling bitterness, proceeded to review *The Raven and Other Poems* in the next number of the *Knickerbocker*.[61] A possible explanation of Clark's failure to review the *Tales* is that the book was successful, selling more than fifteen hundred copies in less than three months,[62] and that Clark did not wish to fly too obviously in the face of public opinion. His review, as might be expected, was hardly a consideration of Poe's poetry so much as a sustained sneer at the poet himself. Clark quoted passages from Poe's preface, the better to mock at him. Then, singling out the famous declaration, "With me poetry has not been a purpose, but a passion," he noted how pitiable and meager were the results of that passion, although Poe had reached the age "at which all the great poets produced their great works." He then derided Poe's claim to precocity by saying: "We...are disposed to

60. XXVI, 579–583.
61. XXVII (Jan., 1846), 69–72.
62. According to Poe in the *Broadway Journal,* II (Oct. 25, 1845), 200. Poe's assertion is borne out by the fact that Wiley and Putnam, the publishers of the *Tales,* brought out his poems as well, which indicates that the *Tales* must have more than paid for the publication costs and that the publishers expected additional profits from an edition of the poems.

believe the author, and should believe him if he said the same
of the poems we have read." Then he charged Poe with having
only an "aptitude for rhythm"; said that his criticisms of
poetry seemed written after a very thorough cramming of
Blair's lectures and the essays of Lord Kames; recalled an
earlier assertion made by Poe that "there cannot be such a
thing as a didactic poem,"[63] and from this unqualified premise
deduced the absurd conclusion that Poe thinks a "poem is a
metrical composition without ideas." Not only his best poems,
Clark declared, but many of Poe's criticisms were composed
on this principle, "words being the sole substance in them."
Clark then accused Poe of having drawn upon Tennyson in
writing "Lenore,"[64] and proceeded to find humor in the vague-
ness of some of Poe's titles, as, for example, "To the River
———," "as though there were something mighty private or
naughty in his address to a running stream, which might compromise its character, if known."

Clark continued his gibing by adding that "there are very
few boys who have not written scores of verses like this; but
very rarely do they publish such verses when they become
men." Poe's poetical reputation, Clark contended, rested
mainly on "The Raven," but even that poem "will not bear
scrutiny." Clark then declared how magnanimous he was being
in this "review":

If we were disposed to retort upon Mr. Poe for the exceedingly gross
and false statements which, upon an imaginary slight [!], he made

63. Poe, taking issue with the "heresy of *The Didactic*" in many a review, had
asserted in *Graham's Magazine,* XX (March, 1842), 189–190, that didacticism
as a purpose is detrimental to poetry and that the didactics of Longfellow—
Clark's friend—"are all *out of place.* . . . We do not mean to say that a didactic
moral may not be well made the *under-current* of a poetical thesis; but that it
can never be well put . . . obtrusively forth. . . ." In "The Philosophy of Composition" (1846) Poe took issue with Clark and proceeded to elucidate his "real
meaning, which some of my friends have evinced a disposition to misrepresent."
He explained again that Beauty, not truth, should be the object of a poem, and
that it by no means followed from anything he had said that truth may not be
introduced into a poem, so long as it was properly subordinated to "that Beauty
which is . . . the essence of the poem."

64. The charge that Poe was an imitator of Tennyson was first made in an
anonymous article called "The Poets of America" and appeared in the *Foreign
Quarterly Review,* XLIV (Jan., 1844), 321–322. The article, which is examined
in the next chapter, gained wide notoriety, and Clark, in echoing the accusation,
was simply capitalizing on a ready-made situation.

in his paper respecting this Magazine, we could ask for no greater favor than to be allowed to criticize his volume of poems. Surely no author is so much indebted to the forbearance of critics as Mr. Poe, and no person connected with the press in this country is entitled to less mercy and consideration. His criticisms, so called, are generally a tissue of coarse personal abuse or personal adulation. . . . But criticism is his weakness. . . . In ladies' magazines, he is an Aristarchus, but among men of letters his sword is a broken lath.

Immediately following this treatment of Poe's poems appeared Clark's review of Longfellow's *Poems*. A eulogy of Longfellow, it was at the same time a scarcely veiled attack on Poe who, in the first half of the preceding year, had gained a wide, if mixed, reputation by leveling charges of plagiarism and imitation against Longfellow. The review concluded with this statement:

The pretentious and the self-conceited, the 'neglected' and the soured, among our self-elected poets, may be pardoned for decrying that excellence [of Longfellow's poetry] they cannot reach. Again we commend Mr. Longfellow's beautiful volume to a wide public acceptance. A more appropriate and admirable present for the new year, let us add 'in season,' could no where be found.[65]

Poe was aware of these comments but he saw fit to ignore them. In the meantime, he had obtained an appointment to read a poem before the Boston Lyceum. Whether Poe could not write a poem to order for the occasion or whether he wanted to hoax the Bostonians is a question that need not detain us at this point, except to note that the episode created a furor and was editorially discussed in numerous journals, in and against Poe's favor. Clark, always alert for material that could be quoted to Poe's disparagement, picked up this item and published it in the February number of the *Knickerbocker*: "The *Boston Morning Post*, in commending the review of Mr. Poe's poems in our last number, takes exception to the inference which might be drawn from our remarks, that Mr. Poe really *'humbugged'* the courteous people of Boston. . . . In justice to the Bostonians, we make the annexed extract from the 'Post's['] notice. . . ." The extract stated that Poe spoke before a large audience; that he recited in a "baby voice"; that few could

65. *Knickerbocker*, XXVII (Jan., 1846), 72–73.

tell whether it was prose or poetry he was delivering, "had it not been for the sing-song reading of the author"; that the reaction of those who heard the poem was "expressed by nods, winks, smiles and yawns"; and that almost half the audience had left the hall before Poe concluded. The extract Clark quoted ended: "Let us hear no more of this 'humbugging' the Bostonians, who from kindly feelings to a stranger heard in silence that which they knew was balderdash, or who silently left a place from which they felt the 'poet' ought to have been expelled. And yet he boasts of his conduct!"[66]

Shortly afterward, Poe's "Literati of New York City," ominously subtitled, "Some Honest Opinions at Random Respecting Their Autorial Merits, with Occasional Words of Personality," was awaiting publication in *Godey's Lady's Book*. When in May, 1846, the first series appeared, it created such a demand that Godey had to put out extra editions of the magazine and finally reprint the series along with the second series in the June number. Only two of the eight articles that constituted this first series could have offended Clark. The first was the introduction in which Poe touched upon Longfellow, who, he alleged, had a "whole legion of active quacks at his control"—an allusion to Clark, who had puffed Longfellow continually in the *Knickerbocker*. The second was the sketch of Charles F. Briggs ("Harry Franco"), in which Poe said that Briggs was "grossly uneducated" and a contributor to the *Knickerbocker*.

But what offended Clark most was the news that he himself was to be included in the *Literati* papers. He had heard the information from Louis Godey himself. As Godey reported the incident in "A Card" published in the *New York Evening Mirror* on May 8, 1846:

When during a recent visit to New York, the subscriber [Godey] informed Mr. Lewis Gaylord Clark that Mr. Poe had him 'booked' in his 'Opinions of the New York Literati,' he supposed that he was giving Mr. Lewis Gaylord Clark a very agreeable piece of information; as it must have been quite apparent to the gentleman himself, that

66. *Ibid.*, XXVII, 184. The article appeared in the *Boston Post* on Jan. 14, 1846.

his natural position was not among the literati, but *sub-literati* of New York; and he ought to have been greatly surprised and gratified to find himself placed in such agreeable company. But it seems that, on the contrary, the information that Mr. Lewis Gaylord Clark received has put him in a perfect agony of terror.

Thus apprised, Clark had his attack on Poe ready for the May number of the *Knickerbocker*:

There is a wandering specimen of '*The Literary Snob*' continually obtruding himself upon public notice; today in the gutter, tomorrow in some milliner's magazine; but in all places, and at all times, magnificently snobbish and dirty, who seems to invite the 'Punchy' writers among us to take up their pens and impale him for public amusement. Mrs. Louisa Godey [a slur on Mr. Louis Godey] has lately taken this snob into her service in a neighboring city, where he is doing his best to prove his title to the distinction of being one of the lowest of his class at present, infesting the literary world. The '*Evening Gazette and Times*' speaks of our literary 'snob' as one 'whose *idiosyncrasies* have attracted some attention and compassion of late;' and adds: 'We have heard that he is at present in a state of health which renders him not completely *accountable* for all his peculiarities!' We do not think that the 'ungentlemanly and unpardonable personalities of this writer,' of which our contemporary complains, are worthy of notice simply because they are so notoriously false that they destroy themselves. The sketch, for example, of Mr. Briggs, ('Harry Franco,') in the paper alluded to, is *ludicrously* untrue, in almost every particular. Who that knows 'Harry Franco,' (whose prose style Washington Irving pronounced 'the freshest, most natural and graphic he had met with,') would recognize his *physical* man from our 'snob's' description? But after all, why should one speak of all this? Poh! Poe! Leave the 'idiosyncratic' man 'alone in his glory.'[67]

The "Card" in which Godey had advertised the fact that he had informed Clark of his inclusion in the *Literati* papers was, of course, a rebuke of Clark for this scurrilous attack. Godey went on to say in that card that Clark's "desperation is laughably exhibited in the insane attack he has made on Mr. Poe, in the Knickerbocker for May, where Mr. Poe is represented as

---

67. XXVII, 461. Despite all efforts to find the article in the New York *Evening Gazette and Times* which Clark alluded to, nothing remotely corresponding to Clark's "quotation" from that paper can be found, either by myself or by two other persons who were kind enough to double- and triple-check my own fruitless searches. Was the item faked? The passage beginning, "There is a wandering specimen . . . ," and ending, "infesting the literary world . . . ," was copied with minor typographical differences in the *Boston Evening Transcript*, May 5, 1846.

imbecile from physical infirmity, and at the same time is threatened with impalement. It would undoubtedly afford the public much amusement to witness an attempt on the part of Mr. Lewis Gaylord Clark to impale Edgar A. Poe. . . ." Godey then said that it takes a *"born* blockhead" to make the blunder of asserting that Mr. Poe's personalities are not worthy of notice and that they destroy themselves, and then proceed to make them the subject of special notice in an attempt to destroy the writer, "even descending to the heartless and cruel insinuation, that illness has weakened the powers of his mind." Godey concluded:

> The subscriber has been repeatedly advised to discontinue the publication of 'Mr. Poe's articles on the New York Literati.' It will be readily perceived, however, that such a course on his part would be as indelicate and unjust towards Mr. Poe, as it would be ungrateful towards the public, who have expressed distinct and decisive approbation of the articles in that unmistakeable [*sic*] way which a publisher is always happy to recognize.

The unmistakable way, of course, was sales, and according to Griswold, who had no reason to favor Poe, "three editions were necessary to supply the demand for some numbers of the magazines containing them."[68]

In September, Poe's attack on Clark appeared, even as Godey had promised. He began with the familiar gibe that *"Mr. Clark* is known principally as the twin brother of the late *Willis* Gaylord Clark" and added: "He is known, also, within a more limited circle, as one of the editors of 'The Knickerbocker Magazine.' " Poe spoke of the "editorial scraps" to be found at the back of each number of the *Knickerbocker*—an allusion to Clark's own "Editor's Table," a famous feature of the magazine—as "the joint composition of a great variety of gentlemen," which it was in the sense that Clark was in the habit of quoting in that Table, as we have seen, items from newspapers, magazines, and correspondents. "Were a little more pains taken in elevating the *tone* of this 'Editors' Table,' (which its best friends are forced to admit is at present a little Boweryish),"

---

68. Memoir to *The Literati,* pp. xxii–xxiii. Godey in his magazine, XXXII (May, 1846), 240, also reprinted the "S.T." article to indicate, among other things, that Clark's suggestion that Poe was insane was typical of his attacks.

Poe went on, deliberately misplacing the apostrophe and, at the same time, alluding to such vulgar attacks as those that appeared there on Cornelius Mathews and himself, "I should have no hesitation in commending it . . . as a specimen of . . . easy writing and hard reading." Then, speaking of Clark's other contributions to the magazine, Poe remarked that the style of them "has its merits, beyond doubt, but I shall not undertake to say that either 'vigor,' 'force' or 'impressiveness' is the precise term by which that merit should be designated. Mr. Clark once did me the honor to review my poems [an allusion to Clark's recent treatment of *The Raven* volume], and—I forgive him."

When Poe turned to a discussion of the *Knickerbocker* itself, he said that it seemed "to have in it some important elements of success": its title was good, it had some eminent contributors, "although none of these gentlemen, continue their contributions"; the printing and paper have been excellent; and—a loaded remark—"there certainly has been no lack of exertion in the way of what is termed 'putting the work before the eye of the public.'"

Still some incomprehensible *incubus* has seemed always to sit heavily upon it, and it has never succeeded in attaining *position* among intelligent or educated readers. On account of the manner in which it is necessarily edited, the work is deficient in that absolutely indispensable element, *individuality*. As the editor has no precise character, the magazine, as a matter of course, can have none. When I say "no precise character," I mean that Mr. C., as a literary man, has about him no determinateness, no distinctiveness, no saliency of point;—an apple, in fact, or a pumpkin, has more angles. He is as smooth as oil or a sermon from Dr. Hawks; he is noticeable for nothing in the world except for the markedness by which he is noticeable for nothing.

Poe then mischievously speculated about the current circulation of the *Knickerbocker* and arrived at the ridiculously low figure of "some fifteen hundred copies."[69]

In a final paragraph, Poe offered a description of Clark, his characteristic way of ending all these sketches. In doing this,

69. Spivey, whose Ph.D. dissertation was a study of the *Knickerbocker*, states in "Poe and Lewis Gaylord Clark," p. 1131, that the circulation of the *Knickerbocker* was very much greater than five thousand in 1846.

he overestimated Clark's age by four or five years, said that his "forehead is, phrenologically, bad—round and what is termed 'bullety' [and that] . . . the smile is too constant and lacks expression."[70]

Considering Clark's recent remarks on Poe in his "review" of *The Raven* volume and in "The Literary Snob," this sketch was less harsh than Clark had reason to expect. Nevertheless, Poe seems to have irritated all the sore points of Clark, for when Clark prepared his retort for the October number of the *Knickerbocker,* he was fouler than he had been:

Our thanks are due to 'J. G. H.,' of Springfield (Mass.,)[71] for his communication touching the course and the capabilities of the wretched inebriate whose personalities disgrace a certain Milliner's Magazine in Philadelphia; but bless your heart, man! you can't expect us to publish it. The jaded hack who runs a broken pace for common hire, upon whom you have wasted powder, might revel in his congenial abuse of this Magazine and its Editor from now till next October without disturbing our complacency for a single moment. He is too mean for hate, and hardly worthy scorn. In fact there are but two classes of persons who regard him in *any* light— those who despise and those who pity him; the first for his utter lack of principle, the latter for the infirmities which have overcome and ruined him. Here is a faithful picture, for which he but recently sat. We take it from one of our most respectable daily journals:

'It is melancholy enough to see a man maimed in his limbs, or deprived by nature of his due proportions; the blind, the deaf, the mute, the lame, the impotent, are all subjects that touch our hearts, at least all whose hearts have not been indurated in the fiery furnace of sin; but sad, sadder, and saddest of all, is the poor wretch whose want of moral rectitude has reduced his mind and person to a condition where indignation for his vices and revenge for his insults are changed into a compassion for the poor victim of himself. When a man has sunk so low that he has lost the power to provoke vengeance, he is the most pitiful of all pitiable objects. A poor creature of this description called at our office the other day, in a condition of sad imbecility, bearing in his feeble body the evidences of evil living, and betraying by his talk such radical obliquity of sense, that every

---

70. *Godey's Lady's Book,* XXXIII, 132.
71. "J. G. H." of Springfield, Mass., may have been Josiah Gilbert Holland (1819–1881) or merely a crank. It is curious to note that an "H. G. J." (a reversal of these initials), also of Springfield, Mass., was respectfully informed in *Godey's Lady's Book,* XXXIII (Nov., 1846), 240, "that we cannot republish any article in our 'Book,' especially the one he refers to—biographical notice of L. Gaylord Clark. He is referred to the September number of our magazine, which he can either buy or borrow."

spark of harsh feeling toward him was extinguished, and we could not even entertain a feeling of contempt for one who was evidently committing a suicide upon his body, as he had already done upon his character. Unhappy man! He was accompanied by an aged female relative [Poe's mother-in-law, Mrs. Maria Clemm?], who was going a weary round in the hot streets, following his steps to prevent his indulging in a love of drink; but he had eluded her watchful eye by some means, and was already far gone in a state of inebriation. After listening awhile with painful feelings to his profane ribaldry, he left the office, accompanied by his good genius, to whom he owed the duties which she was discharging for him.'

Now what [Clark asked] can one gain by a victory over a person such as this? If there are some men whose enemies are to be pitied much, there are others whose alleged friends are to be pitied more. One whom this 'critic' has covered with what *he* deems praise, describes him as 'a literary person of unfortunate peculiarities, who professes to know many to whom he is altogether unknown.' Can it then be a matter of the least moment to us, when the *quo animo* of such a writer is made palpable even to his own readers, that he should underrate our circulation by thousands, overrate our age by years, or assign to other pens the departments of this Magazine which we have alone sustained, with such humble ability as we possessed, through nearly twenty-six out of its twenty-eight volumes? As well might Carlyle lament that he had called him an 'unmitigated ass,' or Longfellow grieve at being denounced by him as 'a man of no genius, and an inveterate literary thief.'[72] And as to his literary *opinions,* who would regard *them* as of any importance?—a pen-and-ink writer, whose only 'art' is correctly described by the *'London Athenaeum'* to 'consist in conveying plain things after a fashion which makes them hard to be understood and commonplaces in a sort of mysterious form, which causes them to sound oracular.' 'There are times,' continues the able critical journal from which we quote, 'when he probably desires to go no farther than the obscure; when the utmost extent of his ambition is to be unintelligible; that he approaches the verge of the childish, and wanders on the confines of the absurd!' We put it to our Massachusetts correspondent, whether such a writer's idea of style is at all satire-worthy? And are we not excused from declining our friend's kindly-meant but quite unnecessary communication?[73]

Here for the first time—three years before his death—we have in print the allegations so familiar these days—that Poe

---

72. Although in quotation marks, the statement respecting Longfellow is not Poe's. On the contrary, Poe repeatedly declared that Longfellow had genius, but that he abused it with imitativeness and, at times, with outright plagiarism, as well as with didacticism. Similarly, but of far less consequence, Poe did call Carlyle an ass, but not an unmitigated one.

73. XXVIII, 368–369.

was a "wretched inebriate"; that he was a "hack ... for common hire," which is to say that he tailored critical opinions to order for a price; that he had an "utter lack of principle"; that he had certain unspecified "infirmities" that had ruined him; and that his friends, whom he witlessly maligned in praising, were aware of his "unfortunate peculiarities." Lest readers of the *Knickerbocker* should regard these views of Poe as aroused and distorted by rancor, Clark "corroborated" them by citing apparently impartial opinions to indicate that his views were universally held. He alluded to an unnamed correspondent, "J.G.H." He "quoted" an article from an unidentified "respectable" newspaper (whether Poe actually "sat" for such a portrait is questionable, since no mention of Poe appears in the extract that Clark purported to quote and since a diligent search has failed to uncover the article in question). And he cited the London *Athenaeum*. Thus, J. G. H.'s view of Poe is by implication so much harsher than Clark's and even, perhaps, so obscene that "man! you can't expect us to publish it." Thus, from the second source, real or invented, there are further charges: "imbecility," "evil living," "radical obliquity of sense," and "suicide" upon body and character. Moreover, Poe is shown to be in the care of a keeper, and that an "aged female relative," whose task is to prevent him from drinking—a woman upon whom he is utterly dependent but whom he should be comforting if he had any conscience at all—all of which so pains the compassionate writer that he proceeds to smear the "poor creature" in his "respectable" paper. And thus, in the third and only identified source, there appear to be further heinous charges, but ones which only assert that Poe was pretentious at times or obscure or even absurd in his stories, though Clark fobbed off these adjectives, not in relation to Poe's stories and poems, as the *Athenaeum* had, but to his "literary opinions."[74] What Clark failed to mention is just as illuminating, that the *Athenaeum* habitually found fault with American writers, especially with their addiction to English

---

74. See the *Athenaeum*, No. 957 (Feb. 28, 1846), pp. 215–216.

models, and that, for example, only recently the *Athenaeum* had accused Longfellow of imitation.[75]

Thus wrote, quoted, and commented the editor of the *Knickerbocker* whose complacency, so he averred, was not ruffled for a moment. So unruffled was he that he added this controversial footnote, obviously to assign a discreditable motive to Poe's attacks on him in the *Literati* series, that of vengeance for the rejection of a number of his manuscripts by Clark:

> He is equally unknown to those whom he abuses. The Editor hereof has no remembrance of ever having seen him save on two occasions. In the one case, we met him in the street with a gentleman [Chivers?], who apologized the next day, in a note now before us, for having been seen in his company 'while he was laboring under such an *excitement*;' in the other, we caught a view of his retiring skirts as he wended his 'winding way,' like a furtive puppy with a considerable kettle to his tail, from the publication-office, whence— having left no other record of his tempestuous visit upon the publisher's mind than the recollection of a coagulum of maudlin and abusive jargon—he had just emerged, bearing with him one of his little narrow rolls of manuscript, which had been previously submitted for insertion in our 'excellent Magazine,' but which, unhappily for his peace, had shared the fate of its equally attractive predecessors.

For reasons given earlier, the first of Clark's statements— that he had rejected a manuscript of Poe's—is extremely doubtful. And if the second statement implies that Clark repeatedly rejected a number of Poe's manuscripts, then the statement is plainly false and casts even greater doubt on the veracity of the first statement. Moreover, Clark claimed to have met Poe on only two occasions—both, as he described them, decidedly unfavorable to Poe. He may have been merely forgetful in neglecting to mention a time when he and Poe, among others, proposed toasts at the booksellers' dinner held in New York City on March 30, 1837.[76]

75. See, for instance, *ibid.*, No. 950 (Jan. 10, 1846), pp. 35–36, and No. 959 (March 14, 1846), pp. 266–267.
76. See the *New York Commercial Advertiser*, XL (April 3, 1837), which shows that Clark's toast preceded Poe's by only eight short toasts. The toasts Clark and Poe offered are revealing: Clark proposed "Protection to Home Manufactures, whether of the hands or of the intellect." Poe proposed, with

But Poe had not discharged all his cannon. *Godey's Lady's Book* carried in its next number Poe's paper on Charles Fenno Hoffman. Here Poe wrote:

Mr. Hoffman was the original editor of "The Knickerbocker Magazine," and gave it while under his control a tone and character, the weight of which may be best estimated by the consideration that the work thence received an impetus which has sufficed to bear it on alive, although tottering, month after month, through even that dense region of unmitigated and unmitigable fog—that dreary realm of outer darkness, of utter and inconceivable dunderheadism, over which has so long ruled King Log the Second, in the august person of one Lewis Gaylord Clark.[77]

Clark retaliated the following month by discharging two attacks on Poe. One was in the form of doggerel, no doubt written by Clark himself, since he had referred to Poe as "Aristarchus" and "Poh" in many of his diatribes. The subtitle seems to be a strained pun on *Poe, pooh,* and *pro* in the expression *pro pudor* (for shame):

> Epitaph on a Modern 'Critic.'
> 'P'oh' Pudor!'

> 'Here Aristarchus lies!' (a pregnant phrase,
> And greatly hackneyed, in his early days,
> By those who saw him in his maudlin scenes,
> And those who read him in the magazines.)
> Here Aristarchus lies, (nay, never smile,)
> Cold as his muse, and stiffer than his style;
> But whether Bacchus or Minerva claims
> The crusty critic, all conjecture shames;
> Nor shall the world know which the mortal sin,
> Excessive genius or excessive gin![78]

The second attack[79]—not only on Poe, but on Simms, Duyckinck, and Mathews as well—began with a quotation

---

what appears to be his usual taste for hoaxing, "The Monthlies of Gotham— Their distinguished Editors, and their vigorous *Collaborateurs*."

77. XXXIII (Oct., 1846), 158.

78. *Knickerbocker,* XXVIII (Nov., 1846), 425.

79. *Ibid.,* XXVIII, 452. The article from which Clark quoted may be found in the *North American Review,* LXIII (Oct., 1846), 357–381. The *North American* noticed the *Knickerbocker* only to condemn it. It appears that Clark had published an article disparaging C. C. Felton, a professor of Greek literature at Harvard and a favorite and apparently an assistant editor of the *North American Review.* In retaliation, the *North American* wrote: "But we cannot express our astonishment that . . . it should have been allowed to appear in a magazine *once* so respectable as The Knickerbocker" (LXV, July, 1847, 242). For a similar instance, see the *North American Review,* XLIV (Jan., 1837), 270–272.

from the *North American Review,* whose favorite poet—Long-fellow—Poe had attacked during 1845. First of all, Clark, quoting and agreeing with the *North American,* charged that the *Library of American Books* (edited by Duyckinck and published by Wiley and Putnam) "with the exception of a few of the volumes, is not likely to do much honor to American literature." Secondly, Clark suggested in a footnote, Duyckinck, for the sake of helping his friend Mathews, had been dishonest with his employers in that, "through a misunderstanding, or without their knowledge," *Big Abel* had been announced as a forthcoming book in the series. Clark, together with the *North American Review,* wondered

what can have seduced these respectable publishers into printing, as one of the series, that indescribably stupid imitation of Dickens, entitled and called 'Big Abel and Little Manhattan;' a contribution to the patriotic native American literature a good deal worse than the very worst things of 'The Yemassee' and 'Guy Rivers.' Surely, surely, this dismal trash cannot have been seriously chosen as a fit representation of American originality, in a 'Library of American Books'. . . .

In "justice to the enterprising publishers," Clark explained in the footnote alluded to, Mathews had insisted upon the publication of *Big Abel,* even though Wiley and Putnam had offered him a hundred dollars to release them from an obligation they had inadvertently incurred.

Having disposed of Mathews in this way, Clark turned to Simms, again quoting the *North American* but omitting its praise:

The author of these novels means to be understood as setting up for an original, patriotic, native American writer; but we are convinced that every judicious reader will set him down as uncommonly deficient in the first elements of originality. He has put on the cast-off garments of the British novelist, merely endeavoring to give them an American fit; and . . . there is in his literary outfits a decided touch of the shabby genteel.

Clark continued:

These works, with the 'Tales of Edgar A. Poe,' who is described [by the *North American Review*] as 'belonging to the forcible-feeble and shallow-profound school,' are pronounced 'poor materials for an American Library.'

. . . Now the preceding forcible and candid comments upon the productions of Mr. Simms, and those of a writer or two of kindred pretensions ... are quite coincident with our own expressed opinions in these pages.

The last of Poe's *Literati* papers appeared in the October number of *Godey's*. He ended them, he wrote his young admirer, George W. Eveleth, because they were considered "elaborate criticisms when I had no other design than critical *gossip*," and because the "unexpected circulation of the series, also, suggested to me that I might make a hit and some profit, as well as proper fame, by extending the plan into that of a *book* on American Letters generally, and keeping the publication in my own hands." Poe also commented in that letter:

My reference to L. G. Clark, in spirit but not in letter, is what you suppose. He *abused* me in his criticism—but so feebly—with such a parade of intention & effort, but with so little effect or power, that I —forgave him:—that is to say, I had little difficulty in pardoning him. His strong point was that I ought to write well, because I had asserted that others wrote ill—and that I *didn't* write well because, although there had been a great deal of fuss made about me, I had written so little—only a small volume of 100 pages. Why he had written more himself![80]

Having blackened Poe to the limits of his ability, and Poe refraining from giving further offense, Clark seemed satisfied to let the quarrel lapse. Only once before Poe died did Clark mention him again, and then only under the exigency of having to defend himself against charges of personal malice toward Mathews, Simms, and Poe. That occasion was in January, 1848, when Clark found an article in *Blackwood's Magazine* that, he thought, would acquit him of the charges and prove him an honest editor. He wrote:

In connexion with two or three of our contemporaries, we have been accused of having been actuated by personal prejudice in our notices of ... Mr. Cornelius Mathews, and of ... Mr. W. Gilmore Simms. This, as our readers are aware, we have not only disclaimed, but have repeatedly shown, by passages from other reviews of these writers, that our own impression of their characteristics was held in common with the public and the highest literary authorities of the country. We have quoted, for example ... the '*North-American Review*,' ... and we now find our opinions fully confirmed on the other side of the water, by a journal obviously as uninfluenced by personal bias as

---

80. Letter dated Dec. 15, 1846 (Ostrom, *Poe's Letters*, II, 332).

have been the judgments of the 'North-American' and the Knickerbocker.

Having suggested that a universal opinion could be adduced
from two instances, Clark then quoted the article in *Blackwood's* to discredit Mathews and Simms and to redeem himself. Finished with those authors, he turned to Poe:

> Of Mr. Poe's 'Tales' the reviewer remarks, that while they cannot
> be called common-place, they evince little taste and much analytic
> power. One is not sorry to have read them—one has no desire to read
> them twice. His style 'has nothing peculiarly commendable; and
> when the embellishments of metaphor and illustration are attempted,
> they are awkward, strained, and infelicitous. The effect of his de-
> scriptions, as of his story, depends never upon any bold display of
> the imagination, but on the agglomeration of incidents, enumerated
> in the most veracious manner.' Such is the tenor of the article in
> Blackwood, which is written in an evident spirit of candor, and with
> much discrimination.[81]

Poe died on October 7, 1849, and Griswold, friend of Clark,
began to edit his works. The first two volumes entitled *The
Works of the Late Edgar Allan Poe: With Notices of His Life
and Genius by N. P. Willis, J. R. Lowell, and R. W. Griswold*
appeared in January, 1850. The "Notice" by Griswold was
simply a republication of the "Ludwig" smear of Poe, now acknowledged, that had originally been printed in the *New York
Tribune* two days following Poe's death. This edition, if we are
to credit such articles as that which appeared in the March,
1850, number of the *Southern Literary Messenger,* was, ironically enough, used for the very kind of humbuggery that Poe
had decried throughout his critical career. Written by
John M. Daniel, editor of the *Richmond Examiner* and a man
whom Poe claimed to have challenged to a duel, the article,
scathing as it was of Poe, was scathing of his editor also, although Daniel made the mistake of assuming that Willis and
Lowell were co-editors. With vitriol, Daniel asserted that
Griswold, Willis, and Lowell

> felt quite pitifully sentimental at his dog's death; and with the ut-
> most condescension they hearkened to the clink of the publisher's
> silver, and agreed to erect a monument to the deceased genius, in the
> shape of Memoir and Essay preliminary to his works. Their kindness

81. *Knickerbocker,* XXXI, 68–71.

and their generosity has been published to the world in every news-paper. The bookseller's advertisement, that all persons possessing letters and correspondence of Poe should send them straightway to him has gone with the news. The publication of the works of Poe were kept back from the public for a long time, that they might be brought out in a blaze of glory.... Here it is at last—and duty com-pels us to say, that this is the rawest, the baldest, the most offensive, and the most pudent humbug that has been ever palmed upon an unsuspecting moon-calf of a world. These three men ... have prac-ticed in the publication as complete a swindle on the purchaser as ever sent a knave to the State prison.[82]

In addition to such reports, violent protest was aroused against the two-volume edition by such men as George R. Graham, who knew Poe far better than Griswold and who felt that Griswold had not only betrayed a trust but had taken re-venge upon a dead man. In his magazine, he published an open letter to Nathaniel Willis, in which he declared the Griswold Notice of Poe to be *"unfair and untrue....* It is Mr. Poe, as seen by the writer while laboring under a fit of the night-mare...."* He then inquired into the reasons for this vilifica-tion of Poe:

Mr. Griswold ... has allowed old prejudices and old enmities to steal ... into the coloring of his picture. They were for years totally un-congenial, if not enemies.... He had, too, in the exercise of his func-tions as critic, put to death, summarily, the literary reputation of some of Mr. Griswold's best friends; and their ghosts cried in vain for him to avenge them during Poe's life-time—and it almost seems, as if the present hacking at the cold remains of him who struck them down, is a sort of compensation for duty long delayed—for reprisal long desired but defered [*sic*].[83]

He added that literature was a religion to Poe and that, as its high priest, he scourged the money-changers from the temple with a whip of scorpions.

---

82. XVI, 173. See also *ibid.*, p. 192, in which the owner and editor of the *Messenger,* John R. Thompson, apologized to Willis and Griswold, making a conspicuous exception of Lowell, who had become an active abolitionist, for the article's appearing during his absence. Thompson and Clark seem to have been friends. In the *Messenger,* XVI (Feb., 1850), 127, Thompson acknowledged "with pleasure the handsome manner in which our friend of *The Knickerbocker* is pleased to speak of us. Praise from such a source is worth something. If it were necessary, we could have the heart to give it back tenfold." And Clark in the *Knickerbocker,* XLVI (Oct., 1855), 424, spoke of "our friend ... John R. Thompson, Esq., of the *'Southern Literary Messenger'....* "
83. *Graham's Magazine,* XXXVI (March, 1850), 224–226.

Clark, who publicly stated that he had known Griswold for nearly the entire period of his connection with the *Knickerbocker*, and with whom Griswold almost became an associate editor on that magazine, felt impelled, as usual, to aid his friend, and what better way than to vilify Poe still further? Yet it must have posed something of a dilemma to Clark to have to defend the editor and, at the same time, to attack his subject. He began his review quite promisingly: "The intellectual character of the late Mr. Poe may now be examined, and its qualities decided upon, without any of those disadvantages which his personal conduct constantly presented as barriers to the fair appreciation of his genius." But the promise failed. Clark pointed out that Poe was "destitute of moral or religious principle," and that, although "very few of our American authors have possessed more of the creative energy or of the constructive faculty," Poe was "frequently a plagiarist of both thoughts and forms."[84] Then, significantly, he stressed "literary thefts" which Griswold himself did not point out in print until his greatly enlarged biographical sketch of Poe appeared in the third volume of the edition: *The Literati: Some Honest Opinions about Autorial Merits and Demerits, With Occasional Words of Personality ... By Edgar A. Poe ... with a Sketch of the Author, by Rufus Wilmot Griswold.*[85] This volume was issued about the middle of September, 1850, more than half a year after Clark's review appeared. Clark asserted that "The Pit and the Pendulum" was plagiarized from "Vivenzio, or Italian Vengeance" and from a tragic scene of the German, E. T. A. Hoffmann. An investigator has shown, however, that a "careful search through the tales of Hoffmann reveals no story of a pendulum used as an instrument of torture," and that if Poe borrowed in this instance, it was not from "Vivenzio," but from a tale called "The Iron Shroud" by

---

84. *Knickerbocker*, XXXV (Feb., 1850), 163–164.

85. This sketch "was transferred to the first volume on the publication of a second edition in 1853, and it continued to occupy this position on the publication of an edition of four volumes in 1856." See Campbell, *The Mind of Poe*, p. 74 n. 1, which also gives his reasons for dating the sketch "about the middle of September, 1850."

William Mumford. The conclusion is that the *Knickerbocker's*
"reviewer's wish was evidently father to the thought."[86]

Clark then maintained that Poe's "charge of plagiarism
against Professor Longfellow, we happen to know, was so false
that the plagiarism was on the other side [*sic*]." Longfellow,
although he recognized the accusation to be absurd, did not
protest this statement until September 28, and then not to
Clark, who originally made it in print, but to Griswold.[87]

As to Poe's criticisms, Clark found them "acute and ingenious, in some respects; but for the most part [they] are
carping, and entirely worthless, for any judgments they embrace of books or authors; he was so much the creature of
kindly or malicious prejudice, or so incapable of going beyond
the range of the grammarian."

When the third volume of Poe's works appeared, containing
the Griswold version of the *Literati* series, Clark was not
happy. He found himself and many of his friends being served
up again for public amusement. It was inevitable that he
should write: "On the score of entertainment of any sort . . .
or of good taste, we trust these disjointed criticisms . . . are not
considered by their editor as presenting any considerable claim
to the regard of the public. Indeed, we have his implied judgment in this respect." Then he remarked that, having "in a
notice of the first and second volumes of the present series" already expressed his judgment of Poe's writings, he would now
content himself with a "synopsis of the extraordinary career
of the author as furnished us by Dr. Griswold in a biography
accompanying the work." [88]

We may well question the authenticity of the "synopsis" by
"Dr." Griswold, a man who had balked at little to malign Poe.
He had circulated stories that Poe had had "criminal rela-
tions" with his mother-in-law, Mrs. Clemm.[89] He had seized an

---

86. D. L. Clark, "The Sources of Poe's 'The Pit and the Pendulum,' " *Modern
Language Notes,* XLIV (June, 1929), 349–356. See also the Griswold sketch in
The Literati volume, p. xxxii, in which Griswold repeated the identical charges.
87. See Quinn, *Poe,* p. 674, for Longfellow's letter to Griswold.
88. *Knickerbocker,* XXXVI (Oct., 1850), 370–372.
89. Quinn, *Poe,* p. 680.

opportunity, two days after Poe's shocking death, to publish in the *Tribune* a pseudonymous smear of the man in the form of a characterization of Poe, much of which was, in fact, taken almost verbatim from Bulwer's characterization of Francis Vivian in *The Caxtons*. He had tailored a dead man's text for his own purposes so as to alienate by intent even such a friend of Poe as Duyckinck.[90] He had twisted some strands of truth with so many falsifications and half-truths in the Memoir he prefixed to *The Literati* volume that no one has yet quite untangled the snarl. And finally, though it has not yet been conclusively proved, he had probably pocketed a profit from the sales of the works of the very man he had so used. Such vilification no literary figure ever suffered; and when we consider that this Memoir, coming as it did from the "approved" editor of Poe, was reproduced "as authentic in all save a very few of the contemporary notices of Griswold's edition," as well as in "virtually every other edition of Poe's writings that appeared during the first two decades after the poet's death,"[91] we can understand how far-reaching and deep-rooted became the calumny, and how it must have exceeded Griswold's most sanguine expectations.

Clark, having reiterated many of the Griswold villainies, then repeated precisely what he himself had charged in his earlier review, and for which he now pretended to find support

90. Whatever reasons Griswold had—to hurt Duyckinck, to make him hostile to Poe's memory, to forestall the charges he must have anticipated were forthcoming from him, or to defame Poe by showing him to be treacherous—he interpolated a phrase in one of the Poe letters he quoted: "The last selection of my tales was made from about seventy by [one of our great little cliquists and claquers] Wiley and Putnam's reader, Duyckinck." (Compare the Griswold distortion in his Memoir in *The Literati* volume, p. xxxi, with the original phrasing in Ostrom's edition of the *Letters,* II, 328.) Sad to say, Griswold succeeded to the extent that Duyckinck declared in a review of *The Literati* volume (*Literary World,* VII, Sept. 21, 1850, 228) that Poe was "a literary attorney, who pleaded according to his fee"—a charge that had not occurred to him before and one that, together with similar statements, has helped in shaping the Poe myth. Nevertheless, in the same article, Duyckinck asked this embarrassing question, which waited until 1941 for Arthur Hobson Quinn to answer in his biography of Poe, when he proved that Griswold had not only tampered with Poe's text, but had published forged versions of some of Poe's letters: Why, if Griswold was purporting to present an accurate record of Poe's opinions, was the record "purged of any unhandsome references to Dr. Griswold?"

91. Campbell, *The Mind of Poe,* p. 77.

in the Griswold Memoir: "... Poe's plagiarisms are ... pronounced by his biographer as 'scarcely paralleled in literary history.' He accused Mr. Longfellow, for example, of a plagiarism from *himself*, when it turned out that the poem of Longfellow was written two or three years before the publication of that by Poe, and was, during a portion of that time, in Poe's possession. His unsupported literary opinions [note the *non sequitur*] could rarely be received with credit."

Clark was referring here to Griswold's charge that Poe's "Haunted Palace," which had been widely circulated in "The Fall of the House of Usher," was plagiarized from Longfellow's "Beleaguered City." Poe, as early as 1841, had anticipated such a charge in the prospect of having his poem published with Longfellow's in Griswold's edition of *Poets and Poetry of America* (1842), and had called Griswold's attention to Longfellow's possible plagiarism from him, even citing proof of prior publication.[92] Nevertheless, Poe must have appeared so hateful to Griswold personally—granted that Poe had given him some provocation—that Griswold had an overmastering compulsion to make Poe universally hated. Thus, despite the evidence in his possession, he made Poe appear to be the plagiarist of Longfellow.

Longfellow himself, much as he had reason to dislike Poe, balked at the deception. In his letter to Griswold, dated September 28, 1850, he denied the charge made in the Memoir, saying that "The Beleaguered City" "was written on the nineteenth of September, 1839. I marked the date down at the time."[93] But Longfellow's denial is not needed on this point, except to demonstrate that both Clark and Griswold were colluding in "hacking at the cold remains," to use Graham's phrase. "The Haunted Palace" had appeared in the *Museum* as a separate publication in April, 1839. Clearly, both Clark and Griswold were parties to deliberate falsehoods. To concur in a truth is simple; to concur in a lie betrays collaboration.

92. The letter is dated May 29, 1841 (Ostrom, *Poe's Letters*, I, 160–161).
93. For the dating of these poems and for Longfellow's letter to Griswold, see Quinn, *Poe*, pp. 271, 674.

In November, 1856, after a passage of six years, Clark quoted the *North American Review,* since it contained a harsh article on Poe. The passages Clark reprinted were only re-phrasings of the charges trumped up by Clark and Griswold. A significant passage which Clark omitted to quote reads:

Cliquism was the citadel of wrong against which he brought to bear all the power of his editorial battery whenever he could command the use of a press. Cliquism was the one thing which he hated more intensely than he could express (he never happened to be one of a powerful clique); and the suspicion that certain literary circles looked upon him with disfavor or contempt so embittered his feelings and distorted his vision, as to make him no less unjust to them, than he fancied they were disposed to be towards him.

This omitted passage also states that Poe approached "the American Parnassus ... with all the enginery he could command or invent,—by sapping, mining, blasting, bombardment, stratagem, and storm; his shafts being ever the more keen and swift when aimed at the highest heads."

Having quoted the now familiar allegations against Poe, Clark appended his approval: "True, every word of it: as is also the subsequent remark that the secret of 'Poe's impotency over the public taste'—for he had *no* literary influence what-ever—'lies in the fact that his critical reviews, like all that he wrote, were destitute of moral sentiment.' " The writer in the *North American Review* had concluded with a prayer for some "potent chemistry to blot out from our brain-roll for ever be-yond the power of future resurrection, the greater part of what has been inscribed upon it by the ghastly and charnel-hued pen of Edgar Allan Poe. Rather than remember all, we would choose to forget all that he has written." Clark concluded by recommending the number of the *North American Review* "most cordially to our readers."[94]

Godey, in whose magazine the *Literati* papers, as well as a number of other Poe articles and stories, had first appeared,

94. *Knickerbocker,* XLVIII, 517–518. The review which Clark quoted in part appeared in the *North American Review,* LXXXIII (Oct., 1856), 427–455. Mott (*American Magazines,* II, 243) attributed this article to a Mrs. E. V. Smith. No one by that name has been located; I think it a pseudonym, and not a woman's but a man's. Quinn (*Poe,* p. 685) referred to the writer as "he," and I think legitimately.

wrote to Clark to say that he was not to be counted among those to whom Poe was alleged to have been faithless. Clark replied by evading responsibility for the accusation, and used his typographical tricks to imply that Godey was certainly exceptional: "Mr. L. A. Godey . . . writes us to say, that *he* is not to be 'counted in' among those in Philadelphia to whom the late Edgar A. Poe proved faithless, in his business and literary intercourse. His conduct toward Mr. Godey was in all respects honorable and unblameworthy. The remark which elicits the note of Mr. Godey was copied as a quotation into our pages from the 'North-American Review' in a recent notice of that venerable and excellent Quarterly."[95]

Clark's last public strike at Poe was made four years later when he reviewed Sarah Helen Whitman's defense of Poe, *Edgar Poe and His Critics* (1860). A widow, she had been engaged to Poe in 1848, but the notoriety he had gained during his crack-up period and his strange behavior at the time caused her to break the engagement. Poe, pleading with her, had written:

And you ask me *why* men so *mis*judge me—*why* I have enemies. If your knowledge of my character and of my career does not afford you an answer to the query, at least it does not become *me* to suggest the answer. Let it suffice that I have had the audacity to remain poor that I might preserve my independence—that, nevertheless, in letters, to a certain extent and in certain regards, I have been "successful"—that I have been a critic—and unscrupulously honest and no doubt in many cases a bitter one—that I have uniformly attacked—where I attacked at all—those who stood highest in power and influence—and that, whether in literature or in society, I have seldom refrained from expressing, either directly or indirectly, the pure contempt with which the pretensions of ignorance, arrogance, or imbecility inspire me.—And you who know all this—*you* ask me *why* I have enemies.[96]

Belatedly contrite, Mrs. Whitman had written her small volume in defense of Poe's personal and literary reputation. Clark, in reviewing the work, said that the opinions of the *Knickerbocker* in regard to Poe had been recorded "frankly and conscientiously" several years earlier, and that "it would give us

95. *Ibid.,* **XLIX** (Jan., 1857), 106.
96. The letter is dated Oct. 18, 1848 (Ostrom, *Poe's Letters,* II, 394).

pleasure to add, that Mr. Poe's biographers had since given us occasion to change them," implying, of course, that his opinions remained justifiably unchanged. Then, as usual, he resorted to quoting, this time the *Baltimore Methodist Protestant*. That paper had called Mrs. Whitman's book a noble effort, "but it does not wipe out the ... dishonorable records in the biography of Dr. Griswold.... After reading it, we turned to Dr. Griswold's Memoir, and for the first time were able to peruse it without impatience and a sense of wrong to its subject."[97]

It is true that Poe sometimes played favorites in his criticism and praised writers hardly better than those he derided; that he mistook cruelty for candor; that he sometimes attacked from the ambush of anonymity. But on the whole, allowing for these and similar gross faults, he began his journalistic career as a critic of high principles, and fearlessly asserted and applied those principles, whatever the occasion, the author, the publisher, or the coterie involved. But the literature in America of that time was, for the most part, incredibly bad. One need only read at random in the leading periodicals of the period— in *Godey's*, in *Graham's*, in the *Knickerbocker*, in the *Mirror*— to be convinced of that. To borrow a phrase from George E. Woodberry, no quotation can do sufficient justice to the writers of that time—they must be read to be properly damned. Moreover, the great books of the period were bound for commercial failure. We are told by the authority in the field that not a "single literary work of genuine originality published in book form before 1850 had any commercial value to speak of until much later, and most of our classics were financial failures."[98] Such mediocrity prevailed, in fact, that it seemed a necessary qualification for commercial success. All this considered, it is hardly possible to believe that Poe and Hawthorne, Melville and Emerson, Thoreau and Whitman, could have survived as artists. As a practicing critic, a critic whose profession was criticism and who earned his livelihood chiefly by his criticism,

97. *Knickerbocker*, LV (April, 1860), 429.
98. Charvat, *Literary Publishing in America*, p. 23.

Poe continually received from publishers and individual authors the books they were marketing. Bad as most of them were, it was inevitable that Poe, given his standards and taste, should react to them in indignation, that he should slash at them in his reviews, and that his indignation should be exacerbated by those groups who imposed such works upon the public as monuments of American literature. Nothing, unless Poe abandoned his principles or his profession, could have stopped his clash with the authors, the publishers, and the cliques who wrote, published, and logrolled such works.

Graham, who knew Poe well, recognized Poe's essential critical integrity and the enmity he aroused by maintaining that integrity when he wrote, somewhat exaggeratedly, that his "pen was regulated by the highest sense of duty." Graham also recognized, as few of us do today, that if Poe had compromised himself and puffed the authors he condemned and toadied to the coteries he despised, the doors of fortune would have swung open to him. In Graham's own powerful language:

Could he have stepped down and chronicled small beer, made himself the shifting toady of the hour, and with bow and cringe, hung upon the steps of greatness, sounding the glory of third-rate ability with a penny trumpet, he would have been feted alive, and, *perhaps*, been praised when dead. But no! his views of the duties of the critic were stern, and he felt that in praising an unworthy writer, he committed dishonor.[99]

The clash came with Poe's slashing review of *Norman Leslie* in 1835 and continued throughout his life. The men such as Clark who contended with him were, at first, only trying to starve him out as a writer by curtailing the sale of such works as *Arthur Gordon Pym,* or to destroy him as a critic, as they had destroyed Dr. James McHenry. Failing that, and finding that he was bringing the battle into their very camp, they then attacked him, not as a writer and critic any longer, but as a man, in order to bring him into such disrepute that his critical charges would not be credited. Then, and only then, were such rumors circulated as those alleging him to have carnal relations with his mother-in-law; then was he called a literary snob,

99. *Graham's Magazine,* XXXVI (March, 1850), 226.

today in the gutter and tomorrow in some milliner's magazine; then was he labeled a dirty critic who infested the literary world—a man tainted with alcoholism, immorality, plagiarism, and insanity.

The truth is that Poe, with all his failings, was as a critic successful to the point of his own undoing. Having allowed his enemies no ground on which to stand, he drove them to discredit his criticism by discrediting him as a human being—the familiar *argumentum ad hominem* whose fallaciousness we may all recognize but to whose contagion few of us are immune. In this they succeeded and so well that it may be forever impossible to deflate the Poe myth to its proper proportions.

The final irony is that the man most guilty of creating and circulating calumnies of Poe while Poe was alive enjoyed a reputation for humor and kindliness. In the words of Thomas Bangs Thorpe, a friend of Clark and a contributor to the *Knickerbocker:* "The intellectual peculiarity of Lewis Gaylord Clark was humor; with him it was, of course, instinctive and genuine. He was never else to the world than light-hearted, always kindly disposed, and ever discovering amusement.... He viewed every thing, if you please, from a delicate, truly refined, and humorous stand-point. Nothing to him was really serious, yet he *never* was irreverent, unfeeling, or sarcastic."[100]

100. *Harper's New Monthly Magazine,* XLVIII (March, 1874), 587–592.

5

CULMINATION OF A CAMPAIGN

Poe and Longfellow

> ... I am but defending a set of principles which no honest man need be ashamed of defending, and for whose defence no honest man will consider an apology required.——*Edgar A. Poe*

Poe's encounters with Longfellow have aroused so much emotionalism in Poe and Longfellow partisans that to look at the evidence afresh and with detachment requires the utmost self-discipline. To forestall such emotionalism from prejudicing the evidence, let it be repeated here that our purpose is not so much to defend Poe as a critic but to understand him in that capacity; to consider this "battle" as we have considered earlier ones, in the context of his critical career and literary milieu; and, finally, to draw judgments from the evidence, whether those judgments happen to be favorable or unfavorable to Poe or, in this instance, to Longfellow. Thus, let it be acknowledged at once that in his notices of the Cambridge poet Poe was blunt and quarrelsome at times; that he made serious errors of judgment on occasion; that he was not unwilling to use Longfellow for sensational purposes to enlarge the subscription lists of the magazines he was serving; that the last of his protracted replies to "Outis" may even betray the first symptoms of a mental disturbance that became obvious in the following year; and, having acknowledged this, let us proceed to as impartial an examination of the available evidence as is possible in the circumstances.

Poe first took critical notice of Longfellow when his prose tale, *Hyperion: A Romance* (1839), came to his attention as reviewer for *Burton's Gentleman's Magazine*. This was Longfellow's second published work, if we regard the three editions of *Outre-Mer* as one and ignore his textbooks.

The thin autobiographical narrative was, in the persona of Paul Flemming, an account of his second European trip—from the death of his first wife following a miscarriage to his frustrated romance with Frances Appleton (Mary Ashburton). Steeped in German Romanticism, Longfellow responded to his wife's death and to Frances Appleton in a pretentiously literary style which he later abandoned. Thus, in *Hyperion*, his dead wife was the bough which had broken under the burden of the unripe fruit, and Frances Appleton is the wraith who haunts his dreams "with her pale, speaking countenance and holy eyes." The literary influences manifest in the work are many, but Jean Paul's is most obvious.[1] But the story, however derivative its manner, was essentially a frame on which to hang all sorts of miscellaneous materials: anecdotes, legends, travel notes, translations of German poems, and even discussions of literary topics, some drawn from his Harvard lectures on German literature.

Poe, who insisted time and again that "totality, or unity, of effect" is a desideratum of a literary work and who repeatedly held that "than the true originality there is no higher literary virtue," was bound to be unhappy with the book:

> Were it possible [he wrote] to throw into a bag the lofty thought and manner of the "Pilgrims of the Rhine," together with the quirks and quibbles and true humour of "Tristram Shandy," not forgetting a few of the heartier drolleries of Rabelais, and one or two of the Phantasy Pieces of the Lorrainean Callot, the whole, when well shaken up, and thrown out, would be a very tolerable imitation of

1. See, for instance, Thompson, *Longfellow*, p. 405 n. 5; Edward Wagenknecht, *Longfellow: A Full-Length Portrait* (New York, 1955), p. 5; and James Taft Hatfield, *New Light on Longfellow, with Special Reference to His Relations with Germany* (Boston, 1933), p. 140.

"Hyperion." This may appear to be commendation, but we do not intend it as such. Works like this of Professor Longfellow are the triumphs of Tom O'Bedlam, and the grief of all true criticism. They are potent in unsettling the popular faith in Art—a faith which, at no day more than the present, needed the support of men of letters. . . . A man of true talent who would demur at the great labour requisite for the stern demands of high art . . . make[s] no scruple of scattering at random a profusion of rich thought in the pages of such farragos [sic] as "Hyperion." Here, indeed, there is little trouble—but even that little is most unprofitably lost. . . . We are indignant that he too has been recreant to the good cause.[2]

Such criticism of *Hyperion* was by no means unusual then or now. Longfellow himself observed: "The Boston papers are very savage, and abuse me shockingly. . . ."[3] One such "abusive" review was written by Orestes A. Brownson, editor of the *Boston Quarterly Review*, whose reaction to *Hyperion* was similar to Poe's: "I do not like the book. It is such a journal as a man who reads a great deal makes from the scraps in his table-drawer. . . . You cannot guess why the book was written. . . ."[4] Another "abusive" reviewer confessed in the Boston *Mercantile Journal* of September 27, 1839, that one "book" of the four "books" of *Hyperion* was a dose as large as he could swallow because he found it a "mongrel mixture of descriptions and criticism, travels and bibliography, commonplaces clad in purple, and follies 'with not a rag to cover them.'" Amusingly enough, Frances Appleton, unhappy at being served up to the public under the persona of Mary Ashburton, remarked privately: "There are really some exquisite things in this book, though it is desultory, objectless, a thing of shreds and patches like the author's mind."[5]

But not all notices of *Hyperion* were unfavorable, for four of Longfellow's friends—Cornelius Conway Felton, Samuel

2. *Burton's Gentleman's Magazine,* V (Oct., 1839), 227.
3. Letter dated Oct. 1, 1839. Earlier, on Sept. 12, Longfellow had written to Willis Clark in Philadelphia, urging him to send "all notices of Hyperion, particularly the most abusive ones." (For both these statements, see Livingston, *Longfellow Bibliography,* pp. 24–25.) Wagenknecht (*Longfellow,* p. 5) calls *Hyperion* a "disorganized, Jean-Paul Richter kind of Romance," but Hatfield (*New Light on Longfellow,* p. 78) contends that "in spite of all the sweepings which it contains, the work is essentially original."
4. *Boston Quarterly Review,* III (Jan., 1840), 128.
5. Quoted by Wagenknecht, *Longfellow,* p. 233.

Ward, and the Clark brothers—published their reviews of that work too.[6] For the *Boston Courier* Felton wrote a stinging reply to the *Mercantile Journal* reviewer, which he trenchantly titled, "Hyperion to a Satyr" (a reply that Willis Clark reprinted in his *Philadelphia Gazette*),[7] as well as a seventeen-page defense of *Hyperion* for the *North American Review*. In the *North American,* Felton conceded what was already the fact, that *Hyperion* "must encounter a variety of critical opinions"; yet, he maintained, the book "must not be judged by the principles of classical composition"—that is to say, by the principle of unity, as Poe and others had judged it. Readers, he said, who were "attuned to sentiments of tenderness," who had an imaginative turn of mind, and who were "sensitively alive to the influence of the beautiful," would come back to the book again and again. Ward devoted twenty pages of the *New York Review* to affirming that the book is a "lay ... uttered by the scholar with the lips of a minstrel," and "that the appearance of Hyperion is an event in the annals of our scholarship and literary taste." Willis Clark, who pronounced the work great, promised to review it "with liberal extracts, some Saturday" for his *Philadelphia Gazette*. And Lewis Clark, declaring in the *Knickerbocker* that the Romance "is an exquisite production and will be so pronounced by every reader of taste," urged his subscribers to "possess themselves at once of 'Hyperion,' and sit down to a feast of calm philosophy, poetry, and romance."

Encouraged by the reception of *Hyperion*—he oversanguinely remarked that a large edition of the book had been sold in a few weeks[8]—Longfellow created another opportunity

6. Felton's reviews appeared in the *Boston Courier* of Oct. 2, 1839, and in the *North American Review,* L (Jan., 1840), 145–161; Ward's in the *New York Review,* V (Oct., 1839), 438–457; Willis Clark's in his *Gazette,* unlocated but see Dunlap, *The Clark Letters,* p. 53; and Lewis Clark's in the *Knickerbocker,* XIV (Sept., 1839), 277–280.

7. Unlocated but see Dunlap, *The Clark Letters,* p. 54.

8. Letter to George W. Greene, dated Oct. 1, 1839 (Livingston, *Longfellow Bibliography,* p. 24). On Jan. 2, 1840, however, Longfellow recognized his error: "But see what ill luck with Hyperion; the publisher fails; half the edition is seized by creditors and locked up; and the book has been out of the market for four months." Again, on March 5, 1842, Longfellow wrote, this time to

to appear on the literary market in that same year. He collected his "Voices of the Night" (eight "Psalms," including "Hymn to the Night," "A Psalm of Life," "The Beleaguered City," and "Midnight Mass for the Dying Year," which had appeared in the *Knickerbocker*), sorted through his "Earlier Poems" (from which he selected seven), gathered twenty-three of his "Translations" (some of which had appeared in *Hyperion* and elsewhere), and made a modest, three-sectioned volume of the whole, which he inappropriately christened *Voices of the Night*.

Unlike *Hyperion,* this work was widely acclaimed by the press. As Longfellow wrote, "Every one praises the book. Even the Boston papers which so abused Hyperion, praise this highly."[9] Before the volume appeared in December, Lewis Clark announced in the *Knickerbocker*:

'Voices of the Night.'—Professor Longfellow, of Cambridge, has in press, under the above title, a volume of poems, which is to embrace the several beautiful 'Psalms of Life,' that were written for the Knickerbocker, together with many of the earlier original poems and translations of the author. We would not so far slander the feeling and good taste of the public, as to suppose that the volume will not meet with a large and rapid sale.[10]

And when the book was published, Clark observed:

Perhaps it will be considered altogether a work of supererogation, that we should invite the attention of our readers to a volume of poems from the pen of Professor Longfellow, from whom they have heard so often, and never without delight.... Most cordially do we commend these 'Voices of the Night' to the imaginations and hearts of our readers.[11]

Felton, too, in the *North American,* extolled the volume, especially the title section, saying that they "are among the most remarkable poetical compositions, which have ever appeared in the United States"[12]—a verdict that Clark, not to be

Ward: "All I have received from him [Colman, the publisher of *Hyperion*] is $72.50" (*ibid.,* p. 25).

9. Thompson, *Longfellow,* p. 303.

10. *Knickerbocker,* XIV (Nov., 1839), 470.

11. *Ibid.,* XV (Jan., 1840), 75.

12. L (Jan., 1840), 266–269. The *Hyperion* review is attributed to Felton by Allibone (*Dictionary of Authors*), by Poole (*Index to Periodical Literature*), etc. Evidence for Felton's authorship of the *Voices* review appears in the review itself: "And we shall observe the same general fact, which we have pointed out in our remarks upon the style of 'Hyperion,' " etc. (p. 268).

outdone, quoted in his "Editor's Table," adding that "we are especially gratified to find the praise which has been bestowed in these pages upon . . . 'Hyperion,' . . . and . . . 'Voices of the Night,' reechoed in the deliberate verdict of the 'North American.' "[13]

Such acclamation by the press was in great measure deserved. Reviewers familiar with the run of American poetry were bound to be impressed by the command of language, the freshness of imagery, and the sureness of technique that characterize most of the Psalms. Felton's opinion, that the Psalms were "among the most remarkable poetical compositions, which have ever appeared in the United States," was perfectly sound at the time. Reviewers like Poe, however, who held that the world, not America, "is the true theatre of the biblical histrio"; who refused to let literary patriotism enter into their judgments; who felt compelled to compare Longfellow's accomplishments with those of Coleridge, Keats, and Shelley rather than with John Brainard's, Fitz-Greene Halleck's, and Mrs. Sigourney's, were bound to be more moderate in their acclaim. Thus, in reviewing *Voices* for *Burton's Gentleman's Magazine,* Poe remarked that when he had first seen "Hymn to the Night" in a newspaper, he had been impressed with the "firm belief that a poet of high genius had at length arisen amongst us." No poem, he remarked, ever opened with a beauty more august and the first five stanzas are nearly perfect. Had Longfellow always written this way, Poe continued, "we should have been tempted to speak of him not only as *our* finest poet, but as one of the noblest poets of all time." His perusal of *Voices* had not modified his conviction that Longfellow had genius; it had, however, altered his opinion as to his "capacity for . . . any enduring reputation." For though Longfellow possesses the "loftiest qualities of the poetical soul . . . . he has nothing of unity"—the same observation, Poe added, that *Hyperion* had induced in him. Even the five stanzas of the "Hymn" alluded to have defects consequent upon lack of unity—defects which he considered symptoms of inability to achieve "that perfection which is the result only

13. *Knickerbocker,* XV (Jan., 1840), 81.

of the strictest proportion and adaptation in all the poetical requisites...." Hence, he said, the defects he had pointed out existed not only in the poems but "in the mind of the writer, and thence ineradicable...."[14]

If we can condone Poe's questioning the degree of Long-fellow's talents (and neither in this notice nor in subsequent ones did he fall into the easy fatuity of condemning Long-fellow's poems contemptuously or of admiring them vacuously), we may not be so willing to condone his questioning Longfellow's honesty in the high-handed way he proceeded to do at the close of this review. Copying Longfellow's "Midnight Mass for the Dying Year" and Tennyson's "The Death of the Old Year," he called attention to a plagiarism "too palpable to be mistaken, and which belongs to the most barbarous class of literary robbery: that class in which, while the words of the wronged author are avoided, his most intangible, and therefore his least defensible and least reclaimable property is purloined." Aside from occasional lapses, Poe admitted, "there is nothing of a visible or palpable nature by which the source of the American poem can be established. But then nearly all that is valuable in the piece of Tennyson is the ... conception of personifying the Old Year as a dying old man, with the singularly wild and fantastic *manner* in which that conception is carried out. Of this conception and of this manner he is robbed." Needless to say, Poe ruled out all possibility of coincidence, if he considered it at all.[15]

14. VI (Feb., 1840), 100–103. In *Biographia Literaria* (chap. xv) Coleridge too had remarked of a "man of talents and much reading" that he had "mistaken an intense desire of poetic reputation for a natural poetic genius; the love of the arbitrary end for a possession of the peculiar means. But the sense of musical delight, with the power of producing it, is a gift of imagination; and this together with the power of reducing multitude into unity of effect, and modifying a series of thoughts by some one predominant thought, or feeling, may be cultivated and improved, but can never be learned."

15. A later Poe critique, "Tale-Writing—Nathaniel Hawthorne" (*Godey's,* XXXV, Nov., 1847, 252–256), amplifies many of the points made in this review. In that critique, Poe explained that "to be peculiar is to be original," but that true originality, however, implies a "peculiarity springing from ever-active vigor of fancy—better still if from ever-present force of imagination, giving its own hue, its own character to everything it touches, and especially, *self impelled to touch everything.*" In more modern terms, Poe suggests here that the unmistakable sign of a truly original writer is that he leaves his signature on everything he writes because he has a characteristic and even compulsive vision that selects,

If the puffing lavished on *Hyperion* by the *North American Review*, the *Knickerbocker,* and the *Philadelphia Gazette* had not provided Poe with evidence of logrolling or, to use his expression, the "corrupt nature of our ordinary criticism," and if the phenomenon of *Voices* passing through four printings within the year[16] had not signalized to him that Longfellow was being abetted by the New York and Boston coteries, he must have at least suspected the fact when he ran into an old adversary, Willis Clark, whom he had encountered under similar circumstances in the *Norman Leslie* incident. Most likely in order to stimulate sales of *Burton's Gentleman's Magazine,* Poe called attention to what he deemed Longfellow's plagiarism in *Alexander's Weekly Messenger,* a journal to which he was contributing at the time. In his column for January 29, 1840, he referred to a review in *Burton's* "which shows up Professor Longfellow as a plagiarist of the first water...."[17] The allegation, made so bluntly, reached Longfellow at Cambridge, and he proceeded to deny it to his friend Ward: "My brother told me yesterday that some paragraphs had appeared in some New York paper [*Alexander's* was printed in Philadelphia] saying I stole the idea of the 'Midnight Mass' from Tennyson. Absurd. I did not even know that he had written a piece on this subject."[18] Unfortunately, the evidence does not entirely support Longfellow's statement. "The Fifth Psalm: A Midnight Mass for the Dying Year" first appeared in the *Knicker-*

---

shapes, and orders miscellaneous incidents, ideas, characters, etc.—a statement that becomes clear enough if we think of William Faulkner's fiction or of Robinson Jeffers' poetry. Longfellow, as Poe seems to have seen the matter, had borrowed the "vision" ordering Tennyson's poem, and, to this extent, though he had avoided his language, he was guilty of plagiarizing Tennyson's least defensible property. This further explains too why Poe said that Longfellow had little capacity for any enduring reputation: if his poems have no unity, the poet cannot be said to have a characteristic vision, let alone a compulsive one. And, as Poe pointed out in "Tale-Writing," he did not judge an author "altogether by what he does, but in great measure—indeed, even in the greatest measure— by what he evinces a capability of doing."

16. Livingston, *Longfellow Bibliography,* pp. 26–27. According to the *Knickerbocker,* XIX (Feb., 1842), 181, *Voices* passed through five printings by Feb., 1842, but this claim seems exaggerated.

17. Brigham, *Poe's Contributions to Alexander's,* p. 29.

18. Henry Marion Hall, "Longfellow's Letters to Samuel Ward," *Putnam's Monthly,* III (Oct., 1907), 42. Thompson (*Longfellow,* p. 416 n. 4) states that this letter was written sometime between Feb. 10 and 27, 1840.

bocker in October, 1839. In 1838 Emerson, in correspondence with C. C. Little, who wanted to bring out the first American edition of Tennyson's *Poems* (London, 1833)—the book that contains "The Death of the Old Year"—told that publisher that Longfellow owned a copy.[19] Moreover, Longfellow in a letter to Frances Appleton written sometime in 1837 or 1838 extolled the virtues of Tennyson ("the nicest ear can ask no richer melody:—and the most lively imagination no lovlier [*sic*] picture, nor more true") and even quoted verses and cited page numbers from the very volume containing "The Death of the Old Year."[20] Had Longfellow been candid, Poe's charge would appear today, as it must have appeared then, decidedly unfair; but Longfellow's denial in the circumstances tends to draw suspicion from the accuser to the accused.

Having written to Ward, Longfellow wrote to Willis Clark as well: "Pray who is it that is attacking me so furiously in Philadelphia. I have never seen the attacks, but occasionally I receive a newspaper with a defense of my writings, from which I learn there has been an attack. I thank you for what you have done for me; and for your good thoughts and good words."[21] Clark, responding to Longfellow's letter, wrote: "You ask me who attacks you here? The only ones I have seen against you, have been in *Burton's*.... I have answered *thoroughly,* any attack upon you—and shall continue to do so, whenever they appear."[22] Clark spoke the truth, for he had answered Poe's anonymous articles in *Burton's* and *Alexander's.* On February 4, 1840, he had printed a statement in his *Gazette* designed to acquit Longfellow of plagiarism by

19. John Olin Eidson, *Tennyson in America* (Athens, Ga., 1943), pp. 33 and 210 n. 97.

20. Thompson, *Longfellow,* pp. 413–414.

21. Letter dated July 5, 1840 (*ibid.,* p. 306). Longfellow had reason to thank Clark, for Clark had been helpful on several occasions. The kind of assistance he provided may be inferred from two of his extant letters to Longfellow. The first, dated Feb. 25, 1837, reads: "Have you anything in press, now? If you have command me in the American Quarterly here, for which I am constantly asked to write." The second, dated July 18, 1840, reads: "If you have seen my Gazette . . . you would have found that I missed no chance to offer my testimony in behalf of the master spirit, so far as *deep* poetical *thought* is concerned, of our American Age. . . . I am not through with him yet." See Dunlap, *The Clark Letters,* pp. 39 and 57.

22. Letter dated July 18, 1840 (*ibid.,* p. 58).

convicting Tennyson of stealing from Longfellow, or, failing that, by suggesting that Longfellow, at worst, had only filched from one of his own earlier poems. His defense, based on the error that Tennyson was a Scotsman and on the reduction of Poe's charge to imitation, only evidenced his partiality for Longfellow:

A neighboring periodical, we hear, has been attempting to prove that Professor Longfellow's sublime and beautiful "Midnight Mass for the Dying Year," has been imitated from a poem by Tennyson. Preposterous! There is nothing more alike in the two pieces than black and white, with the exception of the personification,—and *that* was Longfellow's, long before the Scotch writer thought of 'doing' his poem. Who does not remember that striking simile in one of the Professor's earlier lyrics,

> ———"where Autumn, like a faint old man, sits down,
> By the wayside, aweary?"

This same beautiful piece was copied in Edinburgh, from an English periodical where it was *altered*, to suit the scenery of England; and it is fifty times more probable that Tennyson thus got *his* idea, than that Mr. Longfellow should have done more in the "Mass," than repeat a favorite one of his thought. On himself, one of the most strikingly original poets of this country, and the best translator of any nation known to our language, such a charge falls hurtless—and for the reputation of the maker, (acknowledged, we hear, among his friends) should be withdrawn. We ask the Weekly Messenger, who has repeated the charge of *abstraction,* to clip this *caveat,* and give it utterance.

On February 12, his earliest opportunity, Poe did as Clark bade him. He reprinted Clark's caveat in *Alexander's* and added:

The "neighboring periodical," alluded to in so parliamentary a style, is the "Gentleman's Magazine," and the accuser, whose "reputation" is so entirely a matter of hearsay with Mr. Clark, is a Mr. Poe, one of the editors of that very excellent and very popular journal. . . .

Mr. Poe does not say that Professor Longfellow's poem is "imitated" from Tennyson. He calls it a bare-faced and barbarous plagiarism. . . . In support of this accusation he has printed the poems in question side by side—a proceeding, which, we must acknowledge, has an air of perfect fairness about it. . . . We mention that the critic has done all this, because we understand, from the opening words of the paragraph quoted above, that Mr. Clarke [*sic*], is only aware, as usual, through hearsay, of what is really written in the "Gentleman's Magazine."

Matters standing thus, the question is altogether one of opinion. Mr. Poe says the Professor stole the poem; so do we; and so does every body but Mr. Clarke. *He* says the Professor did *not* steal the poem. He says, moreover, that Mr Poe ought to "withdraw" the charge, lest, being persisted in, it may do injury to his own reputation; (Mr. P's) about which he (Mr. C.) is solicitous. Whether Mr. Poe will oblige the editor of the Gazette, remains yet to be seen.[23]

Poe, needless to say, did not oblige the editor of the *Gazette* and the matter lapsed.

All that can be said here is that Poe was still plumping for sales of *Burton's* and that he exercised some restraint by merely reiterating the original accusation. He could easily have strengthened his position by adducing other and far less questionable instances of "plagiarism" in *Voices*—even from the very poem "Autumn" which Clark had cited. Consider the last nine lines of that poem, for example, in respect to ideas, phrases, and even the blank verse of "Thanatopsis":

> O what a glory doth this world put on
> For him who, with a fervent heart, goes forth
> Under the bright and glorious sky, and looks
> On duties well performed, and days well spent!
> For him the wind, ay, and the yellow leaves
> Shall have a voice, and give him eloquent teachings.
> He shall so hear the solemn hymn, that Death
> Has lifted up for all, that he shall go
> To his long resting-place without a tear.

In his original review of *Voices,* however, Poe had said that no author of mature age should desire to have his poetical character estimated by the productions of his mind at immaturity, and "Autumn," like the rest of the "Earlier Poems," was written, as Longfellow had acknowledged, before he was nineteen.

Twice during the next year Poe had occasion to write to Longfellow—the first and last time letters were exchanged between them. As editor now of *Graham's Magazine,* Poe was asked by the proprietor to solicit contributions from Longfellow, who had become, almost overnight on the strength of *Voices,* America's best-selling poet and thus a most desirable contributor. Poe's position was awkward, for however much

23. Brigham, *Poe's Contributions to Alexander's,* pp. 33–34.

he had acclaimed Longfellow as a poet, he had not only pointed out his weaknesses but had accused him of plagiarism, and he felt he could anticipate the poet's response. His letter reflects his dilemma:

Mr Geo: R. Graham, proprietor of "Graham's Magazine", a monthly journal published in this city, and edited by myself, desires me to beg of you the honor of your contribution to its pages. Upon the principle that we seldom obtain what we *very* anxiously covet, I confess that I have but little hope of inducing you to write for us;— and, to say truth, I fear that Mr Graham would have opened the negotiation much better in his own person—for I have no reason to think myself favorably known to you—but the attempt was to be made, and I made it.

Poe added that if Longfellow were interested, he could submit an article every month, whether in poetry or prose, length, subject, and price at his discretion.

In conclusion—I cannot refrain from availing myself of this, the only opportunity I may ever have, to assure the author of the "Hymn to the Night", of the "Beleaguered City" and of the "Skeleton in Armor", of the fervent admiration with which his genius has inspired me:—and yet I would scarcely hazard a declaration whose import might be so easily misconstrued, and which bears with it, at best, more or less, of niaiserie, were I not convinced that Professor Longfellow, writing and thinking as he does, will be at no loss to feel and appreciate the honest *sincerity* of what I say.[24]

Longfellow replied on May 19, refusing the offer and acknowledging Poe's existence. With nice discretion, he avoided mentioning Poe's recent strictures on his work and, at the same time, managed to return the compliment Poe had paid him:

I am much obliged to you for your kind expressions of regard, and to Mr. Graham for his very generous offer. . . . But I am so much occupied at present that I could not do it with any satisfaction either to you or to myself. I must therefore respectfully decline his proposition.

You are mistaken in supposing that you are not "favorably known to me." On the contrary, all that I have read from your pen has inspired me with a high idea of your power; and I think you are destined to stand among the first romance-writers of the country, if such be your aim.[25]

24. Letter dated May 3, 1841 (Ostrom, *Poe's Letters*, I, 158–159).
25. Samuel Longfellow, ed., *Life of Henry Wadsworth Longfellow, with Extracts from His Journals and Correspondence* (Boston, 1891), I, 390–391.

During the next month Poe sought to establish his own journal. Having found Longfellow more agreeable than he had reason to expect, Poe wrote him a second letter in which he discussed his projected magazine and asked again for contributions: "In your former note you spoke of present engagements. The proposed journal will not be commenced until the 1st January 1842."[26] What Longfellow replied, if he replied at all, is not known, but it can hardly be coincidence that, despite his previous objections, he appeared in *Graham's Magazine* for January, 1842, and soon became one of Graham's headliners.

In the meantime Poe, upon request, submitted some of his poems to Rufus Griswold for inclusion in that compiler's anthology, *The Poets and Poetry of America*. Earlier in the month Poe had praised "The Beleaguered City" in his letter to Longfellow; now, he called Griswold's attention to the similarity between the Longfellow poem and his own "Haunted Palace" in what was evidently a private attempt to acquit himself in advance of the charge of plagiarism. "The Beleaguered City" was well known, not only to subscribers of the *Knickerbocker*, but to readers of *Voices*, whereas his own poem had led an obscure, not to say fugitive, existence; and he no doubt felt justified in trying to forestall the charge. It would have been embarrassing, to say the least, to one who had so recently accused Longfellow of plagiarizing from Tennyson to be accused, in turn, of plagiarizing from Longfellow. Thus, Poe furnished Griswold with evidence that "The Haunted Palace" antedated Longfellow's poem. If he could have conceded the possibility of coincidence, his tone would have been less offensive, but Poe typically saw such likenesses only as evidence of plagiarism:

I first published the H.P. in Brooks' "Museum", a monthly journal of Baltimore, now dead. Afterwards, I embodied it in a tale called "The House of Usher" in Burton's Magazine. Here it was, I suppose, that Prof. Longfellow saw it; for, about 6 weeks afterwards, there appeared in the South. Lit. Mess: a poem by him called "The Beleaguered City", which may now be found in his volume [*Voices*]. The identity in title is striking; for by the Haunted Palace I mean

26. Letter dated June 22, 1841 (Ostrom, *Poe's Letters*, I, 166–167).

to imply a mind haunted by phantoms—a disordered brain—and by the Beleaguered City Prof. L. means just the same. But the whole tournure of the poem is based upon mine, as you will see at once. Its allegorical conduct, the style of its versification & expression—all are mine.[27]

As matters turned out, plagiarism was adduced from this evidence only by Poe and, after Poe's death, by Griswold. Though in full possession of the facts, that compiler twisted the charge so that Poe was made to appear the plagiarist of Longfellow. Moreover, using these very poems as evidence, Griswold commented that Poe's "plagiarisms are scarcely paralleled for their audacity in all literary history." Griswold even assigned this as "the first cause of all that malignant criticism which for so many years he carried on against Longfellow."[28]

Before he reviewed another Longfellow volume, Poe alluded to the Cambridge poet on four occasions,[29] twice quite cuttingly and twice quite admiringly, an ambivalence that was to become characteristic of his attitude toward Longfellow. If he could have explained imitation in terms of coincidence, Poe would have been, allowing for his aesthetic reservations, one of Longfellow's strongest advocates, for he never doubted his genius. But unable, for most of his career, to explain imitation in any terms other than intention, he praised the poet but condemned the "plagiarist." His attitude became quite clear in his review of Wilmer's *Quacks of Helicon*. Confronted with Wilmer's indictment that Longfellow "Steals all he can and butchers what he steals,"[30] Poe treated the statement as a half-truth. "Mr. Longfellow *will* steal," he conceded, "but, perhaps, he

27. Letter dated May 29, 1841 (*ibid.*, pp. 160–161). The bibliographical information in this letter is correct. "The Haunted Palace" first appeared in the *American Museum of Science, Literature and the Arts* in April, 1839, and, later, incorporated into "The Fall of the House of Usher," appeared in *Burton's* in Sept., 1839. The Longfellow poem first appeared in the *Southern Literary Messenger* in Nov., 1839. Earlier, in reviewing *Voices*, Poe had said that he regarded "The Beleaguered City" as Longfellow's "finest poem," for he discovered "a certainty of purpose about it which we do not discover elsewhere"—a statement that some may consider as sincere praise but that others, familiar with Poe's penchant for tongue-in-cheek remarks, may want to consider otherwise.
28. "Memoir," *The Literati*, pp. xxxii–xxxiii.
29. These four notices appeared in *Graham's Magazine*, XIX (Aug., 1841), 92; (Nov., 1841), 229; and XX (Feb., 1842), 129 and 120, to note them in the order in which they are discussed in the text.
30. *Quacks of Helicon*, pp. 35–36.

cannot help it, (for we have heard of such thing,) and then it must not be denied that *nil tetigit quod non ornavit*." Similarly, Poe in his signed "Chapter on Autography" declared that Longfellow was "entitled to the first place among the poets of America," but that he was guilty of imitation—"an imitation sometimes verging upon downright theft." Yet twice in February, 1842, Poe praised Longfellow without qualification. In atomizing a poem by Cornelius Mathews, he remarked that the poem had first appeared in *Arcturus,* a magazine co-edited by Mathews, where, insultingly, "it took precedence of some exceedingly beautiful stanzas by Professor Longfellow...." And in another critique he observed that John Brainard has "written poems which may rank with those of any American, with the single exception of Longfellow...."

The publication of Longfellow's second small collection of verse, *Ballads and Other Poems* (1841), which contained four translations and twelve of his own poems, including "The Skeleton in Armour," "The Wreck of the Hesperus," "The Village Blacksmith," and "Excelsior," consolidated Longfellow's literary position and entitled him to be called—as he has been called—America's first professional poet and her unofficial poet laureate. Of the many reviews celebrating the book, Felton's in the *North American Review* is perhaps most pertinent. Longfellow had become so established and the salability of his works so certain that Felton, in his thirty-page discussion, conceded that Longfellow no longer needed puffs— that the mere announcement of a book bearing his name would suffice to guarantee a best-seller. Nevertheless, not to blink at the fact, Felton continued to review almost every one of Longfellow's works and almost always in the *North American*:

> Mr. Longfellow's poetry has become so generally known, and, wherever known, is so universally admired, as to need no aid from the journals of literature.... It is, therefore, with no expectation of adding to its widespread renown, or of increasing the number of its admirers, that we call our readers' attention to this second volume [of poetry] from Professor Longfellow's pen.[31]

31. LV (July, 1842), 114–144. This passage is quoted from p. 114.

In the din of such universal and generally uncritical acclaim, Poe's two reviews of the *Ballads* may be unique for their reservations. In the first of these reviews, Poe remarked that he had space only "to say a few random words of welcome to these 'Ballads,' by Longfellow, and to tender him, and all such as he, the homage of our earnest love and admiration." Nevertheless, the man who had argued early in his career (in his "Letter to B——") that a poem "is opposed to a work of science by having for its *immediate* object pleasure, not truth," and who, at the end of his career (in "The Poetic Principle") charged that the "heresy of *The Didactic*" had "accomplished more in the corruption of our Poetical Literature than all its other enemies combined," felt compelled to qualify his homage. Thus, he said that Longfellow's insistence on didactics was preventing him from realizing his full genius—that his conception of the aim of poetry was, in fact, forcing him to utter conventionalities that, by their nature, seemed imitative and reminiscent. In Poe's words:

Much as we admire the genius of Mr. Longfellow, we are fully sensible of his many errors of affectation and imitation. His artistical skill is great, and his ideality high. But his conception of the aims of poesy *is all wrong;* and this we shall prove at some future date—to our own satisfaction, at least. His didactics are *all out of place.* He has written brilliant poems—by accident; that is to say when permitting his genius to get the better of his conventional habit of thinking. . . . We do not mean to say that a didactic moral may not be well made the *under-current* of a poetical thesis; but that it can never be well put so obtrusively forth, as in the majority of his compositions.[32]

In the following month Poe devoted another review to the *Ballads* to amplify points he had raised here. This second review was no more an attack upon Longfellow than the first. Rather, it was Poe's effort to release him from the trammels of didacticism. For Longfellow's error, Poe contended, is that he regards the inculcation of a moral as essential to his poetry and thereby does violent wrong to his high powers: "His invention, his imagery, his all, is made subservient to the eluci-

32. *Graham's Magazine,* XX (March, 1842), 189–190.

dation of some one or more points . . . which he looks upon as *truth.* . . . Now with as deep a reverence for 'the true' as ever inspired the bosom of mortal man, we would limit, in many respects, its modes of inculcation. . . ." Yet he did not wish to be misunderstood. Poetry "is not forbidden to depict—but to reason and preach of virtue." He then said that the true poet is not concerned with truth but with beauty. He recognized that such a rigorous definition would rule out much of what has been considered poetic—*Hudibras* and the *Essay on Man,* for instance—and he cited Keats as the poet "most fully instinct with the principles now developed. . . . Beauty is always his aim."

We have thus shown our ground of objection to the general *themes* of Professor Longfellow. In common with all who claim the sacred title of poet, he should limit his endeavors to the creation of novel moods of beauty. . . . To what the world terms *prose* may be safely and properly left all else. . . .

Of the pieces which constitute the present volume, there are not more than one or two thoroughly fulfilling the idea above proposed . . . [for] the aim of instruction . . . has been too obviously substituted for the legitimate aim, *beauty.*[33]

Poe was either uncertain of his position or else overstated his views in an effort to make a strong case against the heresy of the didactic, a "heresy" that, needless to say, was an orthodoxy in its time. In his first review of the *Ballads,* he made a mechanical division between the aesthetic and the moral (Poe used the term *didactic* loosely, sometimes in connection with moral truth, more often in connection with conventional doctrine and obtrusive moral tags), saying that a "didactic moral may . . . be . . . the *under-current* of a poetical thesis. . . ." In the second review, however, he declared that poetry has nothing to do with truth (the "obstinate oils and waters of Poetry and Truth" are irreconcilable)—an assertion he repeated to the very words in "The Poetic Principle" when deriding the idea that "the ultimate object of all Poetry is Truth." Yet in both

33. *Ibid.,* XX (April, 1842), 248–251. This and the second review of the *Ballads* caused Lewis Clark, when reviewing *The Raven and Other Poems* in the *Knickerbocker* (XXVII, Jan., 1846, 69–72), to reason that, since Poe claimed "there cannot be such a thing as a didactic poem," a poem, according to Poe, "is a metrical composition without ideas."

reviews of the *Ballads* and in other contexts, Poe suggested that when the moral becomes aesthetic—when, in other words, the moral, far from being an appendage to a poem, becomes implicit in the poem—"Poetry and Truth" are perfectly reconcilable. In discussing, for example, Ludwig Uhland's "Das Glück von Edenhall," which Longfellow had translated and included in the *Ballads,* Poe remarked that the "pointed moral with which it terminates is so exceedingly natural—so perfectly fluent from the incidents—that we have hardly heart to pronounce it in bad taste." His objection, clearly, is to the explicit statement of a moral that should have been made implicit in the poem. Even in "The Poetic Principle" Poe cited among "a few of the simple elements which induce in the Poet himself the true poetical effect. . . . all noble thoughts . . . all holy impulses. . . ." And in his "Marginalia" Poe categorically declared: "I confidently maintain that the *highest* genius is but the loftiest moral nobility."[34]

Though Poe went too far in denying the relation between the moral and aesthetic, we should not lose sight of the significant fact that he was fighting fire with fire and an extreme position with an extreme position. The position he was opposing is that a work of art is never self-justifying: it justifies itself only insofar as it imparts ethical doctrine—a position that even Emerson, for all his brilliance, rigidly adopted in "The Poet." Thus, artistic value is identified with, if not identical to, moral content; therefore, the loftier the moral, the greater the work of art; and, by the same reasoning, a work of art that has no ostensible message must be, a priori, seriously deficient. As Poe stated the case more fully in "The Poetic Principle":

It has been assumed, tacitly and avowedly, directly and indirectly, that the ultimate object of all Poetry is Truth. Every poem, it is said, should inculcate a moral; and by this moral is the poetical merit of the work to be adjudged. We Americans especially have

----

34. *Southern Literary Messenger,* XV (June, 1849), 336. Norman Foerster discusses this problem too in "Poe," *American Criticism: Studies in Literary Theory from Poe to the Present* (Boston, 1928), pp. 8–14, as does Floyd Stovall in "Poe's Debt to Coleridge," *University of Texas Studies in English* 10 (July, 1930), pp. 112–114.

patronised this happy idea; and we Bostonians, very especially, have developed it in full. We have taken it into our heads that to write a poem simply for the poem's sake, and to acknowledge such to have been our design, would be to confess ourselves radically wanting in the true Poetic dignity and force:—but the simple fact is, that, would we but permit ourselves to look into our own souls, we should immediately there discover that under the sun there neither exists nor *can* exist any work more thoroughly dignified—more supremely noble than this very poem—this poem *per se*—this poem which is a poem and nothing more—this poem written solely for the poem's sake.[35]

Whether Poe misrepresented or had failed to synthesize his views, he did not distort Longfellow's, as anyone familiar with the *Voices* and *Ballads* is aware. Earlier, Longfellow had stated the principle implicit in such poems as "The Rainy Day," "A Psalm of Life," "The Village Blacksmith," and "Excelsior," that the "natural tendency of poetry is to give us correct moral impressions, and thereby advance the cause of truth and the improvement of society"[36]—a tendency he reinforced by emasculating the burly Jean Paul Richter and the passionate Heinrich Heine in his "translations, comments, and frequent imitations of these writers. . . ." Thus a poet in whose work "there was always enough easily recognizable middle-class morality . . . to make him seem entirely safe in a country still distrustful of beauty for its own sake,"[37] and who adopted principles associated more with Pope and Gray than with Shelley and Keats, was bound to be received with some reser-

---

35. *Sartain's Union Magazine,* VII (Oct., 1850), 232–233. For an almost identical statement written during the so-called Longfellow war, see Poe's article, "Increase of Poetical Heresy," *Weekly Mirror,* I (Feb. 8, 1845), 281.

36. "Defence of Poetry," *North American Review,* XXXIV (Jan., 1832), 56.

37. Both these quotations are from Odell Shepard's Introduction to *Henry Wadsworth Longfellow: Representative Selections* (New York, 1934), pp. xxxi and xxxix respectively. Whatever may be said about the nature of poetry, Poe's essential criticism holds: didacticism, especially of a truistic nature, is anti-poetic. According to modern critics, Poe was much too gentle with Longfellow in this respect, for he cited (in regard to the *Ballads,* for instance) too many exceptions ("The Village Blacksmith," "The Wreck of the Hesperus," and "The Skeleton in Armour"), despite the fact that he objected to such moral tags as that which concludes "The Village Blacksmith":

> "Thanks, thanks to thee, my worthy friend,
>   For the lesson thou hast taught!
> Thus at the flaming forge of life
>   Our fortunes must be wrought,
> Thus on its sounding anvil shaped
>   Each burning deed and thought."

vation by a Romantic critic like Poe. The fact that Poe could not dismiss him out of hand is indication enough that Longfellow was a force to reckon with. We can only conjure with the idea of what Longfellow might have accomplished had Poe become his literary conscience, as Edmund Wilson became Scott Fitzgerald's, at least to the extent of urging him to reexamine his poetic principles or of listening to his neighbor Emerson when he said in "The Poet": ". . . it is not metres, but a metre-making argument that makes a poem—a thought so passionate and alive that like the spirit of a plant or an animal it has an architecture of its own. . . ." Yet America, needless to say, was hardly prepared to receive poets who wrote "simply for the poem's sake" or whose poems (to use Emerson's phrase) did not contain "the ground-tone of conventional life," despite the efforts by Poe and others to prepare the ground for their reception. Had Longfellow been tempted to write otherwise—had he used ideas less comfortably familiar, sentiments less aseptically decent, didactics less obtrusive, language less explicit and mellifluous—his poems might in their time have shared the fate of *Leaves of Grass* (Whitman, after all, had listened to Emerson) rather than have enjoyed what was probably the greatest popular success that any poems ever had—and success more than greatness seems to have been Longfellow's concern.

Poe did not review Longfellow's next volume, his *Poems on Slavery* (1842), disqualifying himself, perhaps, on the grounds of his antipathy to abolitionism and his avowed prejudice to didactic poetry. But in 1843 he used a stanza from "A Psalm of Life" as an epigraph to his story, "The Tell-Tale Heart,"[38] and in a letter to Lowell he reaffirmed his conviction that "Longfellow has genius. . . ." Yet, however much he admired the poet, he confessed that he did not know "how to understand him at times. I am in doubt whether he should not be termed an arrant plagiarist." He then called Lowell's attention to

---

38. As the tale appeared in *The Pioneer*, I (Jan., 1843), 29–31. In his subsequent reprinting of the story in the *Broadway Journal* of Aug. 23, 1845, Poe dropped the epigraph because, as he said during his quarrel with "Outis," the stanza was a plagiarism.

Longfellow's recent book, *The Spanish Student: A Play in Three Acts* (1843), and mentioned that he had written "quite a long notice of it for Graham's December number. The play," he added, "is a poor composition, with some fine poetical passages."[39]

This notice was never printed in *Graham's* for two reasons. First, Graham would hardly welcome adverse criticism of a work that had originally appeared in his own magazine.[40] Second, both Graham and Griswold (the latter was now editor of *Graham's*) had had trouble with Longfellow and were using their rejection of Poe's adverse review to reconcile their star contributor. The trouble began in 1842 when an artist, Franquinet by name, had painted a portrait of Longfellow while the poet was abroad, which, without Longfellow's approval, was engraved to appear in *Graham's* in May, 1843. When the poet returned from Europe and saw the portrait, he was angry at the thought that Graham and Griswold would allow this "most atrocious libel imaginable; a very vulgar individual, looking very drunk and very cunning," to appear in the magazine and demanded that the painting and the plate be destroyed. Graham, faced with the choice of sacrificing the $405 he had invested or of losing his headliner, decided to concede to Longfellow's demand and begin all over again "with a portrait—the best you have." But Longfellow had none that satisfied him and insisted that he be given time to have one done. Graham refused to wait and the portrait made its scheduled appearance.[41] The "libel" was atrocious enough to impel Lewis Clark to condemn the portrait in the *Knickerbocker* as a " '*counterfeit* presentment,' sure enough"; to assert that "the artist ought to be indicted"; and to describe Longfellow as a "handsome man with 'soft and flowing hair,' touched with the slightest possible tinge of 'sable silver;' an eye with a liquid, interior look," etc.[42]

39. Dated Oct. 19, 1843 (Ostrom, *Poe's Letters,* I, 238).
40. The play appeared in *Graham's* in three instalments: XXI (Sept., 1842), 109–113; (Oct., 1842), 176–180; and (Nov., 1842), 229–234. Poe's review was five pages long and Poe expected to receive $20 for it (see Ostrom, I, 272).
41. Bayless, *Griswold,* pp. 57–58.
42. XXI (June, 1843), 591.

Griswold, who relinquished his editorship of *Graham's* in October of that year, wrote Longfellow in an evident attempt to placate him and smeared Poe in the process. Poe, he said,

has recently written an elaborate review of your "Student" in his customary vein, but if anything a bit more personal and malignant than usual. This was offered to Graham before I left, and has since been *given* to him—so anxious is the poor critic for its appearance; but of course Mr. Graham refused it. I mention the circumstances because it would be very like Poe, since he cannot find a publisher for his "criticism," to attempt to win your friendship with his praise.[43]

Graham also sought to pacify Longfellow by showing a concern for him which he had failed to show before in respect to the portrait:

I have a savage review of your "Spanish Student" from the pen of Poe, which shall *not* appear in Graham. I do not know what your crime may be in the eye of Poe, but suppose it may be a better, and more widely established reputation. Or if you have wealth—which I suppose you *have*—that is sufficient to settle your damnation so far as Mr Poe may be presumed capable of effecting it. . . .

I had to suffer $30 [Poe had asked only $20] for the review of you and you shall have it for as many cents when you come along this way, I do not suppose it will ever be redeemed, and I doubt if the writer of it will be.[44]

As he exaggerated the price, Graham seems to have exaggerated the severity of the review. Soon after Poe had submitted the critique to Graham, he had observed that the *Student* as a play was poor but that it contained fine poetical passages. Moreover, his treatment of that play in his article "The American Drama" fails to justify Graham's statement. In that article Poe stated the crux of his position, that the "great adversary of Invention is Imitation." One must forget the old models and "consider *de novo* . . . the *capabilities* of the drama—not

---

43. Letter dated Dec. 26, 1843 (quoted by Bayless, *Griswold*, p. 76). The statement that Graham refused the review is untrue. In a letter to Longfellow dated March 11, 1845 (quoted by Mary E. Phillips, *Edgar Allan Poe: The Man*, Chicago, 1926, II, 978), Graham acknowledged that Poe had "written demanding return of Review. . . . If he sends money or another article I shall be obliged to let him have it. . . ." Griswold's last statement is merely malice, arising from the fact that Poe had trained his fire on Griswold in a lecture which he delivered on Nov. 25, 1843, in Philadelphia (see Campbell, *Mind of Poe*, p. 65). It was not Poe who attempted to win Longfellow's friendship either by letter or criticism, but Griswold himself.

44. Letter dated Feb. 9, 1844 (quoted by Bayless, *Griswold*, p. 76).

merely ... its conventional purposes." In considering Nathaniel Willis's *Tortesa, the Usurer,* he objected to mere complexity passing for plot. Ideally, he said, a plot "is perfect only inasmuch as we shall find ourselves unable to detach from it or *disarrange* any single incident involved, without *destruction* to the mass...." Practically, a plot may be considered of "high excellence, when no one of its component parts shall be susceptible of *removal* without *detriment* to the whole."

Then he turned to *The Spanish Student,* which had passed through three editions in the first year of its publication and with which Longfellow confessed himself "much disheartened. Neither you [Ward], nor Sumner, nor Ticknor, nor Felton likes it.... I shall probably throw it into the fire."[45] Poe dissented from the general opinion regarding the play. The few, he asserted, who do not have their opinions formed for them "received the play with a commendation somewhat less *prononcée* ... than Professor Longfellow might have desired, or may have been taught to expect." He then quoted the "finer passages.... by way of justice to the poet" and proceeded to criticize the dramatist. He demonstrated that Longfellow was imitative of the old models: he mistook complexity for plot; his incidents were the stock-in-trade of a "thousand and one comedies"; two-thirds of his material was unnecessary and the arrangement of it was random; moreover, the play echoed the "quaint and stilted tone of the English dramatists":

In fact throughout "The Spanish Student," as well as throughout other compositions of its author, there runs a very obvious vein of *imitation.* We are perpetually reminded of something we have seen before ... and even where the similarity cannot be said to amount to plagiarism, it is still injurious to the poet in the good opinion of him who reads. ...

Upon the whole, we regret that Professor Longfellow has written this work, and feel especially vexed that he has committed himself by its republication. Only when regarded as a mere poem, can it be said to have merit of any kind. ... We are not too sure, indeed, that a "dramatic poem" is not a flat contradiction in terms. At all events a man of true genius, (and such Mr. L. unquestionably is,) has no business with these hybrid and paradoxical compositions. Let a poem be a poem only; let a play be a play and nothing more. As for "The

45. Livingston, *Longfellow Bibliography,* p. 35.

Spanish Student," its thesis is unoriginal; its incidents are antique; its plot is no plot; its characters have no character; in short, it is little better than a play upon words, to style it "A Play" at all.[46]

That this is harsh criticism cannot be doubted. The only question is whether the harshness is not an inevitable consequence of Poe's aesthetic principles and critical candor. Poe, of course, thought so. When the New York *Evening Gazette* of August 8, 1845, declared this review a "somewhat sweeping condemnation" and added, "but Mr. Longfellow does not seem to please Mr. Poe in anything that he writes," Poe was indignant. In the *Broadway Journal* of August 16, 1845, he replied that he had been grossly misrepresented by the statement that he could find nothing to admire in Longfellow:

From Mr. L.'s first appearance in the literary world until the present moment, we have been, if not his warmest admirer and most steadfast defender, at least *one* of his warmest and most steadfast. We even so far committed ourselves . . . as to place him . . . at the very head of American poets. Yet, because we are not so childish as to suppose that every book is thoroughly good or thoroughly bad—because we are not so absurd as to adopt the common practice of wholesale and indiscriminate abuse or commendation—because upon several occasions we have thought proper to *demonstrate* the sins, while displaying the virtues of Professor Longfellow, is it just, or proper, or even courteous on the part of "The Gazette" to accuse us, in round terms, of uncompromising hostility to this poet?[47]

These were Poe's major reviews of Longfellow, and before we turn to less literary, more journalistic, matters, we should assess them briefly. With one conspicuous exception—the shot-in-the-dark accusation that Longfellow had plagiarized his "Midnight Mass" from Tennyson, not to mention the occasional harshness of tone that Poe seems to have considered an earmark of critical candor—nothing in the Poe critiques we have examined seems in any way discreditable. In the first

---

46. *American Review*, II (Aug., 1845), 117–131.
47. In the light of such evidence, one is tempted to surmise that Graham was feigning indignation in his letter and was really glad to have the opportunity Poe had given him to appease Longfellow. The fact that Graham continued to publish Poe's contributions, that he remained friends with Poe, and that he militantly came to his defense when Griswold blackened him in the "Ludwig" article and in the "Memoir," seems to lend support to this surmise. In any case, Graham's failure to publish the review was bound to strike Poe as an attempt to grant Longfellow critical indemnity.

of them, Poe pronounced *Hyperion* imitative and disunified, a judgment that can hardly be questioned. In the second, he said that *Voices* evinced poetic genius but not of the highest order—a declaration that errs, if at all, on the side of indulgence. In the two reviews of the *Ballads*, Poe demonstrated that Longfellow, by warping his art for didactic ends, was abusing his high powers, and he attempted, in the process, to perform a service for him, from which, at least for his present reputation, he might have benefited enormously. In his article on the American drama, Poe again stated what seems sufficiently clear, that *The Spanish Student* as a drama is devoid of merit. And in passing, Poe remarked that Longfellow was entitled to the first place among American poets, but that his tendency to imitate sometimes verged on plagiarism.[48]

Poe did not notice Longfellow again until he had joined the staff of the *Mirror* as assistant editor.[49] In reviewing his *Waif* (1844, dated 1845), a collection of about fifty poems to which Longfellow contributed only the "Proem" ("The day is done and the darkness . . ."), Poe made three significant comments. First, that the "Proem" was the best poem in the collection, despite the fact that the anthology contained works by Herrick, Marvell, Shelley, and Browning. Second, that a comparison of "The Death-Bed" by Hood (which also appeared in *The Waif*) and a poem that appeared in Griswold's *Poets and Poetry of*

48. Poe's concern with copyism may strike one as a quirk; yet, to quote the findings of Nelson Adkins, who has published the most thorough study of that problem to date: "Any examination of Poe's principles touching the problem of plagiarism leads, it seems to me, to one conclusion: the man's essential sincerity in the charges he was continually making. In art, Poe stood for *genius*, and what must inevitably be the product of genius, *originality*. This high critical purpose Poe stated unequivocally" (" 'Chapter on American Cribbage': Poe and Plagiarism," *Papers of the Bibliographical Society of America*, XLII, Third Quarter, 1948, 169–210).

49. The *Mirror*, at this time under the ownership of Nathaniel Willis, George Morris, and Hiram Fuller, appeared in two editions—the *Evening Mirror* and the *Weekly Mirror*. The evening edition appeared six times a week and was unpaginated; the weekly edition, consisting largely of items published in the *Evening Mirror*, appeared on Saturday. In the *Weekly Mirror*, I (Oct. 12, 1844), 15, Willis alluded to Poe's connection with the journal for the first time: "We wish to light beacons for an authors' crusade and we have no leisure to be more than its Peter the Hermit. We solemnly summon Edgar Poe to do the devoir of Coeur de Lion—no man's weapon half so trenchant!"

America (which Poe mentioned neither by title nor author) showed that *"somebody is a thief."* Third:

We conclude our notice on the "Waif," with the observation that, although full of beauties, it is infected with a *moral taint*—or is this a mere freak of our fancy? We shall be pleased if it be so;—but there *does* appear . . . a very careful avoidance of all American poets who may be supposed especially to interfere with the claims of Mr. Long-fellow. These men Mr. Longfellow can continuously *imitate* (*is* that the word?) and yet never even incidentally commend.[50]

If there was any single reason for the animus of this final comment, one can find it in an anonymous article that, upon its appearance in the London *Foreign Quarterly Review,* became a *cause célèbre.* Typical of the English view except in its wholesale condemnation, the article insisted that American poets were either imitators or plagiarists. The major exception was "the most accomplished of the brotherhood, Henry Wadsworth Longfellow. But we have some doubts whether he can be fairly considered an indigenous specimen. His mind was educated in Europe. . . . But America claims him, and is entitled to him. . . . He is unquestionably the first of her poets, the most thoughtful and chaste; the most elaborate and finished." Among the imitators and plagiarists was Poe, a "capital artist after the manner of Tennyson; [who] approaches the spirit of his original more closely than any of them." The article concluded with the statement that almost every American poet was "on a level with the versifiers who fill up the corners of our provincial journals, into which all sorts of platitudes are admitted by the indiscriminate courtesy of the printer."[51]

Poe, of course, considered the charge of imitation ridiculous. Writing to Lowell, who had been completely ignored by the

50. This notice, entitled "Longfellow's Waif," appeared in two instalments in the *Evening Mirror,* I (Jan. 13 and 14, 1845). The notice was also republished in its entirety in the *Weekly Mirror,* I (Jan. 25, 1845), 250–251, together with Willis's "disclaimer," "H.'s" reply, and "Post-Notes by the Critic," to be discussed in the text. Since no satisfactory bibliographical notation exists on this "controversy," I have documented the exchanges in detail.

51. "The Poets of America," XXXII (Jan., 1844), 291–324. For an amusing article that returns the compliment by using the same arguments and, at times, the same language, see "The Morals, Manners, and Poetry of England—The Poets and Poetry of America: An Article in the Foreign Quarterly Review, for January, 1844," *North American Review,* LIX (July, 1844), 1–44.

Foreign Quarterly reviewer, Poe asked if he had seen the article:

It has been denied that Dickens wrote it—but, to me, the article affords so strong internal evidence of his hand that I would as soon think of doubting my existence. He tells much truth—although he evinces much ignorance and more spleen. Among other points he accuses myself of "metrical imitation" of Tennyson, citing, by way of instance, passages from poems which were written & published long before Tennyson was heard of:—but I have, at no time, made any poetical pretension.[52]

In answering Poe's letter, Lowell said that the article was written, not by Dickens but by John Forster, Dickens' friend, though Dickens "may have given him hints. Forster is a friend of some of the Longfellow clique here which perhaps accounts for his putting L. at the top of our Parnassus."[53]

In reaction to this information, Poe apparently felt that

52. Letter dated March 30, 1844 (Ostrom, *Poe's Letters,* I, 246–247). That Poe wrote earlier than Tennyson may or may not be true: Poe often claimed to have been precocious. But that he published before Tennyson is an error, since both their first volumes appeared in 1827. The error seems an honest one, however, since Tennyson's first book—*Poems by Two Brothers*—did not reach America until the 1850's. See Eidson, *Tennyson in America,* p. 3.

53. Letter dated June 27, 1844 (quoted by W. M. Griswold, ed., *Passages from the Correspondence and Other Papers of Rufus W. Griswold,* Cambridge, Mass., 1898, p. 151). Woodberry, when he earlier published this letter in "Lowell's Letters to Poe," *Scribner's Magazine,* XVI (Aug., 1894), 170–176, expurgated the last sentence quoted. Lowell's surmise rather than Poe's seems correct, though both surmises could be right if Dickens and Forster had collaborated. Longfellow too felt that Forster had a "hand in" the article, a speculation that does not necessarily exclude Dickens. More than a year after the article appeared, Longfellow wrote to Forster: "I have never yet thanked you directly, though I have commissioned Felton to do it, for the cordial praise of me in the Foreign Quarterly, which I am confident you had a hand in, & for which I beg you now to receive my warmest thanks." To which Longfellow added: "It has had a curious effect here, namely that of making some of the critics very furious against me; but that is of no consequence, as in the end I am confident the result will be good." (Letter dated May 8, 1845, from a typescript supplied by Mr. A. W. Wheen of the Victoria & Albert Museum.) Though Forster answered this letter of Longfellow's on June 3, he conspicuously avoided any denial of having had a hand in the article. (This Forster letter is in the Houghton Library at Harvard University, and I am grateful to Mr. William H. Bond, Curator of MSS there, for finding it for me.) The "Longfellow clique" had entertained Dickens in 1842 when he visited America, and Longfellow had been in correspondence with Dickens and Forster before he became a guest in Dickens' home while on his third European trip, where he renewed his friendship with Forster. The warmth that Forster and Dickens felt for Longfellow is evident in Forster's letter to Longfellow dated Jan. 3, 1843, a year before the article in the *Foreign Quarterly* was published: ". . . here will Dickens and myself be smacking our lips . . . in brimming bumpers in honor of Henry Wadsworth Longfellow" (Samuel Longfellow, *Longfellow,* II, 7).

Longfellow, inadvertently or otherwise, had been instrumental in enlisting a transatlantic journal for the purpose of reducing almost every other American poet's claim to an impertinence so that, relatively, his position would be all the more unquestionable. Moreover, as a consequence, he probably began to see himself as the butt of a bad joke. He who had condemned imitation was now charged with that very sin. The man whose imitativeness he had censured was now held up as an original poet, at least by conspicuous default of any statement to the contrary in an article teeming with charges of imitation and plagiarism. And, as if to make the barb penetrate deeper, the poet he was said to imitate was the very poet he had accused Longfellow of plagiarizing. Whatever the validity of these speculations, Poe found the stigma of imitation so intolerable that, to exculpate himself, he footnoted the section "Poems Written in Youth" in the *Raven* volume (1845) as follows: "Private reasons—some of which have reference to the sin of plagiarism, and others to the date of Tennyson's first poems—have induced me, after some hesitation, to republish these, the crude compositions of my earliest boyhood . . . . the date of which is too remote to be judiciously acknowledged."[54] Thus, to all appearances, the remarks in the *Foreign Quarterly* were still rankling in Poe when he reviewed *The Waif*.

Poe's innuendoes in the *Mirror* drove Hiram Fuller and George Morris, co-editors of that journal, to print a joint disclaimer of them, saying: "For the opinions of the Daily paper, Mr. Willis is alone the gate-keeper, and by himself or by his direction, all its principal articles are written."[55] Poe's allegations, moreover, elicited a letter from a self-acknowledged friend of Longfellow, a Mr. "H.," now known to have been George S. Hillard,[56] one of the members of the

54. The poems in that section, with the exception of "To Helen," were, in fact, selected from his 1827 and 1829 volumes, although they appeared in their revised forms (see Quinn, *Poe*, p. 482).

55. *Weekly Mirror*, I (Jan. 18, 1845), 227. Despite this disclaimer, Poe's *Waif* review also appeared in the *Weekly Mirror* on Jan. 25.

56. This identification was made by R. Baird Shuman, "Longfellow, Poe, and *The Waif*," *Publications of the Modern Language Association*, LXXVI

"Five of Clubs" at Cambridge, which included Henry R. Cleveland, Charles Sumner, Cornelius C. Felton, and Longfellow. The letter, coming from Boston and dated January 15, was published in the *Evening Mirror* on January 20, and was prefaced by Willis, who also disclaimed responsibility for the *Waif* review: "We are willing to take any position to serve our friends, and if, by chance, we play the antagonist to shew another's 'skill of fence' in his behalf, we trust not to be believed less his friend, after the joust is over. The criticisms on the 'Waif' ... were written in our office by an able though very critical hand." Willis also made a point of publishing in this and the next issue of the *Evening Mirror* Lowell's high estimate of Poe as a critic that was to appear in the February number of *Graham's Magazine*.

"H.'s" principal concern was "with the sting in the tail of the second communication [the second instalment of Poe's review of *The Waif*], in which Mr. Longfellow is charged with omitting, from discreditable motives, any extracts from American poets, though he continuously imitates some of them. This is no light accusation; and is one against which his friends feel bound to enter their most emphatic protest." "H." maintained that an anthologist has the privilege of selecting any materials he cares to and declared that the charge of discrimination was wholly untrue, especially in this instance, since he had known the compiler for a long time. "If it be asked," he concluded, "why has he not given public demonstration of this kindness of spirit towards his poetical brethren, the answer is obvious. He is a poet himself, and addresses the public in that capacity, and not as a critic.... The charge of habitually imitating other American poets touches Mr. Longfellow in his public character as a poet, and not his personal character as a man, and therefore requires no especial reply from his friends."

Directly following "H.'s" letter and under the title, "Post-Notes by the Critic," Poe published his rejoinder:

(March, 1961), 155–156. This article also identifies Charles Sumner as the second of Longfellow's defenders.

I did not dispute Mr. L.'s *'right'* to construct his book as he thought proper. I reserve to myself the right of thinking what I choose of the construction. . . .

As 'the charge of habitually imitating other American poets requires no especial reply'—it shall surely rest undisturbed by any reply of mine. . . .

It seems to me that the whole state of the case may be paralleled thus:

A accosts B, with—"My dear friend, in common with all mankind, and the angels, I regard you as a demi-god. Your equal is not to be found in the country which is proud to claim you as a son. . . . but permit me! there is a very—a *very* little speck of dust on the extreme end of your nose—oblige yourself and your friends by brushing it away." "Sir," replies B, "what you have asserted is wholly untrue. . . . I consider you a malignant critic, and wish to have nothing further to do with you—for know that there *are* spots upon the sun, but my proboscis is a thing without spot!"

Nothing more was heard from "H." nor, apparently, was anything to be heard again from Boston or Cambridge on this score; and though, most likely, Poe would have furnished articles on imitation and plagiarism for the *Mirror,* he might have ignored Longfellow indefinitely. Unfortunately, however, a series of episodes occurred which gave a sensational vogue to Poe's comments and made it imperative for Longfellow's friends to rescue the poet from the notoriety which, for a time, threatened him.

On January 25 the Buffalo *Western Literary Messenger* published a letter from "Pi Kappa Rho," who compared Longfellow's translation of "The Good George Campbell from the German of O.L.B. Wolf[f]" (which had appeared in *Graham's Magazine* in February, 1843) with the ballad, "Bonnie George Campbell" (which had appeared in William Motherwell's collection, *Minstrelsy, Ancient and Modern,* Glasgow, 1828). "Pi Kappa Rho," assuming that Wolff, a professor at the University of Jena, had not translated the Scotch ballad, accused Longfellow of a "gross plagiarism" and of impudence in "supposing that he can, undetected, palm off upon us, in a mutilated state, this . . . beautiful ancient Scottish song, as a translation from the German of O.L.B. Wolf."

The charge, apparently unanswerable, became common editorial fare, which brought Longfellow's integrity into question and began to make Poe's recent allegations appear valid. Among the New York papers that carried the *Messenger* charge were *The Rover*, the *Broadway Journal*, and the *Daily Tribune*.[57] *The Rover*, also assuming that the Wolff translation did not exist, noted:

A writer in the Western Literary Messenger has recently detected this gentleman (Longfellow) in one of the most flagrant and unscrupulous pieces of plagiarism that ever occurred in our literature. In a critique upon his "Waif," in the Evening Mirror, a covert allusion was made to a disposition on the part of the "Professor" to thrive upon the hard-earned laurels of others, and the only fault of Willis's [sic] article was, that he merely hit the nail's head. . . .

The editor then printed the Scottish poem and Longfellow's alleged plagiarism side by side and concluded, "Singular *coincidence*, eh?"

The *Broadway Journal* observed: "Charges of plagiarism are very frequently made, and often with good reason, against our popular authors. . . . The 'Rover' . . . contains a very grave charge against Longfellow . . . which, if true, would lead us to distrust everything that came from his pen." The *Tribune*, however, cited a "correspondent of the Boston Post" to explain that Longfellow's error was not one of plagiarism but one of inadvertence:

In a collection of German poems which Mr. Longfellow owned, was a poem called 'Der gute Ritter [sic] Campbell;' this poem happened to be a translation and a plagiarism, as it was given for original, from an old English ballad. Longfellow suspecting nothing, translated it, and has hit so exactly upon a good version, that it is almost word for word with the English original. The remarkable thing is, that Longfellow, celebrated for his acquaintance with ballad literature, should have overlooked this lyric, which is printed in Motherwell's collection of ancient and modern Poems—so far have overlooked it, as to translate it out of German.—Homer occasionally nods.

This was scarcely a vindication. Since the source that Longfellow had used remained unspecified, the charge that Wolff plagiarized instead of merely translated is unsupported. A collection by Wolff that contains the poem is, as Poe later pointed out, *Halle der Völker: Sammlung vorzüglicher Volkslieder der bekanntesten Nationen, grösstentheils zum ersten Male metrisch in das Deutsche übertragen* (Frankfurt, 1837), a title that plainly clears Wolff of plagiarism. Aware that this explanation satisfied few of his critics, Longfellow wrote a letter to Graham, dated February 19, 1845, to explain the situation more convincingly. But mysteriously—and it is only one of the mysteries of this affair—the letter was not published in *Graham's* until May, 1845. The source he had used while abroad in the summer of 1842 was not a collection by Wolff at all, but one by Karl Gollmick. That collection, called *Der Sängersaal: Auswahl von Gedichten zum Komponieren* (Darmstadt, 1842), contained the Wolff translation of "Bonnie George Campbell," where it "appeared as an original poem by Wolf...." Fortunately, Longfellow found that the printer had made an error (actually, the error—or liberty taken—had originated with Wolff) and transcribed the Scottish river *Tay* for the German *Tag,* an error that Longfellow had faithfully translated and that, as he put it, is "an unimpeachable witness of the falsity of the charge brought against me."[58]

In the meantime, with Longfellow's honesty impugned and his reputation at stake, a second defender of Longfellow, now

58. *Graham's Magazine,* XXVI (May, 1845), 240. Another mystery is why, when Griswold, as editor of *Graham's,* explained that the poem was "really an old Scottish ballad" and even gave him some evidence of that fact in a letter dated March 3, 1843, Longfellow withheld an explanation of his mistake. (See Bayless, *Griswold,* p. 58.) Longfellow's diary entry of Sept. 19, 1842, shows that he copied "Der gute George Campbell von O.L.B. Wolf" from Gollmick's work, but no translation of the poem appears in the diary at this time, despite his statement in *Graham's* "that I immediately wrote a translation of it, with a pencil, in my pocketbook...." (I am grateful to Mr. William H. Bond, Curator of MSS of the Houghton Library at Harvard University for this information.) However, now that a copy of the Gollmick edition has been found (in the city library of Mainz, Germany), Longfellow's testimony can receive full corroboration. That collection *does* contain the Wolff translation, faithfully reproduced; Wolff *is* cited as the composer of the poem; and there is *no* suggestion in the compilation that the poem did not originate with Wolff. (I am grateful to Dr. Schneiders and Dr. Middendorf of the Bayerische Staatsbibliothek in Munich, as well as to Dr. Bulling of the Universitäts-Bibliothek in Jena and Dr. Köhler of the Deutsche Staatsbibliothek in Berlin, for assistance in this matter.) I have taken the liberty of making certain corrections and additions in the Longfellow explanation. He did not cite the subtitle of Gollmick's collection or the place and date of publication, and he spelled Gollmick's name with a final *h*.

identified as Charles Sumner, Longfellow's friend, decided to take issue with Poe's innuendoes regarding *The Waif.* Willis reopened the controversy with these words:

> Longfellow's Waif.—A friend, who is a very fine critic, gave us, not long since, a review of this delightful new book. Perfectly sure that any thing from that source was a treasure for our paper, we looked up from a half-read proof to run our eye hastily over it, and gave it to the printer—not, however, without mentally differing from the writer as to the drift of the last sentence....
>
> Notwithstanding the haste with which it passed through our attention (for we did not see it in proof) the question of admission was submitted to a principle in our mind; and, in admitting it, we did by Longfellow, as we would have him do by us. It was a literary charge, by a pen that never records an opinion without some supposed good reason, and only injurious to Longfellow, (to our belief) while circulating, un-replied-to, in *conversation-dom.* In the second while we reasoned upon it [we thought] ... Our critical friend believes this, though we do not. Longfellow is asleep on velvet; it will do him good to rouse him; his friends will come out and fight his battle; the charges (which to *us* would be a comparative pat on the back) will be openly disproved, and the acquittal of course leaves his fame brighter than before—the injurious whisper, in Conversation-dom, killed in the bargain!

Willis then proceeded to quote part of Charles Sumner's letter, though he did not disclose his correspondent's identity to the public:

> It has been asked, perhaps, why Lowell was neglected in this collection? Might it not as well be asked why Bryant, Dana and Halleck were neglected? The answer is obvious to any one who candidly considers the character of the collection. It professed to be, according to the Proem, from the humbler poets; and it was intended to embrace pieces that were anonymous, or which were not easily accessible to the general reader—the *waifs* and *estrays* of literature. To put anything of Lowell's, for example, into a collection of *waifs,* would be a particular liberty with pieces which are all collected and christened.[59]

Clearly, Longfellow was becoming good "copy," and, as editor of the *Mirror,* Willis had reason to encourage the "controversy." Yet, though Poe's remarks had apparently helped *Mirror* sales, Willis felt no need to sully his reputation for geniality by seconding Poe's charges nor, on the other hand,

---

59. *Evening Mirror,* I (Feb. 5, 1845) ; reprinted in the *Weekly Mirror,* I (Feb. 8, 1845), 287.

any urge to diminish those sales by discounting Poe's charges entirely. Graham, however, concerned with protecting the reputation of his drawing card, asked Willis to make his "disclaimer" stronger, a request with which Willis complied by saying that he "dissented from *all* the disparagement of Longfellow" in his assistant editor's review of *The Waif*.[60]

Graham wrote to Longfellow too: "What has 'broke loose' in Poe? I see he is down on you in New York papers and has written demanding return of Review [of *The Spanish Student*] I mentioned he had written for me. If he sends money or another article I shall be obliged to let him have it...." He added in a postscript: "Mr. Willis made a disclaimer of being an endorser of Poe's views, at my request. I cannot see what Poe says *now*, can hurt you."[61] And Mrs. Longfellow wrote to Samuel Longfellow just prior to Willis's publishing his stronger disclaimer: "If you see the *Mirror*, you know how shabbily Willis tries to excuse Poe's insolence. Have you seen a curious poem by the latter entitled 'The Raven,' most artistically rhythmical but 'nothing more,' to quote the burden?"[62]

Despite Willis's disavowal of "*all*" the disparagement of Longfellow," Poe was allowed to continue his criticism of Longfellow, this time indirectly in an article entitled "Imitation—Plagiarism." Having in mind such articles as that which had appeared in the *Foreign Quarterly*, Poe wrote that the "British reviewers have very frequently accused us of imitation, and the charge is undoubtedly well based." He explained why this was true:

60. *Evening Mirror*, I (Feb. 14, 1845); reprinted in the *Weekly Mirror*, I (Feb. 22, 1845), 317. Poe regarded Willis's disclaimer as satirically intended. "Now when we consider that many of the points of censure made by me in this *critique* [of *The Waif*] were absolutely as plain as the nose upon Mr. Longfellow's face—that it was impossible to gainsay them—that we defied him and his coadjutors to say a syllable in reply to them—and that they held their tongues and not a syllable said—when we consider all this, I say, then the satire of the '*all*' in Mr. Willis' manifesto becomes apparent at once. Mr. Longfellow did not see it; and I presume his friends did not see it. I did." (*Broadway Journal*, I, March 8, 1845, 147.)

61. Letter dated March 11, 1845; quoted by Phillips, *Poe*, II, 978.

62. Letter dated Feb. 13, 1845; quoted by Edward Wagenknecht, ed., *Mrs. Longfellow: Selected Letters and Journals of Fanny Appleton Longfellow* (*1817–1861*) (New York, 1956), p. 116. "The Raven" had appeared in the *Evening Mirror*, I (Jan. 29, 1845) and in the *Weekly Mirror*, I (Feb. 8, 1845), 276.

The want of an international copy-right law renders it impossible for our men of genius to obtain remuneration for their labors. Now since, as a body, men of genius are proverbially poor, the want of the international law represses their efforts altogether. Our sole writers, in consequence, are from the class of *dilettanti;* and although among this class are unquestionably many gifted men, still as a class—as men of wealth and leisure—they are imbued with a spirit of conservatism, which is merely a mood of the imitative spirit.

He then made the observation that the

sin of plagiarism involves the quintessence of meanness; and this meanness seems in the direct ratio of the amount of *honor* attained by the theft. A pickpocket is content with his plunder; the plagiarist demands that mankind should applaud him, not for plundering, but for the thing plundered.

He added, with an apparent allusion to Longfellow and his defenders:

When a plagiarism is detected, it generally happens that the public sympathy is with the plagiarist, and his friends proceed to every extreme in the way of exculpation. But how unjust! We should sympathize rather with him upon whom the plagiarism has been committed. Not only is he robbed of his property—of his fame ... but he is rendered liable by the crime of *the plagiarist to the suspicion of being a plagiarist himself.*[63]

Briggs in his magazine, the *Broadway Journal,* objected to Poe's allegation that James Aldrich—a New York editor and sometime poet—had stolen from Hood. The resemblance between the two poems, Briggs contended, was insufficient to warrant such a conclusion, and he urged, though he was in error, that Aldrich's poem had been written before Hood's.[64] Poe's reply, printed under the title "Plagiarism" and introduced by a brief and neutral foreword by Willis, was that there were ten distinct similarities between the two short poems, which he enumerated to support the conclusion that somebody was a thief, and—he added curtly—the "only doubt in our mind is about the sincerity of any one who shall say that somebody is *not.*"[65]

63. *Evening Mirror,* I (Feb. 15, 1845); reprinted in the *Weekly Mirror,* I (Feb. 22, 1845), 306.
64. I (Feb. 15, 1845), 109.
65. *Evening Mirror,* I (Feb. 17, 1845); reprinted in the *Weekly Mirror,* I (Feb. 22, 1845), 310.

On February 28 Poe mounted the platform of the New York Historical Society to deliver his lecture on American poets. The event was sensationally announced in the *Evening Mirror* as follows:

Edgar Poe's Lecture.—The decapitation of the criminal who did not know his head was off till it fell into his hand as he was bowing, is a Poe-kerish similitude, but it conveys an idea of the Damascene slicing of the critical blade of Mr. Poe. On Friday night we are to have his "Lecture on the Poets of America," and those who would witness fine carving will probably be there.[66]

The nature of the lecture can be inferred from the comments it elicited from the editors of the *Daily Tribune,* the *Evening Mirror, The Town,* and the *Democratic Review.*[67] Greeley observed that the lecture embodied "much acute and fearless criticism," but that Poe was often unjust in his censure of American reviewing. Moreover, he objected to Poe's "broad assertion that Longfellow is a plagiarist. Of all critical cant, this hunting after coincidence of ideas, or phrase, often unavoidable, between authors, is the least endurable." Nevertheless, he asked if the lecture might not be repeated. Willis stated that "one of the most readable and saleable of *books* would be a dozen of such Lectures by Mr. Poe, and we give him a publisher's counsel to print them." He mentioned that Poe discussed Bryant, Halleck, Longfellow, Sprague, and Dana and found Longfellow to have more genius than any of the others, but that "his fatal alacrity at imitation made him borrow, when he had better at home." *The Town* reported that the lecture "was worthy of its author—keen, cutting and withering, when it touched on the mountebanks of American literature; and full of faith and hope, when it spoke of the future." John L. O'Sullivan of the *Democratic Review* praised Poe for the

devoted spirit in which he advocated the claims and urged the responsibilities of literature. The necessity of a just independent criticism was his main topic. He made unmitigated war upon the prevalent Puffery, and dragged several popular idols from their pedestals. ... There has been a good deal said about this lecture, which should

66. I (Feb. 27, 1845).
67. *Tribune,* March 1, 1845; *Evening Mirror,* March 1, 1845; *The* Town, I (March 8, 1845), 46; *Democratic Review,* XVI (April, 1845), 413.

be either repeated or printed. If published with proper revision and some additions, it would render our literature, at the present time, an important service.

Poe's own comment on the lecture is of interest too:

In a late lecture on the "Poets and Poetry of America," delivered before an audience made up chiefly of editors and their connexions, I took occasion to speak what I know to be the truth, and I endeavoured so to speak it that there should be no chance of misunderstanding what it was I intended to say. I told these gentlemen to their teeth that, with a *very* few noble exceptions, they had been engaged for many years in a system of indiscriminate laudation of American books—a system which, more than any other one thing in the world, had tended to the depression of "American literature" whose elevation it was designed to effect. I said this, and very much more of a similar tendency, with as thorough a distinctness as I could command. Could I, at the moment, have invented any terms *more* explicit, wherewith to express my contempt of our general editorial course of corruption and puffery, I should have employed them beyond a shadow of a doubt;—and should I think of anything more expressive *hereafter,* I will endeavour either to find or to make an opportunity for its introduction to the public.

And what, for all this, had I to anticipate? In a very few cases, the open, and, in several, the silent approval of the more chivalrous portion of the press;—but in a majority of instances, I should have been weak indeed to look for anything but abuse. To the Willises—the O'Sullivans—the Duyckincks[68]—to the choice and magnanimous few who spoke promptly in my praise, and who have since taken my hand with a more cordial and more impressive grasp than ever—to these I return, of course, my acknowledgements, for that they have rendered me my due. To my villifiers [*sic*] I return also such thanks as they deserve, inasmuch as without what they have done me the honor to say, there would have been much point wanting in the compliments of my friends.[69]

---

68. In the *American Review,* I (Feb., 1845), 146–151, Duyckinck had called for the year 1845 to be one "of Rebellion . . . against all shabbiness and unworthiness in literature," and urged that authors who had hitherto fought the system single-handedly unite in this cause. Moreover, in the *New York Weekly News,* I (Feb. 1, 1845), 2, Duyckinck declared that whenever Poe's name was mentioned, "it has been with the comment that he is a remarkable man of genius." He extolled the imaginative power displayed in his tales and criticisms —criticisms, he added, that were "profoundly constructed and original . . . , and calling forth the same faculties as the production of the best books themselves."

69. Letter "To the Editor of the Broadway Journal," *Broadway Journal,* I (March 8, 1845), 159. Briggs, the editor, in a letter to Lowell dated March 8, 1845, remarked that he too had attended the lecture and felt that Poe's comments had gained for Poe a "dozen or two of waspish foes who will do him more good than harm" (quoted by Woodberry, *Poe,* p. 228).

The opportunity Poe promised to find or make was already awaiting him. A pseudonymous correspondent, "Outis," moved by Poe's editorial, if not forensic, attack upon his friend Longfellow, entered the lists on March 1.[70] Asking Willis for fair play and the privilege of having his remarks published in the *Mirror*, he argued that "identities" between poems do not necessarily imply plagiarism, for if plagiarism was the only inference to be drawn from identities, then every author was liable to the charge, since no one could possibly read everything that was published. To clinch his argument, he added:

Who, for example, would wish to be guilty of the littleness of detracting from the uncommon merit of that remarkable poem of ... Mr. Poe's ... entitled "The Raven," by charging *him* with the paltriness of imitation? And yet, some snarling critic, who might envy the reputation he had not the genius to secure for himself, might refer to the frequent, very forcible, but rather quaint repetition ... as a palpable imitation of ... *the Ancient Mariner*.

Outis then submitted excerpts from an "anonymous" poem, "The Bird of the Dream," and, comparing it with "The Raven," pointed out eighteen similarities, outnumbering the ten similarities which Poe had noted in comparing the Aldrich and Hood poems. Outis concluded: "Such criticisms only make the *author* of them contemptible, without soiling a plume in the cap of his victim."[71]

Poe did not reply to Outis in the *Mirror*. Though on excellent terms with Willis, he severed connections with him to accept the more promising position of co-editor of the *Broadway Journal*. Briggs, in charge of the *Journal*, recognized in Poe a drawing card ("his name is of some authority"; "Wiley and Putnam are going to publish a new edition of his

70. Phillips (*Poe*, II, 956 ff.) has speculated that Poe created a defender of Longfellow out of whole cloth, assigning him the name of Outis (Gk. "Nobody"), the better to assail the poet. But see Killis Campbell, "Who Was 'Outis'?" in *University of Texas Studies in English*, VIII (1928), 107–109, for a refutation that concludes with the statement that if Outis was not Cornelius Conway Felton, Longfellow's colleague, he was certainly not Poe. Anyone who troubles to read Poe's replies to Outis must conclude, I think, that Poe was thoroughly embarrassed by him and was, in fact, driven to his wits' end to vindicate himself.

71. *Evening Mirror*, March 1, 1845.

tales and sketches"; "Everybody has been raven-mad about his last poem, and his lecture"). Moreover, though Briggs regarded the "very ticklish hobby" of detecting plagiarisms unfortunate for Poe's reputation, he felt that such articles, together with the replies they might provoke from journals avid for scandal, would serve as advertisements of the *Journal* and enlarge its subscription list.[72]

Poe, as expected, replied to Outis as soon as he became associated with the weekly *Journal*, for the innuendoes in Outis's letter were as embarrassing to him as his in the review of *The Waif* must have been to Longfellow. Abandoning editorial anonymity, he began by summarizing the history of the controversy, even reprinting the "documents" in the case—his, Briggs's, Willis's, and those of Longfellow's defenders. Then, proceeding to the matter at hand, he said that he admired the chivalry that prompted Outis's reply, but nothing else, and that he especially disliked the "desperation of the effort to make out a case." Poe then questioned whether a critic might make a charge of plagiarism, not from "littleness" or "envy," but from strictly honorable and even charitable motives. To answer his own question, he reasoned that if the possibility of plagiarism is admitted at all, then the chances are that an established author steals from an obscure one. The obscure author is thus falsely accused of plagiarism, which makes the real culprit guilty on two counts: that of the original theft, which would alone deserve exposure, and that of foisting his crime upon the guiltless struggler. He summed up this phase of the argument by saying that because he, for one, wished to convict the guilty to exonerate the innocent, the charge of "carping littleness" was brought against him. He paused here for want of space, but promised to resume the discussion in the next number of the *Journal*.[73]

72. See Briggs's letters to Lowell dated March 8, 16, and 19, 1845 (Woodberry, *Poe,* pp. 227–229).
73. "Imitation—Plagiarism—Mr. Poe's Reply to the Letter of Outis—A Large Account of a Small Matter—A Voluminous History of the Little Longfellow War," I (March 8, 1845), 147–150.

Poe's remarks began to arouse newspaper and magazine editors, among them J. Hunt, Jr., of the *National Archives*:

As a critical tattler, we know of none other which seems to give a more condid [*sic*] review of the works of *authors* [than the *Broadway Journal*]. We own, notwithstanding, that we have cherished rather of a sour feeling towards one of the editors—Mr. Poe in times past, for his sarcastic, and what to us then appeared malicious criticism on other's [*sic*] production. All who have read "Graham" for the last two or three years—will corroberate [*sic*] our statement, and there breathes not a man, having any pretensions to authorship, who so flinchingly squirms at the strictures of others, than does Mr. Poe. This may be seen in the No. now before us. . . . One quarter of the paper is made use of by Mr. Poe, endeavoring to smooth over and give diminutiveness to what a writer for the Mirror, calling himself "Outis," and some of the other papers have said of him, respecting his late lecture . . . and his Plagarisms [*sic*]. It is a very true remark, that a Joker will rarely ever receive one in return, good naturedly; and this is to a great extent true of Mr. Poe.

But we will 'pass all his imperfections by' and to show that we are not blind to his good qualities, we will say that, as a writer, on general topics, Mr. Poe, undoubtedly, stands on an equal with the best of his class. Among all the reading which we receive, there is no weekly which more claims our attention than does the Broadway Journal. Every article in it shows the scholar, and yet the language is such that a child may read and understand.[74]

On March 17 Poe, without respect for the full truth, answered the editor of the *National Archives,* but the magazine had become defunct in the meantime:

Let me put it to you as to a frank man of honor—Can you suppose it possible that any human being could pursue a strictly impartial course of criticism for 10 years (as I have done in the S.L. Messenger and in Graham's Magazine) without offending irreparably a host of authors and their connexions?—but because these *were* offended, and gave vent at every opportunity to their spleen, would you consider my course an iota the less honorable on that account? Would you consider it just to measure my deserts by the yelpings of my foes, indepently [*sic*] of your own judgment in the premises, based upon an actual knowledge of what I have done?

You reply—"Certainly not," and, because I feel that this *must* be your reply, I acknowledge that I am grieved to see any thing (however slight) in your paper that has the appearance of joi[n]ing in with the outcry so very sure to be made by the 'less['] honorable portion of the press under circumstances such as are my own.

74. I (March 13, 1845), 2.

Poe then explained his reasons for commenting upon the Outis letter at length: "...it demanded an answer & no proper answer could be given in less compass—...the subject of imitation, plagiarism, &c is one in which the public has lately taken much interest & is admirably adapted to the character of a literary journal—and...I have some important developments to make, which the commonest principles of self-defence demand imperatively at my hands."[75]

As he had promised, Poe resumed his discussion of plagiarism on March 15. He agreed with Outis that identities between poems might exist by coincidence but that the admission of such a possibility would by no means eliminate the possibility of plagiarism, particularly as in the case of the Aldrich and Hood poems when "in the compass of eight short lines" there are "ten or twelve peculiar identities of thought and identities of expression." To demonstrate, as Outis had demonstrated, that in another instance two writers by coincidence had used an identical metaphor did not by any means prove that "Mr. Longfellow is innocent of the imitation with which I have charged him, and that Mr. Aldrich is innocent of the plagiarism with which I have *not* charged him...." He added that he would "continue, if not conclude this subject, in the next 'Journal'...."[76]

In his third reply, Poe said that Outis suffered from the misapprehension that one accusation cancels another—that by insinuating that Poe had committed plagiarism, it could be reasoned that Aldrich and Longfellow had not. When he had accused Aldrich or Hood of plagiarism, Poe said, he printed their poems together and in full, but he had not been accorded such treatment by Outis. Instead,

an *anonymous* gentleman rebuts my accusation by telling me that there is a certain similarity between a poem of my own and an *anonymous* poem which he has before *him,* and which he would like to transcribe if it were not too long. He contents himself, therefore, with giving me, from the too long poem, three stanzas which are shown

75. Ostrom, *Poe's Letters,* I, 282–283.
76. "A Continuation of the Voluminous History of the Little Longfellow War —Mr. Poe's Farther Reply to the Letter of Outis," *Broadway Journal,* I, 161–163.

... to have been *culled,* to suit his own purposes, from different portions of the poem, but which (again to suit his own purposes) he places before the public in consecutive connexion!

Then, registering a doubt as to the existence of the poem, he examined the eighteen identities that Outis had pointed out, only to discover that the poems failed to tally except on two points.

In considering plagiarism, Poe continued, one must regard, not only the number of coincidences, but the peculiarity of each one; and not only that, but "the antagonistic differences, if any, which surround them—and very especially *the space* over which the coincidences are spread, and the number or paucity of the events, or incidents, from among which the coincidences are selected." He then used the Aldrich and Hood poems again to explain in greater detail why he considered one of them a plagiarism. He summarized this analysis by remarking:

Now the chances that these fifteen coincidences [in his examination he added five to the original ten], so peculiar in character, and all occurring within the compass of eight short lines, on the one part, and sixteen on the other—the chances, I say, that these coincidences are merely accidental, may be estimated, possibly, as about one to one hundred millions. ...

He concluded by saying that he would endeavor to bring this subject to an end in the next number of the *Journal.*[77]

In his fourth reply to Outis,[78] Poe declared:

... if Outis has his own private reasons for being disgusted with what he terms the "wholesale mangling of victims without rhyme or reason," there is not a man living, of common sense and common honesty, who has not better reason (if possible) to be disgusted with the insufferable cant and shameless misrepresentation practised habitually by just such persons as Outis, with the view of decrying by sheer strength of lungs—of trampling down—of rioting down—of mobbing down any man with a soul that bids him come out from among the general corruption of our public press, and take his stand upon the open ground of rectitude and honor.

77. "More of the Voluminous History of the Little Longfellow War—Mr. Poe's Third Chapter of Reply to the Letter of Outis," *ibid.,* I (March 22, 1845), 178–182.
78. "Imitation—Plagiarism—The Conclusion of Mr. Poe's Reply to the Letter of Outis," *ibid.,* I (March 29, 1845), 194–198.

The Outises who practise this species of bullyism are, as a matter of course, anonymous. They are either the "victims without rhyme or reason who have been mangled by wholesale," or they are the relatives, or the relatives *of* the relatives of the "victims without rhyme or reason who have been mangled by wholesale." Their watchwords are "carping littleness," "envious malignity," and "personal abuse." Their low artifices are insinuated calumnies, and indefatigable whispers of regret, from post to pillar, that "Mr. So-and-So, or Mr. This-and-That *will* persist in rendering himself so dreadfully unpopular."

For himself, he said:

. . . I am but defending a set of principles which no honest man need be ashamed of defending, and for whose defence no honest man will consider an apology required.

He continued:

. . . not even an Outis can accuse me . . . of having ever descended, in the most condemnatory of my reviews, to that personal abuse which, upon one or two occasions, has indeed been levelled at myself, in the spasmodic endeavours of aggrieved authors to rebut what I have ventured to demonstrate. . . . no man can point to a single *critique,* among the very numerous ones which I have written during the last ten years, which is either wholly fault-finding or wholly in approbation; nor is there an instance to be discovered, among all that I have published, of my having set forth, either in praise or censure, a single opinion upon any critical topic of moment, without attempting, at least, to give it authority by something that wore the semblance of a reason. . . . If, to be brief, in what I have put forth there has been a preponderance of censure over commendation,—is there not to be imagined for this preponderance a more charitable motive than any which the Outises have been magnanimous enough to assign me—is not this preponderance, in a word, the natural and inevitable tendency of all criticism worth the name in this age of so universal an authorship, that no man in his senses will pretend to deny the vast predominance of good writers over bad?

Poe then objected to Outis's supposing him to make certain charges against Longfellow and then holding him responsible for them. Thus, he proceeded to cite his own charges. First, as he had in 1839, Poe compared the "Midnight Mass" and the "Death of the Old Year" and repeated that this imitation was too palpable to be mistaken and belongs to the most barbarous class of literary piracy. Second (with Longfellow's explanation still unpublished in *Graham's*), he compared Longfellow's translation of "Der gute George Campbell" from Wolff with the original in Motherwell's and commented: "Professor Longfellow defends himself (I learn) from the charge of *imitation* in this case, by the assertion that he *did* translate from Wolff, but that Wolff copied from Motherwell. I am willing to believe almost anything rather than so gross a plagiarism as this seems to be—but there are difficulties which should be cleared up." How did it happen, "in the translation from the Scotch into the German, and again from the German into the English, not only the versification should have been rigidly preserved, but the *rhymes* and *alliteration*?" Why had Longfellow, "with his known intimate acquaintance with 'Motherwell's Minstrelsy,'" failed to recognize at once "so remarkable a poem when he met it in Wolff"? What was the source that Longfellow had used in retranslating from Wolff? It seemed clear to Poe that the Wolff translation must have appeared in a work "plainly acknowledged as a translation, with its original designated," a work whose subtitle Poe footnoted but a copy of which he had been unable to obtain. Third (and Poe seemed driven to his wits' end here), he argued that Longfellow had modeled a scene in his *Spanish Student* upon his own *Politian,* the thirteen coincidences he pointed out textually being "sufficiently noticeable to establish at least the *imitation* beyond all doubt." Finally, he found certain lines in Longfellow coincidental with lines in Bryant, Sidney, Milton, and Henry King.[79] Poe concluded by remarking that he could point out a "score or two" of such imitations, and that, therefore, Longfellow's friends, instead of charging him with carping littleness, should credit him with great moderation for accusing Longfellow only of imitation: "Had I accused him, in loud terms, of manifest and continuous plagiarism, I should but have echoed the sentiment of every man of letters in the land beyond the immediate influence of the Longfellow *coterie*." Further evidence of his moderation, he said, was the fact that he himself had submitted "to accusations of plagiarism for the very sins

---

79. This last charge involved the stanza from "A Psalm of Life," which Poe had used as an epigraph for his "Tell-Tale Heart." The fact that he considered it "at least an imitation" accounts for his dropping the epigraph from the reprinting of the story in the *Broadway Journal*, II (Aug. 23, 1845), 97–99.

of this gentleman against myself," but that, despite this, he had set "forth the *merits* of the poet in the strongest light, whenever an opportunity was afforded me." Yet the moment that he ventured "an infinitesimal sentence of dispraise" of Longfellow, he received—under what he claimed was Longfellow's instigation—"ridiculous anonymous letters from his friends" and, in the *Boston Evening Transcript,* "prickings with the needles of Miss Walter's innumerable epigrams, rendered unnecessarily and therefore cruelly painful to my feelings by being first carefully deprived of the point."[80]

There was a postscript to these replies to Outis still to appear, but, in the meantime, the *Aristidean,* a New York monthly newly founded by Thomas Dunn English, Poe's acquaintance from the Philadelphia days, published the harshest indictment of Longfellow ever made. The article affirmed that Longfellow was vastly overrated by the Boston clique. "In no literary circle out of Boston—or, indeed, out of the small coterie of abolitionists, transcendentalists and fanatics in general, which is the Longfellow junto—have we heard a seriously dissenting voice on this point." Outside of this "knot of rogues and madmen," his real virtues are simply a

80. Poe seems to have exaggerated the number of this editress's prickings. The only pricking of Poe I have found in the *Transcript* prior to the time Poe wrote this reply appeared on March 5, 1845. Miss Walter copied the Boston *Atlas's* curt reply to the *Daily Tribune's* notice of Poe's lecture, which, deploring the fact that only some three hundred of the four hundred thousand people in New York had attended the lecture, added: "Any dancing dog or summerseting [*sic*] monkey would have drawn a larger house." The *Atlas* article of March 4, copied into the *Transcript,* affirmed: "The Tribune may think as it pleases— but we commend the taste of the 399,700 people, as far preferable to that of the 300, in this case. We should much prefer the dancing dog, or sommer-seting [*sic*] monkey, to the man who could make such remarks as this Poe is said to have made, in reference to the poetry of Sprague [also a Boston poet] and Longfellow. If he was to come before a Boston audience with such stuff, they would *poh* at him at once." To which Miss Walter added: "Somebody sent us the other day, an epitaph on a man named Poe, of which the above has reminded us. We know not in what burial place the record is made, but it runs as follows:

"There lies, by Death's relentless blow,
A would-be critic here below;
    His name was Poe
    His life was woe.
You ask, 'What of this Mister Poe?'
Why nothing of him that I know;
But echo, answering, saith—'Poh.' "

"sufficient scholarship, a fine taste, a keen appreciation of the beautiful, a happy memory, a happier tact at imitation or transmutation, felicity of phrase and some fancy." The anonymous writer, turning to Poe's recent lecture, confessed surprise to hear that Poe had claimed for Longfellow a "pre-eminence over all poets of this country on the score of the 'loftiest poetical quality—imagination.'" He believed that an opinion so crude must have arisen from "want of leisure or inclination to compare the works of the writer in question with the sources from which they were stolen." However, a letter written by "an unfortunate wight who called himself 'Outis,' seems to have stirred up the critic to make the proper examination...." For himself, he felt that, "whatever may be the talents of Professor Longfellow, he is the Great Mogul of the Imitators," and that he had achieved his eminent position by "accident or chicanery."

The minute analysis and the charges of plagiarism that followed indicate that Poe had more than a hand in the article and that he planted the article in the *Aristidean* to gain corroboration of his own judgments—a corroboration so devastating that his statements in the *Broadway Journal* would appear mild by comparison. The writer pointed out that such rhymes as *angel* and *evangel* are inadmissible because identical. He cited a passage from "Hymn to the Night" to demonstrate that Longfellow had such a strong tendency to imitation "that he not unfrequently imitates himself." He argued that "A Psalm of Life" is "chiefly remarkable for its containing one of the most palpable plagiarisms ever perpetrated by an author of equal character.... Mr. Poe, in his late *exposé,* has given some very decisive instances of what he too modestly calls *imitations* on the part of Mr. Longfellow from himself (Mr. Poe)." But there are others that can be adduced: Longfellow's "Footsteps of Angels" has lines taken from Poe's "The Sleeper"; "The Beleaguered City" is a palpable imitation of Poe's "Haunted Palace".... "We do not like to be ill-natured; but when one gentleman's purse is found in another gentleman's pocket, how did it come there?" *The Spanish Student* as a poem "is meritorious at points—as a drama it is one of the most lamentable failures." Longfellow, it is true, acknowledged that it was "taken, *in part,* from the 'Gitanilla' of Cervantes. *In part,* also, it is taken from 'Politian . . . by Edgar A. Poe' . . . no acknowledgement, however, is made in the latter instance." Longfellow "has stolen . . . much from Mr. Poe. . . . There are other plagiarisms of Mr. Longfellow which we might easily expose, but we have said enough. There can be no reasonable doubt in the mind of any, out of the little clique, to which we at first alluded, that the author of 'Outre Mer,' is not only a servile imitator, but a most insolent literary thief."[81]

Thus, however often Poe had opposed such malicious attacks as this, however often he had inveighed against a reviewer's remaining anonymous, and however often he had objected to "personalities" in critical articles, he resorted to all the arts of literary assassination for his self-justifying purposes. In commenting on this article in the *Broadway Journal,* Poe only remarked: "There is a long review or rather running commentary upon Longfellow's poems [in the *Aristidean*]. It is, perhaps, a little coarse, but we are not disposed to call it unjust; although there are in it some opinions which, by implication, are attributed to ourselves individually, and with which we cannot altogether coincide."[82]

If Poe acted in his own defense against the ire of editors, O'Sullivan of the *Democratic Review* came to his aid voluntarily:

Mr. Poe has been for some weeks past engaged in a critical discussion in the *Broadway Journal* on the subject of plagiarism. . . . There is no literary question which requires more discrimination, greater nicety of apprehension and occasionally more courage. We appreciate the latter quality in Mr. Poe; it is especially necessary in a country which numbers some thousand poets, and not one, *in the highest sense,* worthy the name among them all. It is something for a man to

81. I (April, 1845), 130–142. See also the glowing review in the *Aristidean,* I (Oct., 1845), 316–319, which hailed Poe's *Tales* as original and which reiterated the familiar charge that Longfellow had stolen all that was worth stealing of the "Haunted Palace" for his "Beleaguered City."
82. I (May 3, 1845), 285.

encounter so formidable an opposition in this day of newspapers and public opinion, when the opportunities for the gratification of a whim or prejudice, to say nothing of malice and disappointed hate, are so ready at hand. Yet it is necessary that a man should respect himself and tell the truth.... Of all pursuits in the world we know of none more humiliating, more dastardly, or less comfortable to an honest man than the aimless, shifting, puffing, practice of literature ... [which imparts] complacency to a certain number of fools, and persecute[s] a certain number of supposed enemies.... It is for the interest of literature that every man who writes should show his honesty and not bring letters into contempt. If in doing this he should happen to fall on the other side of harshness or rudeness ... let him be pardoned, for it is better both for the cause of truth and virtue that this should be the case than that a man should be always dull and complaisant.[83]

On April 5 Poe concluded his reply to Outis with an effort at dignity, but if he accomplished that effect, it was at the cost of misrepresentation and special pleading. His purpose in replying to Outis at such length, he said, had been "to place fairly and distinctly before the literary public certain principles of criticism for which I have been long contending, and which ... were in danger of being misunderstood.... The thesis of my argument, in general, has been the definition of the grounds on which a charge of plagiarism may be based, and of the species of ratiocination by which it is to be established: that is all." He had not intended to be malevolent or discourteous, whatever one might suspect; and if anyone would take the trouble to read what he had written, he would see that he had made "*no* charge of moral delinquency against either Mr. Longfellow, Mr. Aldrich, or Mr. Hood:—indeed, lest in the heat of argument, I may have uttered any words which may admit of being tortured into such an interpretation, I here fully disclaim them upon the spot."[84]

Poe's sudden reversal of position, not to mention the fact that these remarks were in the form of a postscript, suggests that he had finally found an explanation for imitation other than one of intention—an explanation with which he seemed

83. *Democratic Review*, XVI (April, 1845), 413.
84. "Plagiarism—Imitation—Postscript to Mr. Poe's Reply to the Letter of Outis," *Broadway Journal*, I (April 5, 1845), 211–212.

delighted, for he used it again on several occasions[85] and here for the first time. Thus, he proceeded to acquit Longfellow of "moral delinquency"—that is, of wilful plagiarism—and to explain his unconscious plagiarism—imitation—in these terms:

the poetic sentiment (even without reference to the poetic power) implies a peculiarly, perhaps abnormally keen appreciation of the beautiful, with a longing for its assimilation, or absorption, into poetic identity. What the poet intensely admires, becomes thus, in very fact, although only partially, a portion of his own intellect. It has a secondary origination within his own soul—an origination altogether apart, although springing from its primary origination from without. The poet is thus possessed by another's thought, and cannot be said to take of it, possession. But, in either view, he thoroughly feels it as *his own*—and this feeling is counteracted only by the sensible presence of its true, palpable origin in the volume from which he has derived it—an origin which, in the long lapse of years it is almost impossible *not* to forget—for in the meantime the thought itself is forgotten. But the frailest association will regenerate it—it springs up with all the vigor of a new birth—its absolute originality is not even a matter of suspicion—and when the poet has written it and printed it, and on its account is charged with plagiarism, there will be no one in the world more entirely astounded than himself. Now from what I have said it will be evident that the liability to accidents of this character is in the direct ratio of the poetic sentiment—of the susceptibility to the poetic impression; and in fact all literary history demonstrates that, for the most frequent and palpable plagiarisms, we must search the works of the most eminent poets.

Though Poe "exonerated" Longfellow, he raised more questions than he answered. Agreed that the poetic sentiment and the poetic power coexist in the poet. Agreed too that poetic power compels the poet to render his own vision of the beautiful ("primary origination"), which, by definition, is original, and that the poetic sentiment compels the poet, all unawares, to reproduce reproductions of such visions ("secondary origination"), which, again by definition, are unoriginal. Still, crucial problems remain—and Poe, neither here nor elsewhere, solves them, which may account for his dropping the entire "explanation" by 1847. Do the works of the "most eminent

85. See, for instance, "Marginalia," *Democratic Review*, XVI (April, 1846), 97, in which he exonerates both Longfellow and Aldrich on the same grounds as he exonerates them here.

poets" (and Poe in the Marginalia article means the greatest) really contain "the most frequent and palpable plagiarisms"? Does not greatness imply primary origination, as every Romantic critic thought, including Poe himself? Is plagiarism— a sign of the poetic sentiment—rendered negligible by the poetic power evinced in such "plagiaristic" works as *Hamlet* and *The Waste Land*? And, by the same token, is plagiarism to be censured only when the poetic sentiment, acting independently of the poetic power, produces merely a copy? In his article on James Aldrich in the *Literati* papers, Poe seems to suggest as much when he said that "*A* Death-Bed" is indefensible because both "in matter and manner it is nearly identical with . . . '*The* Death-Bed,' by Thomas Hood." And in his "Marginalia," Poe remarked that "Imitators are not, necessarily, unoriginal—except at the exact points of imitation." And what are we to do with the fact of coincidence, which Poe entirely ignored—the kind of coincidence that caused Longfellow to remark, when he chanced upon a simile in Brainard's "Mocking Bird" identical with one in "Excelsior": "Of a truth one cannot strike a spade into the soil of Parnassus, without disturbing the bones of some dead poet."[86]

With this, the "war," precipitated by a single, ill-advised paragraph concluding Poe's *Waif* review, came lamely to a halt, as far as Poe was concerned. True, he would fire Parthian shots at Longfellow from time to time, but he would never review another book of his—neither his *Belfry of Bruges and Other Poems* (1845), nor the *Estray: A Collection of Poems* (1846), nor the new edition of *Outre-Mer* (1846), nor *Evangeline* (1847), nor *Kavanagh: A Tale* (1849). Only in his essay, "The American Drama," when he struck again at the problem of imitation, did he consider Longfellow once more at any length.

Yet, if only to conclude the "war" with a flourish, it seemed necessary to atomize the *North American Review*, which had felt duty-bound to acclaim the literati of Massachusetts and,

86. Journal entry dated Dec. 8, 1846 (Samuel Longfellow, *Longfellow*, II, 66).

in particular, to expatiate upon the virtues of almost every Longfellow book, whether in A. P. Peabody's review of *Outre-Mer*, in Felton's reviews of *Hyperion, Voices, Ballads,* and *Poems*, in Francis Bowen's review of *Poets and Poetry of Europe*, or in various unidentified reviews devoted to the Cambridge poet, including one of *The Waif*. Simms, badly treated by the *North American*, furnished the occasion for that attack in his *Southern and Western Magazine*, and an anonymous writer, presumably Thomas Dunn English, possibly with Poe's assistance, did the devoir for the *Broadway Journal*.[87] The writer in the *Journal* called attention to Simms's observations concerning the "parochial review" and quoted passages from Simms's article so that Northerners "may see in what estimation the North American is held at the South." Simms's theme was that the *North American*, in its thirty years of existence, was guilty of the most flagrant literary sectionalism:

That the "North American Review" has worked religiously for New England, her sons, her institutions, her claims of every sort, there is no . . . question. . . .
We do not know that the Middle States have fared very much better than those of the South, in the treatment which they have received at the hands of this journal. Their favorite writers are not employed upon its pages, and their publications are noticed slowly and with evident reluctance. When reviewed, it is very certain that the New England critic employs in the case of the New-Yorker, a very different and less indulgent standard of judgment than that which regulates his criticism when one of his own writers is under analysis. . . .

The writer in the *Journal* reaffirmed Simms's charges and added "that the North American is held in as little reverence in Boston as in South Carolina," and that "we have not seen, in the pages of this journal, a single instance where it has shown the slightest solicitude in behalf of any young writer,— always assuming that he is not a sprout of New England. . . ."[88]

87. II (May 31, 1845), 337–339. Simms's article was entitled, "A Passage with 'The Veteran Quarterly,'" I (May, 1845), 297–311. Mott, *American Magazines*, I, 756, calls this criticism too bitterly expressed but just.
88. Such remarks, of course, reflect Poe's sentiments as expressed in his various articles and stories. In "The Literary Life of Thingum Bob, Esq.," he alluded to the "North American Quarterly Hum Drum." He advised Hawthorne

Poe's views of Longfellow, though he ceased to express them at any length, were now voiced by others, who had apparently become emboldened by his example. Simms, for instance, remarked:

Longfellow is an artist . . . in all the respects of verse-making. . . . but it strikes us that it would not be difficult to point to the ear-mark of another in the thoughts contained in every sentence which he ever penned. . . . It is the grace and sweetness of his verse, and that extreme simplicity of the thought which taxes no intellect to scan—which we read as we run—that constitutes his claims upon the reader.[89]

Another independent critic, Margaret Fuller, wrote:

We must confess to a coolness toward Mr. Longfellow, in consequence of the exaggerated praises that have been bestowed upon him. When we see a person of moderate powers receive honors which should be reserved for the highest, we feel somewhat like assailing him and taking from him the crown which should be reserved for grander brows. And yet this is perhaps ungenerous. It may be that the management of publishers, the hyperbole of paid or undiscerning reviewers, or some accidental cause which gives a temporary interest to productions beyond what they would permanently command, have raised such an one to a place as much above his wishes as his claims, and which he would rejoice, with honorable modesty, to vacate at the approach of one worthier. We the more readily believe this of Mr. Longfellow, as one so sensible to the beauties of other writers and so largely indebted to them, *must* know his own comparative rank better than his readers have known it for him. . . . Still we must acquit him of being a willing or conscious plagiarist. Some objects in the collection [*Poems*] are his own; as to the rest, he has the merit of

---

(*Godey's*, XXXV, Nov., 1847, 252–256) to "throw out of the window to the pigs all his odd numbers of 'The North American Review,' " for the "criticism of the conservatives, of the hackneys, of the cultivated old clergymen of the 'North American Review,' is precisely the criticism which condemns originality." And just before his death, he wrote (*Southern Literary Messenger*, XV, April, 1849, 221): "I cannot say that I ever fairly comprehended the force of the term '*insult*,' until I was given to understand, one day, by a member of the '*North American Review*' clique, that this journal was 'not only willing but anxious to render me that justice which had been already rendered me by the "*Revue Française*" and the "*Revue des Deux Mondes*" '—but was 'restrained from so doing' by my 'invincible spirit of antagonism.' I wish the 'North American Review' to express *no* opinion of me whatever—for I have none of it."

89. From the *Broadway Journal*, II (Dec. 6, 1845), 339–341. Earlier, in a letter, Simms had observed that Poe was "more than half right" in his charges against Longfellow. In another, Simms thought Longfellow's *Waif* a "poor compilation. I had almost said a dishonest one." In a third, Simms spoke of Longfellow as a "man of nice taste, a clever imitator—simply an adroit artist." Letters dated June 6, 8, and July 15, 1845 (Oliphant *et al.*, *Simms's Letters*, II, 68, 74, 90).

appreciation, and a rearrangement, not always judicious, but the result of feeling on his part.

Such works as Mr. Longfellow's we consider injurious only if allowed to usurp the place of better things. The reason of his being overrated here, is because through his works breathes the air of other lands with whose products the public at large is but little acquainted.... Twenty years hence when he stands upon his own merits, he will rank as a writer of elegant, if not always accurate taste, of great imitative power, and occasional felicity in an original way, where his feelings are stirred.[90]

In the meantime, Longfellow's edition of the *Poets and Poetry of Europe* had appeared. Poe merely noticed the volume in passing, reporting that the "translations are from a great variety of sources" and that "the professor receives three thousand dollars for editing the work."[91] Simms, however, was quite harsh, declaring that the anthology had not been a labor of love with its editor:

He has not expended much of his own time or talent upon it.... He has been content to compile it from whatever materials have been most convenient—has helped himself, without scruple, to the riff-raff translations of beginners, who, learning the several languages, have sent their crude exercises to the magazines. Mr. Longfellow's own hands do not sufficiently appear in these translations, and the work might just as well have been executed by a common workman. Now, it is as a translator, that Mr. Longfellow's chief excellence appears ... and his own reputation, no less than the public expectation, required that he should have given himself up more thoroughly to this performance.[92]

Though suddenly a target for the independent critics, Longfellow maintained silence, except to explain the mistake he had made in respect to "The Good George Campbell." His friends, however, were hardly silent. Lewis Clark, for instance, replied to Longfellow's assailants, abusing Poe personally, as

---

90. *Daily Tribune*, Dec. 10, 1845. Poe reprinted detached passages from this review in the *Broadway Journal*, II (Dec. 13, 1845), 359–360.

91. *Broadway Journal*, I (June 14, 1845), 382.

92. *Southern and Western Magazine*, II (Nov., 1845), 349–350. Such comments were in sharp contrast with those in the *North American Review*, which praised the work in general and the editor in particular. Francis Bowen, the writer of the review, remarked: "In this great crowd of translations by different hands, certainly very few appear equal to Professor Longfellow's in point of fidelity, elegance, and finish," and concluded that the "book abounds with material for the gratification of a cultivated taste, and for the instruction of every mind of a generous and inquiring nature" (LXI, July, 1845, 199–231).

we have seen in an earlier chapter, and now, in answering
Simms's review, he remarked:

We are sorry to see . . . the Parthian arrows which are aimed at Mr.
Longfellow, one of our most popular poets. . . . Of the writings of his
detractors and sneering commentators, how much is remembered, or
laid up in the heart? Edition after edition of Longfellow's writings,
in prose and verse, are demanded by the public; and it is *The Public*
who constitute his tribunal. As to the 'riff-raff translations' to which
Mr. Longfellow is said to have 'helped himself' in the 'Poets and
Poetry of Europe,' it must strike the sensible reader, we think, that
valid condemnation of them should proceed from critics conversant
with the languages from which they are rendered.[93]

Clark's sentiment that the public constituted the literary
tribunal was shared by Longfellow himself, for on December
30, 1845, he wrote in his journal: "The Belfry [of Bruges
and Other Poems] is succeeding famously well. . . . This is
the best answer to my assailants." And Longfellow was quite
aware of his assailants. On December 9, 1845, he noted: "Read
a very abusive article upon my poems by Mr. Simms, the
novelist. I consider this the most original and inventive of all
his fictions." The next day he observed: "In Graham's Magazine for January, received this morning, is a superb poem by
Lowell,—'To the Past.' If he goes on in this vein, Poe will
soon begin to pound him." The following day he recorded:
"Miss Fuller made a furious onslaught upon me in The New
York Tribune. It is what might be called 'a bilious attack.' "[94]

In summary, it must be said at once that the "sting in the
tail" of Poe's *Waif* review and his need, in consequence, to

<hr />

93. *Knickerbocker,* XXVI (Dec., 1845), 585.
94. These journal entries appear in Samuel Longfellow's *Longfellow*, II, 28,
26, 27 respectively. It was not Poe who "pounded" Lowell for the poem alluded to, but Bryant, who intimated that the poem was suggested by one of
his own with the same title (see Horace Elisha Scudder, *James Russell Lowell:
A Biography*, Boston, 1901, I, 245–246 n. 1). Poe, willing, as he said, to praise
an enemy or damn a friend, had already remarked in the *Broadway Journal*
(II, Aug. 16, 1845, 88) that a stanza of Lowell's "To the Future" was a "palpable plagiarism" from Wordsworth. On March 6, 1844, Lowell had written Poe:
"You might cut me up as much as you pleased & I should read what you say
with respect, & with a great deal more of satisfaction, than most of the praise
I get, affords me" (Woodberry, "Lowell's Letters to Poe," p. 174). Nevertheless, Lowell—as Poe charged in reviewing *A Fable for Critics*—retaliated in that
poem, not only upon him, but upon Bryant and Margaret Fuller, who some
years earlier had remarked: "But his verse is stereotyped: his thoughts sound no
depth, and posterity will not remember him" (Scudder, *ibid.*, p. 244 n. 1).

defend himself against *his* assailants has obscured the real
importance of his encounters with Longfellow. He was the first
American critic who, in recognizing Longfellow's real gifts,
had the hardihood to tell the poet that his poems were sometimes weak, or warped for didactic purposes, or suspiciously
imitative—statements which are safe and easy enough to make
now, but which to make then was, as we have seen, to risk
one's critical reputation, to have one's motives questioned,
and to be charged with envy and spite.[95] Longfellow, if he
understood the uses of criticism at all,[96] preferred to ignore
Poe's strictures, however he may have regarded his praise.
For he was not a poet in the sense that the Romantic critic
understood the term. He was, to borrow a phrase from Coleridge, a man of talents and much reading who had acquired
poetry as a trade. Weak in inspiration, conventional though
cultivated in taste, and full of bookish ideas and sentiments,[97]

95. That Poe should be considered envious of Longfellow is such a naïve notion that I, at least, am mystified that it has gained credence among scholars.
The argument in favor of this notion is that Longfellow, after all, had achieved
a reputation sufficient to inspire envy in a man who was himself aspiring to
literary eminence—an argument that ignores the fact that Poe vociferously admired many writers whose reputation could have filled him with envy—William
Cullen Bryant and Nathaniel Hawthorne, to name only two—and whom he
could have easily maligned, if, as the argument implies, malignancy is the inevitable consequence of envy. Moreover, the argument ignores a second significant
fact, that Bryant cherished a positive dislike for Poe, which extended even to
his excluding him from his *Selections from the American Poets* (1840), and
that Hawthorne satirized him as a critic in "The Hall of Fantasy" (1843).

96. Shepard (*Longfellow*, p. xi) thinks it is doubtful that Longfellow "ever
quite understood what criticism aims at or is good for," and Wagenknecht
(*Longfellow*, p. 164) states that the "most disappointing thing about Longfellow's attitude toward criticism is that he never seems to have recognized its
importance."

97. Both in his time and in ours, Longfellow's weaknesses as a poet have
been pointed out. Margaret Fuller, for example, in the *Tribune*, Dec. 10, 1845,
and in her *Papers on Literature and Art* (New York, 1846), which repeats much
of this criticism, wrote: "Mr. Longfellow has been accused of plagiarism. We
have been surprised that any one should have been anxious to fasten special
charges of this kind upon him, when we had supposed it so obvious that the
greater part of his mental stores were derived from the works of others. He
has no style of his own growing out of his own experiences and observations of
nature. Nature with him, whether human or external, is always seen through
the windows of literature. There are in his poems . . . very few showing him
as an observer, at first hand, of the passions within, or the landscape without."
And Thompson (*Longfellow*, p. 264) observed that Longfellow's fundamental
weakness was an "inability to work out ideas for himself and the consequent
necessity for leaning on his . . . favorite authors for support." Elsewhere, Thompson notes that Longfellow, throughout his life, "drew far more material from
books than he ever drew from his head or heart" (p. 177), and that "Experi-

he was nevertheless possessed by an intense desire for literary reputation, and his poems as well as his career suggest that poetry was all too often a means to that end than an end in itself.[98]

If Poe was harsh in his criticism, he was so because he continually overrated Longfellow's powers (he was only on occasion the genius that Poe from his first notice to his last insisted he was) and pointed out faults in his work that Longfellow did not or perhaps could not correct. Only belatedly —and Poe was dealing with the emergent poet—did he realize that Longfellow was not debasing his talents wilfully; his talents were simply limited. He came to understand at last that Longfellow's imitations, which he had supposed premeditated, were really accidental—that his highly cultivated taste caused him to assimilate ideas, images, and sentiments in other poets' works and, unconsciously at the moment of creation, to adapt them to his own purposes—and he exonerated Longfellow for a tendency he apparently could not help. Even Lewis Clark agreed with this explanation, the evidence became so clear and the charges so persistent. "Much has been said, at sundry times and in diverse places," he wrote, "concerning Longfellow's alleged plagiarisms. . . . There is such a thing . . . as *unconscious* plagiarism."[99] Yet if Poe could forgive Longfellow for his proneness to imitation, he could as a critic scarcely condone the all too apparent fact that his imitations were acclaimed and the poet himself venerated for them.[100]

---

ence rarely moved him to an expression of his own emotions or thoughts" (p. 165). For similar commentary, see Shepard, *Longfellow,* pp. xi–lv.

98. Shepard ("The New England Triumvirate: Longfellow, Holmes, Lowell," in *Literary History of the United States,* ed. Robert E. Spiller *et al.,* pp. 590–591) states that Longfellow's "career suggests a cool calculation, not to say an opportunism, seldom found in poetic minds," and in support of this impression he cites Longfellow's "choice and rejection of poetic themes, the timing of his publications, his dealings with publishers, and most of all his accurate knowledge of the public taste. . . ."

99. *Knickerbocker,* XXVII (Jan., 1846), 72–73.

100. In a paragraph entitled "Plagiarists" ("The Blank Book of a Country Schoolmaster," *ibid.,* IV, Sept. 1834, 216), Longfellow raised this apparently soul-searching question: "We read in an old story book . . . that a law once prevailed in a certain city, requiring that every knight should be buried in his armor; and that if any one should rob the grave, and deprive the dead man of his armor, he should suffer death. It once happened, when this city was closely

His explanation no more canceled the fact that Longfellow often imitated than the explanation of kleptomania annuls the charge of continual theft.

There were other matters, of course, that complicated the critic's attitude, especially from the time he wrote the *Waif* review until he took his final notice of the poet. He could not help being aware that Longfellow was a favorite of the two magazines which, because of their cliquishness, were the special objects of his detestation—the *Knickerbocker* and *North American Review*. Nor could he help knowing that Longfellow had "a whole legion of active quacks at his control,"[101] to use his exaggerated statement—a legion, as it must have seemed to him, that even managed to use the *Foreign Quarterly Review* to extol his virtues and to deny the merits of other American poets. Nor could he help noticing that Longfellow was being accorded critical indemnity by American critics, a fact that hardly needed the attestation provided by the suppression of his *Spanish Student* review and the animosities aroused by his comments upon Longfellow's poems. Nor, finally, could he help realizing that, though Longfellow was creating an audience for poetry the like of which had never been known in America, readers were being conditioned to receive only the kind of poetry written by a Longfellow and, later, devoid of Longfellow's artistry and culture, a James Whitcomb Riley and, still later, an Edgar A. Guest—that second-, third-, and fourth-rate poetry is not a way toward first-rate poetry but a substitute for it.

Longfellow, no doubt, found Poe's strictures disagreeable, but he must have also found that they served to advertise his books. When Fields, for example, was contemplating lawsuits

---

besieged, that a poor cavalier transgressed the law, by borrowing the harness of a dead knight from his sepulchre, and though he thereby saved the city from destruction, he was nevertheless condemned to death, in order to satisfy the noisy populace, who were jealous of his fame. . . . Will it not . . . bear a literary application? Let the reader say, whether an author, who robs the grave, and borrows the weapons of the dead, even to do his country service, does not deserve to be put to death as a literary felon, and is not in danger of suffering such a fate."

101. "Author's Introduction" to "The Literati of New York City," *Godey's Lady's Book*, XXXII (May, 1846), 194.

to blanket derision of *Hiawatha,* Longfellow told his publisher: ". . . don't you think we had better let those critics go on advertising it?" Whatever the case, Longfellow's attitude toward Poe may be summed up by two statements he made about him after his death. The first, made publicly a month after Poe had died, was kinder for the reason that it was almost accurate: "The harshness of his criticism I have never attributed to anything but the irritation of a sensitive nature, chafed by an indefinite sense of wrong."[102] The second, made privately, was reported by William Winter, a young friend of the poet. Longfellow, Winter wrote, had indicated to him that "Poe had grossly abused and maligned him," but that he felt sorry for his "unfortunate and half-crazed adversary." He attributed Poe's remarks "to a deplorable literary jealousy," and concluded: "My works seemed to give him much trouble, first and last; but Mr. Poe is dead and gone, and I am alive and still writing—and that is the end of the matter."[103]

Whatever may be said of Poe's encounters with Longfellow, Poe was on the side of genius and on the side of a free criticism, where he belonged. One can deplore his harshness, his bad taste, his occasional poor judgment, but one cannot condemn his over-all verdict in respect to Longfellow, nor the principles upon which he based that verdict, nor the cause for which he struggled, even at the cost of such statements as those that Winter attributed to Longfellow.

102. Quoted by James R. Thompson, ed., *Southern Literary Messenger,* XV (Nov., 1849), 696.
103. "In Memory of Longfellow," *English Rambles and Other Fugitive Pieces in Prose and Verse* (Boston, 1884), pp. 102–103. When Winter revised this essay for inclusion in *Old Friends: Being Literary Recollections of Other Days* (New York, 1909), he bowdlerized this version to make Longfellow appear charitable.

6

EPILOGUE

The End of a Career

Is it any wonder that I was driven *mad* by the intolerable sense of wrong?——*Edgar A. Poe*

Three events combined to cause Poe's downfall as a critic—his Boston Lyceum "hoax," his sentimental episode with Mesdames Osgood and Ellet, and the publication of his papers on the literati of New York City. The exchanges consequent upon these events can be described as literary battles only by semantic generosity. They would be better described as occasions for Poe's enemies to expose and exaggerate his failings as a human being—failings that became quite pronounced in 1845 and that reached pathological proportions by 1846. For this was the period of Poe's crack-up, a crack-up from which he never fully recovered and in the throes of which he behaved quite unfortunately, when not irresponsibly. Unhappily, this is the period that has been taken to characterize Poe's entire career—indication enough that his enemies wrought better than they knew. Admittedly, Poe created those enemies with his acidulous criticism and editorial comment; and not only created them, but supplied them with the materials to ruin him. And ruin him they did, with a vengeance, trumpeting his weaknesses and discrediting his opinions until he was disgraced and all but barred from the magazines which represented the fountainhead of his existence. Though somewhat tangential to the tracing of Poe's work as a critic, an account of these events is necessary if we are to see Poe's critical career in its entirety, if we are to understand how so seasoned a veteran of controversy could have been destroyed as a critic, and if we are to discern the origins of the Poe legend.

As we have seen, Poe had achieved a wide reputation as a critic, and in 1845 testimonies of his critical genius were not infrequent and came from such respected sources as Lowell, Duyckinck, and Greeley. Moreover, "The Raven," published on January 29, 1845, proved so popular that Wiley and Putnam, eager to capitalize on Poe's fame, brought out two Poe volumes, his *Tales* (June) and *The Raven and Other Poems* (November) in that year, from the first of which he received a royalty of eight cents a copy, though copies sold for only fifty cents—a sure sign that Poe had arrived. Also, and what could not but impress him, Poe became a lion of the New York salons, much sought after and admired by the literary ladies. But what must have struck Poe as the final certification of his arrival was the fact that the officers of the Boston Lyceum invited him to help dignify the thirteenth anniversary of that institution by appearing on the same platform with the Honorable Caleb Cushing, the distinguished Massachusetts statesman who had lately returned in triumph from his commission to China— an invitation offered him though he had only recently concluded his quarrel with Longfellow and the Bostonians.[1]

Not everyone, of course, suddenly forgot old and recent animosities in 1845—not with the Longfellow war to keep those animosities alive and to demonstrate that Poe had not

---

1. Lowell had been instrumental in getting Poe the invitation. In his letter dated March 6, 1844, he wrote: "I spoke to the secretary of the Boston Lyceum . . . about engaging you for next year & he seemed very much pleased with the plan & said that the Society would be glad to do it" (Woodberry, "Lowell's Letters to Poe," p. 174). In this letter, Lowell also suggested that Poe "write an article now and then for the North American Review," whose editor Lowell knew and who, he thought, "would be glad to get an article." Poe thanked Lowell on March 30 for the trouble he had taken, said he would be "very glad to avail myself, next season, of any invitation from the 'Boston Lyceum,' " and that he would bear "the hint about the North A. Review . . . in mind" (Ostrom, *Poe's Letters*, I, 247).

sheathed his critical sword. If anything, men like Lowell, Duyckinck, and Greeley constituted only an impressive minority. In a review of Poe's *Tales,* for instance, George H. Colton, editor of the *American Review,* felt the need to plead that personal enmity should not enter into a judgment of the volume. As he remarked:

> We fear that Mr. Poe's reputation as a critic, will not add to the success of his present publication. The cutting scorn with which he has commented on many authors, and the acrimony and contempt which have often accompanied his acuteness, must have provoked enmities of that kind, which are kept warm by being assiduously "nursed." It might be too much to expect praise from those, on whose brows he has been instrumental in fixing the brand of literary damnation; but still we think that even an enemy would be found to acknowledge, that the present volume is one of the most original and peculiar ever published in the United States, and eminently worthy of an extensive circulation, and a cordial reception. . . . Few books have been published of late, which contain within themselves the elements of greater popularity. This popularity it will be sure to obtain, if it be not for the operation of a stupid prejudice which refuses to read, or a personal enmity, which refuses to admire.[2]

And of *The Raven* volume, Margaret Fuller wrote: "A large band of . . . offended dignitaries and aggrieved parents must be on the watch for a volume of poems by Edgar A. Poe, ready to cut, render, and slash in turn."[3]

Well known Poe no doubt had become, whatever notoriety he had gained in the process, but he was desperately poor, and the stipend offered him by the Boston Lyceum was sufficient to lure him into the enemy camp, despite the warnings issued by such Boston papers as the *Atlas* and *Evening Transcript* during the Longfellow war, that if "he was to come before a Boston audience with such stuff, they would *poh* at him, at once."[4]

For about two weeks, announcements appeared in Boston papers that Cushing was to deliver an address and Poe was to

---

2. *American Review,* II (Sept., 1845), 306.
3. *New York Tribune,* Nov. 26, 1845.
4. *Atlas,* March 4, 1845, and *Transcript,* March 5, 1845. Lowell in his letter of March 6, 1844, said, "The Lyceum pays from fifty to a hundred dollars, as their purse is empty or full," but Poe stated without question or complaint that the sum he received was $20. See his letter to Duyckinck dated Nov. 13, 1845 (Ostrom, *Poe's Letters,* I, 301).

"pronounce" a poem, presumably one written for the occasion. Thus, on the evening of October 16, Cushing spoke to a crowded house, and Poe, apparently unable to write a poem for the occasion,[5] perversely read the obscure "Al Aaraaf." Leaving it to be inferred that the poem was new (he seems to have called it "The Messenger Star"), he introduced it with characteristic remarks about didacticism and followed it, upon request, by a recitation of "The Raven." Some members of the audience, whether restless from having listened for reportedly three hours to Cushing, or frankly bewildered by the poem, or simply hostile to Poe for his treatment of Boston literary figures, began to leave. That night, when the doors of the Odeon had been locked, Poe, anticipating exposure of his "hoax" and wanting to vindicate an unsatisfactory performance,[6] made the absurd "confession" to four Bostonians—the critic Edwin Percy Whipple, the publisher James T. Fields, the Shakespearean lecturer Henry Norman Hudson, and Cushing—that the poem he had foisted off as a new one was written before he was twelve years old.

As has been noted, Cornelia Wells Walter, editress of the *Boston Evening Transcript,* had a grievance against Poe for his recent treatment of Longfellow. Thus, on October 17, she printed this editorial in her paper:

A Failure. The anniversary exercises before the Boston Lyceum last evening were heavy and uninteresting, and illy adapted as introductory to a course of lectures. Mr. Cushing's address was one long laudation upon America at the expense of Great Britain—a composition that seemed written rather for popular effect, than for the influence of sound judgment or the development of that high moral tone

5. In his Memoir in *The Literati*, p. xxii, Griswold cited a letter purported to be written by Poe, in which Poe is made to implore Mrs. Frances Osgood to compose the poem for him. "You compose with such astonishing facility, that you can easily furnish me, quite soon enough, a poem that shall be equal to my reputation. For the love of God I beseech you to help me in this extremity." This letter appears neither in Ostrom's nor Harrison's edition of Poe's letters, and Mrs. Osgood could hardly have attested that Poe wrote such a letter, since she was dead when Griswold printed it.
6. There is little question that Poe's performance was poor. The *Boston Daily Times* that on Oct. 16, 1845, called for a full house to "testify the public appreciation of these distinguished writers," on Oct. 18 said that Poe "made what is called a 'no go' of it, and even when he mounted his Pegasus, the *Raven,* Mr Poe didn't go down with the audience at all."

which should ever characterize all public exercises having for their theme any subject of national importance.

The address had been announced in the papers "to be followed by a poem," and, when the orator had concluded, an officer of the society introduced to the assembly a gentleman, who, as we understood him to say, possessed a *raven*-ous desire to be known as the author of a particular piece of poetry on a celebrated croaking bird well known to ornithologists. The poet immediately arose; but, if he uttered poesy in the first instance, it was certainly of a most prosaic order. The audience listened in amazement to a singularly didactic exordium, and finally commenced the noisy expedient of removing from the hall, and this long before they had discovered the style of the measure, or whether it was rhythm or blank verse [*sic*]. We believe, however, it was a prose introductory to a poem on the "Star discovered by Tycho Brahe," considered figuratively as the "Messenger of the Deity," out of which idea Edgar A. Poe had constructed a sentimental and imaginative poem. The audience now thinned so rapidly and made so much commotion in their departure that we lost the beauties of the composition. We heard the prefatory exordium, however (which we took to be *in prose*) and our thoughts upon it ran as follows:

'Twixt truth and poesy they say, there is a mighty schism
I'd like to be a *moral* man, and preach *"didacticism"*
But as truth and taste do not agree and I do surely know it,
Let truth and morals go and be a *critic* and a poet.

As in some "lower deeps" there lies another deep, so one poem was found to involve another last evening. The "Star discovered by Tycho Brahe" was no sooner out of sight, than the terrestrials who had watched its disappearance and were about to follow the same course, were officially urged to a further delay, and another small poem succeeded. This was *"The Raven"*—a composition probably better appreciated by its author than by his auditory, and which has already gone the rounds of the press, followed by a most felicitous *parody* from another source. The parody, however, had not been announced as "part of the entertainment," and was "unavoidably omitted."

We are sorry to record a *failure* in these opening exercises of the Lyceum, though if the expression should seem too severe, we will retract the application and announce only a *'suspension'*—a suspension of interest merely, until the next lecture by Henry Norman Hudson.

Two days after the event, on October 18, Miss Walter exposed Poe's "hoax":

A Prodigy. It has been said by "those who know," that the poem delivered by Edgar A. Poe before the Lyceum, on Thursday evening, was written *before its author was twelve years old.* If the poet felt "doubts of his ability in preparing a poem for a Boston audience" at that early age, it is not to be wondered at that they were openly *expressed* (as a correspondent of a morning paper states) on Thursday evening. A poem delivered before a literary association of adults, as written by *a boy!* Only think of it! Poh! Poh!

In another column of that same issue, Miss Walter printed a communication from a correspondent who signed himself "P" and who had been present at the anniversary exercises. Crudely satirical, "P" remarked that the chief merit of Poe's "apologetic preface" was its length; that his poem, *"at whatever age it may have been written, and for what purpose soever he may have given it in Boston,* was fully equal to anything we have ever seen from him"; that his "system of criticism is ... applicable to nobody's poetry but his own"; and that, as a critic, he "writes for nobody's sense or understanding but his own." "P" then added this garbled statement: "Mr. Poe, we are told, has a great horror of plagiarism. It is about the only literary vice of which he is guilty, and no one can charge him with plagiarism without charging somebody else." He concluded that Poe's "productions are eminently *new* ... and all of them are replete with the same kind of life as a watch."[7]

In this way, Miss Walter and later, by his own admission, Henry Norman Hudson anonymously baited Poe from time to time, a baiting in which many Boston editors joined.[8] An ex-

7. I am indebted to Joseph Edgar Chamberlin's chapter, "The Lady Editor," in his *Boston Transcript: A History of Its First Hundred Years* (Boston, 1930), as well as to his article, "Edgar A. Poe and His Boston Critic, Miss Walter," *Boston Evening Transcript,* Book Section, Jan. 26, 1924, p. 2, for calling attention to the Walter attacks upon Poe.

8. In a letter to Duyckinck dated Nov. 24, 1845, Hudson confessed, in order to exonerate Miss Walter, that the most offensive remarks about Poe in the *Transcript* had been written by him. (See Phillips, *Poe,* II, 1058–1059, for the letter.) There were conceivably two reasons for Hudson's animosity toward Poe. One was to avenge Miss Walter whom Poe was eventually driven to bait in retaliation for her thrusts at him, for Miss Walter had been kind enough to puff the series of Shakespeare lectures Hudson had given in Boston (see *Transcript* for Jan. 13, 17, 27, March 1, Nov. 6, 8, 14, 19, Dec. 3 and 20, 1845, for such puffs). The second reason was that his Shakespeare lectures given in February in New York were a failure—a failure which a writer, whom Hudson and Miss Walter probably thought to be Poe, did nothing to alleviate. Miss Walter admitted Hudson's failure (*Transcript,* April 28, 1845) when she wished him better success in Providence than he had met with in New York. The writer in the *Broadway Journal* had remarked in part: "Mr. Hudson was expected to make

ception was the *Boston Daily Courier* which, on October 18, carried this editorial, "Mr. Poe's Poem":

On Thursday evening, Mr. Poe delivered his poem before the Boston Lyceum, to (what we should have conceived, from first appearances) a highly intelligent and respectable audience. He prefaced it with twenty minutes of introductory prose, showing that there existed no such thing as didactic poetry.... "The poem," called the "Messenger Star," was an elegant and classic production, based on the right principles, containing the essence of *true* poetry, mingled with a gorgeous imagination, exquisite painting, every charm of metre, and a graceful delivery.... The delicious word-painting of some of its scenes brought vividly to our recollection, Keat's [*sic*] "Eve of St. Agnes," and parts of "Paradise Lost."

That it was not appreciated by the audience, was very evident, by their uneasiness and continual exits in numbers at a time. Common courtesy, we should think, would have suggested to them the politeness of hearing it through, though it should have proved "Heathen Greek" to them; after, too, the author had expressed his doubts of his ability, in preparing a poem for a Boston audience.

That it was inappropriate to the occasion, we take the liberty to deny.... We (too often) find a person get up and repeat a hundred or two indifferent couplets of words, with jingling rhymes and stale witticisms, with scarcely a line of *poetry* in the whole.... If we are to have a poem, why not have the "true thing," that will be recognized as such....

We hope Mr. Poe will publish his poem, and give an opportunity for those that were not present, to read and admire.

Friendly as this writer was, he too must have become resentful of Poe when he discovered that he had been hoaxed. For the only thing new about the poem was the title. It had been printed in 1829; it had been revised and published in 1831; and it was scheduled to appear in November again in its original form in *The Raven* volume.

Goaded from day to day by the Boston papers, Poe promised to retaliate: "We have been quizzing the Bostonians," he remarked, "and one or two of the more stupid of their editors and editresses have taken it in high dudgeon. We will

---

a sensation. He had made a sensation in Boston .... [but]what is a thirty-two pounder in the provinces is a mere pop-gun here ... " (I, Feb. 22, 1845, 123). Poe later learned about Hudson's hand in the *Transcript* attacks, most likely from Duyckinck, and took his revenge upon him in the *Broadway Journal* (II, Dec. 13, 1845, 359): "His bad parts are legion— ... an elocution that would disgrace a pig, and an odd species of gesticulation of which a baboon would have excellent reason to be ashamed."

attend to them all in good time."[9] Undaunted, Miss Walter or Hudson quoted this statement on October 28 and commented: "The promise conveyed in this last line is certainly very poe-tential. We thought the poet might possibly be *poedagrical*, but it seems he is intending to take time enough to become a poe-ser!" The next day Miss Walter ran this item in her paper:

> That poem. We showed our readers yesterday that the editor of The Broadway Journal called his childish effort for the amusement of the members of the Lyceum a *"quizz"* upon the Bostonians. . . . We would gently hint, however, to the editor of The Broadway Journal, that while he is perfectly at liberty to think he has quizzed the Bostonians, the quizzer sometimes turns out to be the *quizzee*. . . . The public have had some fun, and so let it pass. Should Mr Poe be desirous of knowing further what is thought of the matter in these parts, we refer him to the pleasant adventure of the immortal Barabello, the "Broadway poet of Rome," who was crowned with cabbage in the Capitol.

In another column in that issue, Miss Walter or Hudson observed that Poe, in announcing his sole control of the *Broadway Journal*, had asked for the support of his friends. With what was apparently intended as a sneer at his reputation for insobriety, the writer remarked: "What a question to ask! Edgar A. Poe to be in a position to require *support*! It is indeed remarkable."

The next day too Miss Walter squibbed Poe:

> "Quizzing the Bostonians." In "E. A. Poe's Poems," *second edition*, published in New York in 1831, is the entire poem recently delivered before the Lyceum of this city, and for the attempt of speaking before which association, the author made an apology as regards his *capacity*. This capacity, it seems, has been deteriorating since Mr Poe was ten years of age, his best poems having been written before that period. Mr Poe may have quizzed *the* Bostonians in his own estimation, but *one* Bostonian was not *quizzed* who had the above-named book of poems in his pocket during the late delivery of the "Messenger Star," and who sat quietly reading it in the gallery, prepared to act *the prompter* if its author by any unaccustomed bewilderment of memory should have lost the cue!

Again on the following day Miss Walter printed these comments from a correspondent:

9. *Broadway Journal,* II (Oct. 25, 1845), 248.

Mr Editor: It seems that Mr Edgar A. Poe is claiming for his *poe*tical soul, the flattering unction that a Gotham Editor has at last succeeded in "quizzing the Bostonians." It must be confessed that he did *out-Yankee* the managers of the Lyceum since he not only emptied their pockets but emptied the house. Still, the thing was worth all its cost, since several *"jeu d'esprits"* were founded upon the results of his antic gallopings [*sic*] about Mount Parnassus.

Subjected to this continual baiting, Poe decided to answer Miss Walter and other hostile Boston editors. He had little choice in any case. There were few editorial friends disposed or militant enough to defend him; he had allowed two weeks to elapse, yet the Boston papers were still clamoring for his head; and his head they were likely to have unless he answered them in kind. To maintain a dignified silence under the circumstances was, he knew, to commit literary suicide. As the Philadelphia editor, John Du Solle, was to remark: "If Mr. P. had not been gifted with considerable gall, he would have been devoured long ago by the host of enemies his genius has created."[10] He began by quoting Major M. M. Noah's comments in the *Sunday Times and Messenger* of October 26:

Mr. Poe's Poem.—Mr. Poe was invited to deliver a poem before the Boston Lyceum, which he did to a large and distinguished audience. It was, to use the language of an intelligent hearer [the *Boston Daily Courier* of October 18], "an elegant and classic production, based on the right principle; containing the essence of true poetry, mingled with a gorgeous imagination, exquisite painting, every charm of metre, and graceful delivery." And yet the papers abused him, and the audience was fidgetty [*sic*]—made their exit one by one, and did not at all appreciate the efforts of a man of admitted ability, whom they had invited to deliver a poem before them. . . . We presume Mr. Poe will not accept another invitation to recite poetry, original or selected, in that section of the Union.

Poe commented that Major Noah had been taken in by Miss Walter, who "has been telling a parcel of fibs about us, by way of revenge for something we did to Mr. Longfellow. . . ." He then reviewed the event and agreed that the audience was large and distinguished; that Cushing preceded him with a very capital discourse; that he himself was most cordially received; that he had occupied some fifteen minutes with an

10. Philadelphia *Spirit of the Times*, Jan. 8, 1847.

apology for not delivering, as is usual in such cases, a didactic poem; and that, after some further words of apology for the "general imbecility" of what he had to offer—"all so unworthy a *Bostonian* audience"—he commenced and, with many interruptions of applause, concluded. "Upon the whole the approbation was considerably more (the more the pity too) than that bestowed upon Mr. Cushing."

When he had finished, Poe continued, the audience, of course, arose to depart, and about one-tenth of them had actually departed when Mr. N. W. Coffin, the corresponding secretary of the Boston Lyceum who was acting as chairman, arrested those who remained by the announcement that the poet had been requested to deliver "The Raven." He had obliged, was again very cordially applauded, "and this was the end of it—with the exception of the sad tale invented to suit her own purposes, by that amiable little enemy of ours, Miss Walters [*sic*]."

Unfortunately, Poe did not leave the matter there, however distortedly he may have presented it. He admitted having been born in Boston, and said that he was heartily ashamed of the fact. The Bostonians "have always evinced toward us individually, the basest ingratitude for the services we rendered them in enlightening them about the originality of Mr. Longfellow." He said that the only reason he had accepted the invitation from the Boston Lyceum was a "curiosity to know how it felt to be publicly hissed—and because we wished to see what effect we could produce by a neat little *impromptu* speech in reply." But, he confessed, he had overrated his own importance or the Bostonian want of common civility. He assured Major Noah that he was wrong: "The Bostonians are well-bred—as *very* dull persons very generally are."

He then created his own parcel of lies to justify his failure to compose an original poem for the occasion. For the price and for "an audience of Transcendentalists," he said, the poem he read was good enough (they understood and especially applauded "all those knotty passages we ourselves have not yet been able to understand")—a poem which he wrote, printed, and published in book form before "we had fairly completed our tenth year." He then explained that the only reason another paper, the *Boston Times,* had become incensed with him was that he had let "some of our cat out of the bag a few hours sooner than we had intended" by confessing to a few "natives who swear not altogether by the frog-pond"—Poe's term of contempt for Boston—"the soft impeachment of the hoax."[11]

Miss Walter's reply on November 4 was to reprint Poe's entire statement, calling attention on another page to "what Edgar A. Poe says of the 'natives' of our *'provincial town'* and of various matters connected with the late poem before the Lyceum. The poet's confession is a most amusing one. Has he done requiring the *support* of his friends?" She also introduced the reprinted Poe article with these remarks:

Poking Fun. We expected something much better than the following after waiting a whole fortnight for Mr Poe's "attention" to the "stupid editors and editresses" of Boston. . . . He determined to do the thing magnanimously however, and if he had but sent a copy of the following to the managers of the Lyceum enclosing the fifty dollars which he *po*-ked out of them for his *childish* effort in versification, he would have exhibited the only proof now wanting of his excessive *po*-liteness.

Simms, who despised Boston cliquism, came to Poe's defense in the Charleston *Southern Patriot.* Poe, he said, was in many respects one of the most remarkable of our literary men and, at the same time, an admirable critic: "he is methodical, lucid, forcible;—well-read, thoughtful, and capable, at all times, of rising from the mere consideration of the individual subject, to the principles . . . by which it should be governed." To these qualities, Simms continued, should be added that Poe "is not a person to be overborne and silenced by a reputation; —that mere names do not control his judgment;—that he is bold, independent, and stubbornly analytical, in the formation of his opinions." Poe has his defects, Simms admitted, which he described as capricious moods that occasionally operate to impair the value and consistency of his judgments.

11. *Broadway Journal,* II (Nov. 1, 1845), 261–262.

Simms then turned to a discussion of the Boston Lyceum affair. Poe, he said, committed three blunders in accepting the invitation. First, such occasions call for moral or patriotic commonplaces in rhyming heroics or merely declamatory verse, and Poe was too highly imaginative to write such a poem. Second, Poe had been exercising himself as a critic at the expense of some of Boston's favorite writers:

The swans of New-England, under his delineation, had been described as mere geese, and these too none of the whitest. He had been exposing the short comings and the plagiarisms of Mr. Longfellow. ... Poe had dealt with the favorites of Boston unsparingly, and they hankered after their revenges. In evil hour then, did he consent to commit himself, in verses to their tender mercies. It is positively amusing to see how eagerly all the little witlings of the press ... flourish their critical tomahawk about the head of their critic. In their eagerness for retribution, one of the newspapers before us actually congratulates itself and readers, on the (asserted) failure of the poet.

Poe's third blunder was in consenting to address an audience in verse who, for three mortal hours, had been compelled to listen to Cushing in prose. "The attempt to speak after this, in poetry, and fanciful poetry too, was sheer madness. . . . But, it is denied that Mr. Poe failed at all. . . . The 'Boston Courier,' one of the most thoughtful of the journals of that city, gives us a very favorable opinion of the performance which has been so harshly treated." Simms concluded by quoting much of that article, which has already been noted.[12]

Poe took advantage of Simms's defense in the *Broadway Journal:* "As we very confidently expected, our friends in the Southern and Western Country . . . are taking up arms in our cause—and more especially in the cause of a national as distinguished from a sectional literature. They cannot see (it appears) any farther necessity for being ridden to death by New-England." Poe then quoted Simms's article in full, demurring at the disparagement of Cushing and perversely commenting that "the most exquisite of sublunary pleasures . . . [is] the

12. I (Nov. 10, 1845), 2.

making of a fuss, or, in the classical words of a western friend, the 'kicking up a bobbery.'" The bobbery he had kicked up may "open their eyes to certain facts which have long been obvious to all the world except themselves—the facts that there exist other cities than Boston—other men of letters than Professor Longfellow—other vehicles of literary information than the 'Down-East Review' [Poe's contemptuous epithet for the *North American Review*]."

Poe then quoted Joseph M. Field, who, as editor of the *St. Louis Reveillé,* agreed with an "exchange paper" on November 9 that if Poe "had as much tact as talent, he would make success for half a dozen papers." But, Field added, he "has too much contempt for tact; he is wrong, but his error makes his career the more remarkable." Then Field called Poe's bluff: Does Poe mean "that his late Boston poem, was intended by him as a *hoax?*" Poe commented:

We had *tact* enough not to be "taken in and done for" by the Bostonians. . . . We knew very well that, among a certain *clique* of the Frogpondians, there existed a predetermination to abuse us under *any* circumstances. . . . We knew that were we to compose for them a "Paradise Lost," they would pronounce it an indifferent poem. It would have been very weak in us, then, to put ourselves to the trouble of attempting to please these people. We preferred pleasing ourselves. We read before them . . . a very "juvenile" poem—and thus the Frogpondians were *had*—were delivered up to the enemy bound hand and foot. . . . They have blustered and flustered—but what have they done or said that has not made them more thoroughly ridiculous?

The fact that the poem was applauded, Poe went on, indicates that

the *clique* (contemptible in numbers as in everything else) were overruled by the rest of the assembly. These malignants did not *dare* to interrupt by their preconcerted hisses, the respectful and profound attention of the majority. . . .

The poem being thus well received, in spite of this ridiculous little cabal—the next thing to be done was to abuse it in the papers. . . . But what have they accomplished? The poem, they say, is bad. We admit it. We insisted upon this fact in our prefatory remarks, and we insist upon it now. . . . It *is* bad—it is wretched—and what then? We wrote it at ten years of age—had it been worth even a pumpkin-pie undoubtedly we should not have "delivered" it to *them.*

He then derided the *Boston Star* which had copied the *"third* edition of the poem" in full, which was "too good . . . by one half" for the occasion, and in several columns said that he really ought to be hanged for perpetrating the hoax. He then mocked "a thing" that the "Frogpondian faction" hired called the *Washingtonian Reformer* to insinuate that he "must have been 'intoxicated' to have become possessed of sufficient audacity to 'deliver' such a poem to the Frogpondians." Why, he said, couldn't "these miserable hypocrites say 'drunk' at once and be done with it?" He was willing to admit anything, including the cutting of his grandmother's throat, if he knew what relevance that admission had to do with his poem. "As for the editor of the 'Jeffersonian Teetotaler' (or whatever it is) we advise her to get drunk—for when sober she is a disgrace to her sex—on account of being so awfully stupid."

In a postscript he noticed what, of course, was not the case, that Miss Walter had been overwhelming him with apologies. He concluded:

The Frogpondians may as well spare us their abuse. If we cared a fig for their wrath we should not first have insulted them to their teeth, and then subjected to their tender mercies a volume of our Poems: *—that,* we think, is sufficiently clear. The fact is, we despise them and defy them (the transcendental vagabonds!) and they may all go to the devil together.[13]

In the next number of the *Broadway Journal,* Poe, in his review of *America and the American People,* properly took issue with Frederick Von Raumer's statement (and he could have cited his own recent rebuttals as evidence) that the "greater American periodical or critical reviews distinguish themselves by propriety, moderation, and dignity," and that "they display an accurate knowledge of all sciences and often contain criticisms which are masterly both in form and substance." He noted with ironic amusement that the moderation of the Down-East Review "must have reference to the applause or attention bestowed upon those insignificant individuals who have the misfortune to reside out of the limits of Massachusetts." In

13. II (Nov. 22, 1845), 309–311.

the same number, he remarked: "The Frog-Pond seems to be dried up—and the Frogs are, beyond doubt, all dead—as we hear no more croaking from that quarter."[14]

But the "Frog-Pond" was hardly dried up. On December 2 Miss Walter printed this item under the heading, "Poe's Poem of 'Al Aaraaff' [*sic*]." "This poem (the same delivered at the opening of the Lyceum of our city) and lately published in a new volume of its author's poetical writings, is mentioned as follows by a Baltimore correspondent of the [Boston] Atlas." She then quoted the correspondent to the effect that the 1831 edition containing the poem failed to sell because people could not understand either that poem or "Tamerlane." Unhappy with her backbiting, Poe maliciously remarked on December 6:

Mr. Edmund Burke, the editress of the "Frogpondian Teetotalle," assures us, with tears in her eyes, that we are mistaken in supposing her "a little old lady in a mob-cap and spectacles."
Our present impression is that she lies. However—we will take another look at her when we pay our next visit to Frogpondium— which will be *soon*—as we have a fine poem that we wrote at seven months—and an invitation to "deliver" it before the Lyceum. They want it immediately—they can't wait.[15]

On that same day the *Harbinger,* edited and printed by the Brook Farm Phalanx, joined the fray. In reviewing *The Raven* volume, that journal made a fair summary of the reputation Poe was beginning to earn by his coarse replies:

Mr. Poe has earned some fame by various tales and poems, which of late has become notoriety through a certain blackguard warfare which he has been waging against the poets and newspaper critics of New England, and which it would be most charitable to impute to insanity. Judging from the tone of his late articles in the Broadway Journal, he seems to think that the whole literary South and West are doing anxious battle in his person against the time-honored tyrant of the North. But what have North or South to do with affairs only apropos to Poe! ... Edgar Poe, acting the constabulary part of a spy in detecting plagiarisms in favorite authors, insulting a Boston audience, inditing coarse editorials against respectable editresses, and getting singed himself the meanwhile, is nothing less than the hero of a grand mystic conflict of the elements. ... The motive of the publication [of *The Raven* volume] is too apparent; it contains

14. II (Nov. 29, 1845), 320–321.
15. *Broadway Journal,* II, 339.

the famous Boston poem, together with other juvenilities, which, he says, "private reasons—some of which have reference to the sin of plagiarism, and others to the date of Tennyson's first poems"—have induced him to republish. Does he mean to intimate that he is suspected of copying Tennyson? In vain have we searched the poems for a shadow of resemblance. Does he think to convict Tennyson of copying *him*?[16]

Poe, after quoting the *Harbinger's* remarks in the *Broadway Journal* of December 13, commented that the *Harbinger* is "the most reputable organ of the Crazyites," that he respected it because it is conducted by well-read persons who mean no harm and whose objects are honorable, "all that anybody can understand of them. . . ." He wondered what he could have done to offend the Brook Farm Phalanx that they should stop the ordinary operations at Brook Farm for the purpose of abusing him. But since the *Harbinger* talked to him like a Dutch uncle, he would reply to it, very succinctly, in the same spirit. "Insanity," he said, "is a word that the Brook Farm Phalanx should never be brought to mention under any circumstances whatsoever." The "old time-honored tyrant of the North" is really "King Log at best." The statement that he insulted a Boston audience was "very true—meant to do it —and did." The charge of "getting singed in return" referred, he presumed, "to the doubling, in five weeks, the circulation of the 'Broadway Journal.'" The statement that his "motive of publication was apparent" is wrong: his poems were in the publishers' hands "a month or six weeks before we received the invitation from the Lyceum." He was happy, however, that the Phalanx could discover no shadow of resemblance between his and Tennyson's poems:

Certainly not—we never could discover any ourselves. Our foot-note . . . has reference to an article written by Charles Dickens in the London "Foreign Quarterly Review" in which Mr. Dickens had paid us some injudicious compliments, among them that "we had all Tennyson's spirituality, and might be considered as the best of his imitators"—words to that effect. Our design had been merely to demonstrate (should a similar accusation again be made) that the poems in question were published before Tennyson had written at all.

16. I (Dec. 6, 1845), 410–411.

"As for the rest," Poe concluded, "we believe it is all leather and prunella—the opinion of 'The Snook Farm Phalanx.' We do trust that, in future, 'The Snook Farm Phalanx' will never have any opinion of us at all."

Lewis Clark, not to be excluded from the altercation, added this tidbit: "The circumstances must indeed be exceedingly unhappy and distressing, which would cause a poet to accept an invitation from a learned society to deliver an original poem at its annual meeting, and after receiving payment therefor, to read a rhapsody composed and published in his tenth year, and afterward bring forward, as a proof of the stupidity of his audience, that they listened to him with civil attention."[17]

Poe could not answer this notice, for on January 3, 1846, his journal having failed, he had published his abrupt valedictory: "Unexpected engagements demanding my whole attention, and the objects being fulfilled, so far as regards myself personally, for which 'The Broadway Journal' was established, I now, as its editor, bid farewell—as cordially to foes as to friends."[18] But his foes were not so easily placated, nor was the storm which he had provoked so easily lulled. Without a journal in which to defend himself, and never again to have another editorial berth, Poe became a stationary target for abuse. On January 2, taking note that the *Broadway Journal* had failed, despite Poe's plea for the support of his friends, Miss Walter wrote this piece of doggerel:

> To trust in friends is but so so,
> Especially when cash is low;
> The Broadway Journal's proved '*no go*'—
> *Friends* would not pay the pen of Poe.

And as late as May 5, 1846, Miss Walter copied from the *Knickerbocker* one of the nastiest pieces of vilification she could find—the piece that declared Poe to be "today in the gutter, tomorrow in some milliner's magazine; but in all places, and at all times, magnificently snobbish and dirty, who seems

17. *Knickerbocker,* XXVII (Jan., 1846), 72.
18. *Broadway Journal,* II, 407.

to invite the 'Punchy' writers among us to take up their pen and impale him for public amusement." To which she added her own choice comment: "This same individual is famous for indulging in gross falsehoods, and these have become so common with him that whenever seen in print they are ever met by the reader, with the simple exclamation, Poh! Poe!"[19] And when, in the eighteenth annual report of the Boston Lyceum, the Board of Trustees recorded their censure of Poe for his conduct at the Odeum as well as in the *Broadway Journal,* Miss Walter published the censure in her paper: "The report says, 'the Board had invited this person on the strength of his literary reputation and were not aware of his personal habits or the eccentricities of his character. For the merit or faults of his literary productions, he, of course, is alone responsible. The public were disappointed as well as ourselves in the poem, and his subsequent abuse of our city and its institutions, show[s] him to be an unprincipled man, while the venom which he ejected against us, only defiled himself.' "[20] With this, the memory of that unhappy episode faded until it was revived by another, equally disagreeable, event.

For in the same year that marked the Boston Lyceum fiasco, Poe—again more by accident than design—precipitated a scandal that by 1846 became ruinous to his reputation. The enemies he had made in the past and of late seized upon and added to the gossip until, by word of mouth, by letter, and by print, Poe's name became anathema, even after his death. By the time the scandal ended, to quote the remark made by Mrs. Elizabeth Frieze Lummis Ellet to Mrs. Frances Sargent Locke Osgood—both of whom may be regarded as authorities in the matter—no one (Mrs. Ellet said neither of us) has "any thing

---

19. Miss Walter was bound to be partial to the *Knickerbocker:* Lewis Clark as systematically supported Longfellow as he derided Poe. In the same issue of the *Transcript* (Jan. 2, 1845) that announced "the advent of a new paper in New York entitled '*The Broadway Journal,*' " Miss Walter commented: "The last number of 'The Knickerbocker' is full of good things, and the 'Editor's Table' plethoric with viands for the laugher and satirist, the man of humor and the man of sense."

20. *Transcript,* May 25, 1846.

to apprehend from . . . a wretch so steeped in infamy as he is now."[21] The sequence of events that led to such a horrendous verdict needs to be reconstructed.

In March, 1845, Poe met Mrs. Osgood, a charming, attractive, and consumptive poetess two years his junior, and the first of the literary ladies with whom he conducted his series of "little poetical episodes"—to borrow Mrs. Osgood's words— "in which the impassioned romance of his temperament impelled him to indulge," despite the fact that Virginia Poe "was the only woman whom he ever truly loved."[22] What must have been a typical salon scene of the period was drawn by Thomas Dunn English about a half-century later in his series called "Reminiscences of Poe":

> In the plainly furnished room at one corner stands Miss Lynch with her round cheery face, and Mrs. Ellet, decorous and lady-like, who had ceased her conversation when Poe broke into his lecture. . . . At my feet little Mrs. Osgood, doing the infantile act, is seated on a footstool, her face upturned to Poe, as it had been previously to Miss Fuller and myself. In the centre stands Poe giving his opinions in a judicial tone and occasionally reciting passages with telling effect.[23]

Impulsively, as seemed to be her nature, Mrs. Osgood engaged in a literary flirtation with Poe, the verses of which Poe published from time to time in the *Broadway Journal*. The first of her verses appeared on April 5, 1845, under the name of Violet Vane, and reveals Poe as the reluctant suitor:

"So Let It Be."

Perhaps you think it right and just,
    Since you are bound by nearer ties,
To greet me with that careless tone,
    With those serene and silent eyes.

So let it be! I only know,
    If I were in your place to-night,
I would not grieve *your* spirit so,
    For all God's worlds of life and light!

21. The letter containing this remark is dated July 8 [1846], and is reproduced in full by Bayless, *Griswold,* pp. 141–142.
22. Mrs. Osgood's letter as printed in Griswold's Memoir in *The Literati,* p. xxxvii.
23. *Independent,* XLVIII (Oct. 29, 1896), 449.

I could not turn, as you have done,
  From every memory of the past;
I would not fling, from soul and brow,
  The shade that Feeling should have cast.

Oh! think how it must deepen all
  The pangs of wild remorse and pride,
To feel, that *you* can coldly see
  The grief, *I* vainly strive to hide!

        .   .   .   .

The fair, fond girl, who at your side,
  Within your soul's dear light, doth live,
Could hardly have the heart to chide
  The ray that Friendship well might give.

But if you deem it right and just,
  Blessed as you are in your glad lot,
To greet me with that heartless tone,
  So let it be! I blame you not![24]

Poe, a victim of gallantry, it seems, rather than of passion, "replied" noncommittally, if flatteringly, to Frances Osgood's advances with a poem he had earlier addressed "To Mary" and "To One Departed," which he initialed with an "E." All that was new was the title, "To F———," and the revisions:

Beloved! amid the earnest woes
  That crowd around my earthly path—
(Drear path, alas! where grows
Not even one lonely rose)—
  My soul at least a solace hath
In dreams of thee, and therein knows
An Eden of bland repose.

And thus thy memory is to me
  Like some enchanted far-off isle
In some tumultuous sea—
Some ocean throbbing far and free
  With storms—but where meanwhile
Serenest skies continually
  Just o'er that one bright island smile.[25]

24. I, 217. The poem later appeared in Mrs. Osgood's *Poems* (Philadelphia, 1850), pp. 403–404. Quinn (*Poe*, p. 478) is responsible for identifying this poem as Mrs. Osgood's. Of the two poems by Mrs. Osgood published in the *Broadway Journal* on April 12, 1845 (p. 231), "Spring" and "Love's Reply" under her pseudonym and her own name respectively, the first has no relevance and the second only the slightest to this literary flirtation.

25. *Broadway Journal*, I (April 26, 1845), 260. This poem appeared under the same title in *The Raven* volume.

Thus encouraged, Mrs. Osgood on September 6, casting off pseudonymity and writing under her own name, responded with her "Echo-Song":

> I know a noble heart that beats
>   For one it loves how "wildly well!"
> *I* only know for *whom* it beats;
>   But I must never tell!
>   Never tell!
> Hush! hark! how Echo soft repeats,—
>   Ah! *never* tell!
>
> I know a voice that falters low,
>   Whene'er one little name 't would say;
> Full well that little name I know,
>   But that I'll ne'er betray!
>   Ne'er betray!
> Hush! hark! how Echo murmurs low,—
>   Ah! *ne'er* betray!
>
> I know a smile that beaming flies
>   From soul to lip, with rapturous glow,
> And I can guess who bids it rise;
>   But none—but none shall know!
>   None shall know!
> Hush! hark! how Echo faintly sighs—
>   But *none* shall know![26]

Still gallant and doubtless pleased by Mrs. Osgood's attentions, if hardly inspired by her, Poe published another "To F————" on September 13, which earlier had borne the title, "To Eliza." Instead of printing all eight lines, however, he printed only four to satisfy the limits of the column and, possibly, to keep the poem innocuous:

> Thou wouldst be loved?—then let thy heart
>   From its present pathway part not!
> Being everything which now thou art,
>   Be nothing which thou art not![27]

26. *Ibid.*, II (Sept. 6, 1845), 129.
27. *Ibid.*, p. 148. When the complete poem appeared in *The Raven* volume, it bore a fuller title, "To F————s S. O————d." The last four lines are:
> "So with the world thy gentle ways,
>   Thy grace, thy more than beauty,
> Shall be an endless theme of praise
>   And love—a simple duty."

Delighted that she seemed a zephyr to Poe's lyre, Mrs. Osgood became even more impetuous, addressing Poe openly for the first time on November 29:

To ———
"In Heaven a spirit doth dwell,
Whose heart-strings are a lute."

I cannot tell *the world* how thrills my heart
To every touch that flies thy lyre along;
How the wild Nature and the wondrous Art,
Blend into Beauty in thy passionate song—

But this *I know*—in thine enchanted slumbers,
Heaven's poet, Israfel,—with minstrel fire—
Taught thee the music of his own sweet numbers,
And tuned—to chord with *his*—thy glorious lyre![28]

If Mrs. Osgood could not "tell *the world*" how thrilled her heart, she seems to have had fair success in apprising the readers of the *Broadway Journal,* for tongues were beginning to wag. When she left New York, whose weather had become inimical to her health, she even wrote letters to Poe, which, according to report, seem to have been quite intimate. Whether Poe answered her confidences is not known—no letters (except perhaps for the note mentioned in note 28) from Poe to Mrs. Osgood have been discovered. Neither Poe's wife nor Mrs. Osgood's husband—Samuel Stillman Osgood, a portrait painter—objected to the friendship. Virginia encouraged the relationship, it seems, feeling that Mrs. Osgood "had a restraining and beneficial effect" upon her husband,[29] and Mr. Osgood, apparently, was used to his wife's impetuous and unconventional behavior.

During Mrs. Osgood's absence, however, another literary lady, Mrs. Ellet, nine years Poe's junior, seems to have come

---

28. *Ibid.,* p. 318. Poe, in an undated note, gingerly addressed to "My Dear Madam" (presumed to be Mrs. Osgood), thanked her "a thousand times for your sweet poem, and for the valued words of flattery which accompanied it," and added—again gingerly, it seems—that he would "not be able to spend an evening with you until Thursday next" because of business pressures. Ostrom, *Poe's Letters,* I, 300. Ostrom dates this note "late October, 1845."

29. From Mrs. Osgood's undated letter as quoted by Griswold in his Memoir in *The Literati,* p. xxxvii.

under his spell, at least according to Poe, and she also seems to have directed a flirtatious poem to Poe under her own name, which Poe also published in the *Broadway Journal*:

COQUETTE'S SONG

Ah yes—gentle sir—I will own
    I ne'er saw perfection till now;
That I never—no never—have known
    A smile such as yours—I'll allow.
And your eyes—Oh, they speak to the soul
    With their glances as bright as the day!
But *I* mean to keep my heart whole—
    So away with your love-vows—away.
        Away—Away—
Away with your love-vows—away!

Ah! ne'er such a voice, I'll confess,
    In its low, murmuring tones have I heard,
So deep with emotion's excess—
    Yet soft as the tones of a bird.
Oh! the thrilling and sweet melody
    Might melt any heart to your sway—
But dearly I love to be free—
    So away with your love-vows—away—
        Away—away—
Away with your love-vows—away!

No, no—I assure you 'tis vain
    To sigh, and to plead, and to woo;
But I'll own, if I *could* wear a chain,
    I would have it—yes—woven by *you.*
Some future time—may be—but now
    I'll be free as a bird on the spray!
I wont—wont be fettered—I vow;
    So away with your love-talk—away—
        Away—away.
Away with your love-talk—away![30]

Though Poe did not respond in verse to Mrs. Ellet, he spoke most highly of her in the *Broadway Journal,* asserting on one occasion that a recent tale of hers was "one of the most exciting

---

30. Poe's statement about Mrs. Ellet's love for him ("whose loathsome love I could do nothing but repel with scorn") appeared in a letter to Sarah Helen Whitman dated Oct. 18, 1848 (Ostrom, *Poe's Letters,* II, 393). That Mrs. Ellet "loved" Poe is partly borne out by this poem. That he scorned her at this time is hardly to be inferred from the fact that he published this poem in the *Broadway Journal,* II (Dec. 13, 1845), 349, or from Mrs. Osgood's reaction to the rumor of Poe's "new romance."

stories we have ever read," and calling her on another occasion "one of the most accomplished of our country-women."[31]

Jealous and forlorn at what seemed Poe's seeking a "prouder prize" (Mrs. Ellet was far more widely known in literary circles), Mrs. Osgood sent him another poem called "A Shipwreck," which Poe had the bad taste to publish in the same number of the *Broadway Journal* that contained Mrs. Ellet's "Coquette's Song":

> I launched a bark on Fate's deep tide—
>   A frail and fluttering toy,
> But freighted with a thousand dreams
>   Of beauty and of joy.
>
> Ah me! it found no friend in them
>   The wave—the sky—the gale—
> Though Love enraptured took the helm—
>   And hope unfurled the sail!
>
> And you, who should its pilot be—
>   To whom in fear it flies—
> Forsake it, on a treacherous sea,
>   To seek a prouder prize.
>
> Alas for Love! bewildered child!
>   He weeps the helm beside,
> And Hope has furled her fairy sail,
>   Nor longer tempts the tide.
>
> Despair and Pride in silence fling
>   Its rich freight to the wave,
> And now an aimless wreck it floats,
>   That none would stoop to save.

Given this situation, it may be inferred that Mrs. Osgood's letters to Poe became more importunate, more intimate. According to Mrs. Ellet's version, at least, when she made one of her visits to the Poe cottage at Fordham, Mrs. Poe "first repeated and afterwards pointed out" to her some "fearful paragraphs" in a letter written by Mrs. Osgood to Poe."[32] Whatever Mrs. Ellet's motivation, whether jealousy or a taste for scandal-mongering, she proceeded to calumniate Mrs. Osgood, intimating that her relation with Poe was far from merely literary and, according to Poe, to so torture his dying wife with

31. II (Oct. 11, 1845), 213, and (Nov. 1, 1845), 258.
32. See n. 21 of this chapter.

anonymous scurrilous letters that Virginia "on her death-bed declared ... Mrs. E. had been her murderer."[33]

Virginia was quite aware of "the tattling of many tongues," since she wrote as much in her 1846 valentine poem to her husband.[34] And that someone was writing poison pen letters to Virginia as early as August, 1845, in all likelihood about Mrs. Osgood's infatuation with Poe, is borne out by Frances Osgood herself in her poem "Slander," which Poe published on August 30. Whether those letters were written, as Poe contended, by Mrs. Ellet is indeterminable.

> A whisper woke the air—
> A soft light tone and low,
> Yet barbed with shame and woe;—
> Now, might it only perish there!
> Nor farther go.
>
> Ah me! a quick and eager ear
> Caught up the little meaning sound!
> Another voice has breathed it clear,
> And so it wanders round,
> From ear to lip—from lip to ear—
> Until it reached a gentle heart,
> And *that—it broke.*
>
> It was the *only* heart it found,
> The only heart 't was meant to find,
> When first its accents woke;—
> It reached that tender heart at last,
> *And that—it broke.*
>
> Low as it seemed to *other* ears,
> It came—a thunder-crash to *hers,*—
> That fragile girl so fair and gay,—
> That guileless girl so pure and true!
>
> 'Tis said a lovely humming bird
> That in a fragrant lily lay,
> And dreamed the summer morn away,
> Was killed by but the gun's *report,*
> Some idle boy had fired in sport!
> The very *sound*—a death-blow came!

33. Letter to Sarah Helen Whitman dated Nov. 24, 1848 (Ostrom, *Poe's Letters,* II, 408).

34. Quinn, *Poe,* p. 497, prints the entire valentine. The only poem that Poe seems to have really written for Mrs. Osgood alone was also "A Valentine"— an acrostic in which "her own sweet name ... nestling, lies / Upon this page" —her middle name, unfortunately, misspelled in the *Evening Mirror* version (Feb. 21, 1846), but corrected in the 1849 version. There is nothing in the poem to reveal that Poe was especially infatuated with Mrs. Osgood.

And thus her happy heart, that beat
With love and hope, so fast and sweet,
   (Shrined in *its Lily* too
For who the maid that knew
But owned the delicate flower-like grace
   Of her young form and face?)
      When first that word
      Her light heart heard,
It fluttered like the frightened bird,
   Then shut its wings and sighed,
   And, with a silent shudder,—*died!*

In any case, Mrs. Osgood on November 22 proclaimed Poe's innocence in the "affair," and innocent he seems to have been:

To ——

Oh! they never can know that heart of thine,
   Who dare accuse *thee* of flirtation!
They might as well say that the stars, which shine
   In the light of their joy o'er Creation,—
Are flirting with every wild wave in which lies
One beam of the glory that kindles the skies.

Smile on then undimmed in your beauty and grace!
   Too well e'er to doubt, love, we know you;—
And shed, from your heaven, the light of your face,
   Where the waves chase each other below you;
For none can e'er deem it *your* shame or *your* sin,
That each wave holds your star-image smiling within.[35]

But now, tormented by the calumnies going the rounds, Mrs. Osgood, in a poem called "To 'The Lady Geraldine,'" reproached Mrs. Ellet for having initiated them. This poem Poe published in the *Broadway Journal* on December 20. The title, an allusion to *Christabel,* is as revealing as the poem itself. In Coleridge's poem, Christabel, while praying in a forest at midnight for her lover, encounters a lady in distress— the lady Geraldine. Moved by the story of her misfortune, Christabel takes Geraldine to her castle, where she is hospitably received. She turns out to be, however, a diabolic creature who has assumed Geraldine's form only to work evil. Though Christabel comes to recognize her true identity, she cannot expose her, for she is silenced by a spell.

35. *Broadway Journal,* II (Nov. 22, 1845), 307.

Though friends had warned me all the while,
  And blamed my willing blindness,
I did not once mistrust your smile,
  Or doubt your tones of kindness.

I sought you not—you came to me—
  With words of friendly greeting:
Alas! how different now I see
  That ill-starred moment's meeting.

When others lightly named your name,
  My cordial praise I yielded;
While *you* would wound with woe and shame,
  The soul you should have shielded.

Was it so blest—my life's estate—
  That you with envy viewed me?
Ah, false one! could you dream my fate,
  You had not thus pursued me.

Perhaps when those who loved me once,
  Beguiled by you, have left me,
You'll grieve for all the hopes of which,
  Your whispered words bereft me.

You'll think, perhaps, the laugh you raised,
  Was hardly worth the anguish,
With which it caused a deep, true heart,
  In silent pride to languish.

You'll think, perchance, the idle jest—
  The joy—will scarce reward you,
For all the blame another's breast
  Must now, in scorn, accord you.

Yet go! 'tis but a darker cloud,
  O'er one fore-doomed to sadness;
I would not change my grief so proud,
  For all your guilty gladness.

Mrs. Ellet responded to "The Lady Geraldine" poem by avowing that she was only trying to keep Mrs. Osgood "safe for heaven" and by assuring her that "cross and thorn" are better than "fruits and flowers"—"fruits and flowers," whether by intent or coincidence, being an allusion to Poe's "To One in Paradise," a poem that appeared in his tale "The Assignation," most recently reprinted in the *Broadway Journal* of June 7 and separately in *The Raven* volume.

I saw thee in thy tender, youthful bloom;
Ah! many then there were who loved thee well,
    And in thy joy, and grace,
    And loveliness rejoiced.

Years since have passed, charged with what freight of gloom!
How art thou changed! pale, woe-worn, hopeless, sad—
    Amid the dismal wreck
    Lives nought but cold Despair!

And thou repinest that thou stand'st apart,

  .   .   .   .

That life to thee is but a sea of woe

  .   .   .   .

Look up, thou lone and sorely stricken one!
Look up, thou darling of the Eternal Sire!
    More blest a thousand fold
    Than they, the idly gay!

For them earth yields her all of bliss; for *thee*
Kind heaven doth violence to its heart of love,
    And Mercy holds thee fast,
    Even in her iron bonds;

And wounds thee, lest thou 'scape her jealous care;
And her *best* gifts—the cross and thorn—bestows.
    They dwell within the vale
    Where fruits and flowers abound;

Those on Affliction's high and barren place;
But round about the mount chariots of fire—
    Horses of fire—encamp,
    To keep thee safe for heaven![36]

Such self-righteousness could only have served to gall, rather than relieve, Mrs. Osgood, who apparently had become quite ill with anxiety, and she ceased her communications to the *Broadway Journal*. When, however, these calumnies of Mrs. Ellet's reached her more aggressive husband, he demanded that Mrs. Ellet formally apologize to his wife or face a court action for libel. So threatened, Mrs. Ellet sent Mrs. Osgood a letter in which she retracted her slanders by fixing the blame entirely on Poe.[37] "The letter shown me by Mrs Poe *must have* been a forgery," a crime which, she wrote, Poe would not hesitate to commit. "It is unfortunate both for you & me

36. *Ibid.,* II (Dec. 27, 1845), 381.
37. See n. 21 of this chapter.

that we ever had any acquaintance with such people as the Poes...." But in the very process of clearing herself, Mrs. Ellet admitted her guilt. If Mrs. Osgood had seen the paragraphs in the "forged" letter she had seen, "you would not wonder I regarded you as I did." She was sorry to have caused pain to one of her own sex by carrying scandal, and she wished that Heaven would forgive her for having done so. She hoped that the injury to Mrs. Osgood's reputation would not be lasting. She assured her that rumors would soon be forgotten. She promised that she and her friends would preserve absolute silence on the subject, except to say, should her name be shamefully mentioned, that she had been wrongfully traduced. And she closed by disowning any ill will toward Mr. Osgood for the harsh things he had said of her and by beseeching God "to guard you in future from danger—and make your life a happy one."

Despite the "explanation" for her gossiping and the "retraction," in both of which Mrs. Ellet regarded herself as the injured party, and despite her prayer to God that Mrs. Osgood's life be a happy one, she did not desist from slandering Mrs. Osgood and Poe, nor did she believe for a moment that the letter was forged. Even as late as 1849, a year before her death, Mrs. Osgood, to stop Mrs. Ellet's incessant tongue, enlisted the aid of Rufus Griswold, who had become infatuated with her. Armed with the retraction, Griswold accosted Mrs. Ellet and told her flatly that "if she ever repeated these falsehoods [he] would print her letter of confession...."[38]

In the meantime the literary ladies, concerned about Mrs. Osgood's reputation and apparently prompted by Mrs. Ellet, sought that persecuted woman's permission to solicit the return of her letters from Poe, which Mrs. Osgood—sick and wanting to end her torment—gave with whatever reluctance. When the committee—Margaret Fuller and Anne C. Lynch—came for the letters, Poe, outraged at the affront and heartily sick of the machinations of Mrs. Ellet, blurted out that Mrs. Ellet had better look after her own compromising letters to him. Though

38. See Phillips, *Poe,* II, 1146, and Bayless, *Griswold,* p. 153.

warrantably provoked, Poe, according to his own statement, felt that his angry words had violated a confidence, not to mention his code of Southern gentleman, and, in contrition, he immediately "made a package of her [Mrs. Ellet's] letters, addressed them to her, and with my own hands left them at her door."[39] Whether Poe on impulse wished those letters into existence, or whether they really existed, will probably never be known, since, if they had existed, they would in all likelihood have been destroyed. There are only two known extant notes from Mrs. Ellet to Poe—an unsigned one addressed to the *Broadway Journal* and postmarked December 16 [1845] which contains only two sentences and reveals nothing. The other, an earlier note, undated and signed "E," is likewise innocuous, but on the verso appear these words in imperfect German: "Ich habe einen Brief fur Sie—wollen Sie gefalligst heute abend nach Uhr den sebben bei mir entnehmen oder abholen lassen?" The letter Mrs. Ellet had for Poe, which she invited him to get, need not, of course, have been written by her. Likewise, there are no known letters of Poe to Mrs. Ellet to cast light upon their epistolary intimacy.[40]

If Mrs. Ellet was vicious before, her vindictiveness became boundless now, for she had been badly compromised by Poe's outburst. Even if her logic—that a correspondence with a married man necessarily implies a relationship other than Platonic—could not be applied to her, as she had made it apply to Mrs. Osgood, she seemed at least exposed as a hypocrite, and, possibly, a jealous one at that, scrupulous about Mrs. Osgood's reputation, which she had not hesitated in damaging, but scarcely about her own. Wanting vindication, which she

---

39. Ostrom, *Poe's Letters*, II, 407–408. English, though a hostile witness, supported this account in one of his *Independent* articles, XLVIII (Oct. 29, 1896), 449, except that he whitewashed Mrs. Ellet. He wrote that the mutual admiration of Poe and Mrs. Osgood became the "town talk, at least among literary people. The coterie thought it should be stopped, and it was suggested to Mrs. Ellet that she should say something to Poe about it. Poe became very much excited at this; and when some of the rest suggested that he should return the lady's letters he accused Mrs. Ellet of having instigated it, and was imprudent enough to say that she had better take care of her own letters which he had, and which compromised herself."

40. Ostrom, *Poe's Letters*, II, 409 n.

knew she could have, since she either had never written letters to Poe or had repossessed her letters, she urged her brother, William M. Lummis, to make Poe prove that he had compromising letters from her or else make him declare himself a slanderer.[41]

Mr. Lummis, obliged to protect his sister's reputation, armed himself with a pistol and went in search of Poe. Poe, no longer having the letters—assuming that he had once had them, or proof that he had received them, and naturally alarmed about his welfare—went to the apartment of Thomas Dunn English to ask for a pistol with which to defend himself against his stalker. English refused, saying that Poe's "surest defense was a retraction of unfounded charges."[42] Such advice, under the circumstances, was the most infuriating that English could have offered. It echoed the charges initiated by Mrs. Ellet and now freely circulating in New York literary circles that Poe was the rankest kind of liar, if nothing worse. Even Simms, living as far from New York as Charleston, South Carolina, wrote to Duyckinck on March 27, 1846: "Your hints with regard to Poe, the Ladies, Billet doux &c quite provoke my curiosity. What is the mischief—who the victims &c."[43] It was no wonder that a fist fight ensued, in which Poe seems to have been beaten.[44]

Unable to free himself from the menace of Mr. Lummis, or, as he may have imagined, a rout of Lummises; helpless to prove he was innocent of slander; and, with his code of chivalry, unwilling, even if he could, to make the accusation stick, Poe, wanting to end the nightmarish episode once and for all, adopted a most desperate solution. He claimed that his statement regarding Mrs. Ellet's letters was made during a seizure

---

41. *Ibid.*, II, 408. In this letter Poe seems to have exaggerated the number of his persecutors. He refers to Mrs. Ellet's brothers and brother-in-law who were sent *"to demand of me the letters."*
42. New York *Evening Mirror*, IV (June 23, 1846).
43. Oliphant *et al.*, *Simms's Letters*, II, 159.
44. See English's article in the *Evening Mirror*, June 23, 1846, and in the *Independent*, XLVIII (Nov. 5, 1896), 4–5; Poe's "Reply to Mr. English and Others" in the Philadelphia *Spirit of the Times*, July 10, 1846; and T. O. Mabbott's article, "Reply to a 'Minor Poe Mystery,'" *Princeton University Library Chronicle*, V (April, 1944), 106–114.

of insanity. If he had not been insane at the time he accused Mrs. Ellet of sending him letters, he had by this time been driven to, if not over, the edge of sanity by this concatenation of events in whose power he was all but helpless. The letters he wrote during this period complain of sickness and mental disturbance; and in his letter to Mrs. Whitman, he frankly expostulates: "Is it any wonder that I was driven *mad* by the intolerable sense of wrong?" Unfortunately, far from ending the crisis, his declaration only provided his enemies with further materials to defame him, and defame him they proceeded to do.

The third event that stemmed from and combined with the previous two events to bring about Poe's downfall was the serial publication from May through October, 1846, in *Godey's Lady's Book* of sketches called, "The Literati of New York City: Some Honest Opinions at Random Respecting Their Autorial Merits, with Occasional Words of Personality."[45] Simms's warning of July 30, 1846—"you are now perhaps in the most perilous period of your career—just in that position— just at that time of life—when a false step becomes a capital error—when a single leading mistake is fatal in its consequences"[46]—was analytic rather than predictive. For Poe's fiasco at the Boston Lyceum had already occurred, the aftermath of which had been climaxed on May 25, 1846, with the censure of him by the Board of Trustees. His disgrace through the instrumentality of Mrs. Ellet was so thoroughly accomplished that, on July 8, 1846, she could declare him to be "steeped in infamy." And three instalments of his *Literati* papers had appeared and three more were forthcoming.

That Poe had prepared papers on New York writers and that Louis A. Godey had accepted them for publication was no secret. Godey, quite aware of Poe's notoriety as a critic, was intent on creating a sensation with the papers, and went to some

45. These papers appeared in six instalments in *Godey's Lady's Book*, XXXII (May, 1846), 194–201; (June, 1846), 266–272, together with a reprint of the May instalment, 289–296; XXXIII (July, 1846), 13–19; (Aug., 1846), 72–78; (Sept., 1846), 126–133; and (Oct., 1846), 157–162.
46. Oliphant *et al., Simms's Letters*, II, 175.

pains to publicize them in advance of publication. According to Hiram Fuller, who, with the departure of Willis and Morris, was now in sole editorial control of the *Mirror*:

> By force of advertisements and placards, Mr. Godey succeeded a month ago in apprising . . . the public . . . that Mr. Poe was coming down, upon the New York literati, in a series of papers in a Philadelphia Magazine, with the force of a 'thousand of brick' and two or three thousand trip hammers, which would infallibly grind them— the literati of New York—into dust and powder, and create a sensation in the world, which it would be impossible to allay, by any possible amount of extra editions of the Lady's Book.[47]

And when Godey published the first of the series, he announced with delighted anticipation that "Mr. E. A. Poe commences No. 1 of the New York Literati. We are much mistaken if these papers of Mr. P. do not raise some commotion in the literary emporium."[48] Godey's expectation of sales was satisfied, for in the June number containing the second instalment, Godey noted that he had "been forced to reprint No. 1 of Poe's Literary Opinions. The demand for the May number we could not supply by some hundreds of copies."[49]

With his reputation for mordancy exploited by Godey's "advertisements and placards," Poe must have sounded threatening indeed in his "Author's Introduction," especially to those writers who felt they might be sketched in subsequent numbers. In that introduction Poe pointed out that two kinds of opinion exist in regard to contemporary authors, the one, popular and clique-manufactured; the other, private and honest. Referring to his article on Bryant which had appeared in the preceding number of *Godey's*[50] and which described the way reputations were made, Poe said that the most "popular" and "successful" authors, being in almost every case "busy-bodies, toadies, quacks," were simply those who profited from a

---

47. Part of a long notice called "Mr Poe and the New York Literati," *Evening Mirror*, May 26, 1846. See this issue also for a number of statements to the effect that Willis and Morris had retired from the *Mirror* and that Fuller (a relative of Margaret Fuller) was in sole charge of both the evening and weekly editions. Augustus W. Clason, Jr., a brother-in-law of Fuller and part owner of the *Mirror*, remained in the background.
48. *Godey's Lady's Book*, XXXII, 240.
49. *Ibid.*, XXXII, 288.
50. *Ibid.*, XXXII (April, 1846), 182–186.

system of chicanery. Citing Hawthorne and Longfellow as examples, he observed that the first *"is not* an ubiquitous quack" and therefore, despite his extraordinary genius, poor;[51] whereas the second, though "a determined imitator and a dexterous adapter of the ideas of other people," is regarded as a "poetical phenomenon," especially since he has "through his social and literary position as a man of property and a professor at Harvard, a whole legion of active quacks at his control. . . ."

Having intimated that justice was to be rendered in the form of an exposé, Poe declared that he would discuss only New York authors and that he would introduce each individual "absolutely at random."

If, to those writers who felt they might be summoned before the critical bar, the introduction made Poe appear both judge and executioner, only his sketches of Charles F. Briggs ("Harry Franco") and, subsequently, of Lewis Clark and Thomas Dunn English confirmed the impression. But the other thirty-five sketches, when they did not damn with faint praise, praised with enough damnation to make the flattery suspect and the portraits unwelcome. There was some obvious, if ill-intended, hoaxing and caricaturing in these papers, which Simms, no doubt prompted by Poe, noted in a letter published in the *Southern Patriot*: "Poe is fond of mystifying in his stories, and they tell me, practices upon this plan even in his sketches; more solicitous, as they assert, of a striking picture than a likeness."[52]

51. Poe was kindly disposed to Hawthorne, despite the fact that in his "Hall of Fantasy" Hawthorne had written: "Mr. Poe had gained ready admittance for the sake of his imagination, but was threatened with ejectment as belonging to the obnoxious class of critics" (*Pioneer,* I, Feb., 1843, 51). Later, however, Hawthorne appears to have modified his opinion of Poe as a critic, notwithstanding that he admired him "rather as a writer of tales than as a critic upon them." In his unique letter to Poe written on June 17, 1846 (from which the above quotation is taken), Hawthorne said: "I presume the publishers will have sent you a copy of 'Mosses from an Old Manse.'. . . I have read your occasional notices of my productions with great interest—not so much because your judgment was, upon the whole, favorable, as because it seemed to be given in earnest. I care for nothing but the truth; and shall always much more readily accept a harsh truth, in regard to my writings, than a sugared falsehood" (Harrison, *Poe's Works,* XVII, 232–233). The book mentioned in the letter contained a second version of "The Hall of Fantasy" with the captious passage deleted.

52. The letter, dated July 15, appeared on July 20, 1846, and is quoted by Oliphant *et al., Simms's Letters,* II, 174 n. 145.

Unhappy with the series, some New Yorkers began writing letters to Godey that were, at turns, anonymous and signed, threatening and wheedling; and some editors such as Hiram Fuller and Lewis Clark began printing vicious remarks about Poe's morals and sanity.[53] What prompted Clark, we know; but it is anybody's guess why Fuller "hated Poe."[54] They had known each other when Poe had been assistant editor of the *Mirror* in the previous year, and Fuller, as we have seen, had blamed Willis and thereby exculpated himself (and Morris) of all responsibility for Poe's attacks on Longfellow. When the second instalment of the *Literati* sketches appeared, Fuller published a long notice in the *Evening Mirror* (a portion of which has already been quoted) called "Mr Poe and the New York Literati," in which he attempted to supply an antidote to Poe's comments that was as nasty as anything Poe was to indite. He began his derisive remarks by saying that, owing to Godey's announcement that Poe was to powder the New York literati, "two milliner's apprentices never slept a wink one whole night," that some students "made a pilgrimage to Bloomingdale to gaze upon the asylum where Mr. Poe was reported to be confined," and that "the New York literati . . . all sat in their garrets shaking in their shoes, with their wives and children clinging to their knees, in fear." Then, becoming coarse, despite his own admission that the sketches were, for the most part, innocuous, Fuller continued:

At last the 'honest opinions' of Mr. Poe, and the Americanized fashions expressed from Paris, appeared together, and Mr. Godey himself says they are creating a great sensation throughout the country,—which we believe. But the sensation, so far as we have had an opportunity of observing, has been one of disgust. We never before saw so much froth on so small a quantity of small beer. . . . People were looking for a furious unbottling of carboy's of vitriol, torrents of aqua fortis, and demi-john's of prussic acid. But instead of these biting, withering and scorching elements, what was our astonishment to find only a few slender streams of sugar house molasses and Godfrey's cordial. . . .

As to the independence for which we have heard Mr. Poe com-

53. *Evening Mirror,* May 26, 1846, and the *Knickerbocker,* XXVII (May, 1846), 461.
54. Alleged by English in the *Independent,* XLVIII (Oct. 15, 1896), 2.

mended, we certainly have never seen so small an amount of that commodity in a literary review as is contained in his 'honest opinions.'. . .

We hope that Mr. Poe gets well paid for his 'honest opinions,' for we are sure that a man must be sadly in want of money who resorts to such methods of raising it. . . . Mr. Poe is the last man in the country who should undertake the task of writing 'honest opinions' of the literati. His infirmities of mind and body, his petty jealousies, his necessities even, which allow him neither time nor serenity for such work, his limited information on local subjects, his unfortunate habits, his quarrels and jealousies, all unfit him for the performance of such a duty, as the specimens already published abundantly prove.

Fuller concluded "after the fashion of our Thersitical Magazinist" by making Poe appear deformed and idiotic. He alleged that Poe was "in height about 5 feet 1 or two inches," and that he weighed about 115 pounds; that "his tongue shows itself unpleasantly when he speaks earnestly, and seems too large for his mouth"; that his forehead, "where phrenology places conscientiousness and the group of moral sentiments," was quite flat; and that "his walk is quick, jerking, sometimes waving." He added that he supposed Poe to be a contributor to the *Knickerbocker,* but of this he could not be certain, and that Poe was the author of *Politian,* "to which Professor Longfellow is largely indebted, it is said by Mr. Poe, for many of his ideas."[55]

The very furor that Godey wanted to excite and had now succeeded in exciting began to frighten him—enough to prompt him to print a disclaimer when the second series of the sketches appeared in June:

The Authors and Mr. Poe.—We have received several letters from New York, anonymous and from personal friends, requesting us to be careful what we allow Mr. Poe to say of the New York authors. . . . We reply to one and all, that we have nothing to do but publish Mr. Poe's opinions, *not our own.* Whether we agree with Mr. Poe or not is another matter. We are not to be intimidated by a threat of the loss of friends, or turned from our purpose by honeyed words.

55. Poe evidently wrote various letters, including ones to Joseph M. Field, editor of the *St. Louis Reveillé,* dated June 15, 1846 (Ostrom, *Poe's Letters,* II, 318–320) and to Simms (letter is lost), asking that this article be condemned and that the impression of his appearance be corrected. Simms sent a letter to the *Southern Patriot* in compliance with the request (see n. 52 of this chapter).

Our course is onward. The May edition was exhausted before the first of May, and we have had orders for hundreds from Boston and New York which we could not supply. . . .

Many attempts have been made and are making by various persons to forestall public opinion. We have the name of one person,—others are busy with reports of Mr. Poe's illness. Mr. Poe has been ill, but we have letters from him of very recent dates, also a new batch of the Literati, which show anything but feebleness either of body or mind. Almost every paper that we exchange with has . . . spoken in high terms of No. 1 of Mr. Poe's opinions.[56]

When the September number of his magazine appeared, containing the penultimate instalment of the series, Godey again ran a disclaimer:

We hear of some complaints having been made by those writers who have already been noticed by Mr. Poe. Some of the ladies have suggested that the publisher has something to do with them. This we positively deny, and we as positively assert that they are published as written by Mr. Poe, without any alteration or suggestion from us.[57]

There is no point in touching upon all the authors Poe treated in the series, authors such as George B. Cheever, Mary Gove, and Henry Carey, but Poe's remarks about Duyckinck, James Aldrich, Margaret Fuller, Mrs. Osgood, and Anne C. Lynch deserve passing mention, since these people have figured in our account. Duyckinck was noted for "his active beneficence, his hatred of wrong done even to an enemy, and especially for an almost Quixotic fidelity to his friends." Aldrich, who had attained brief but unenviable recognition by Poe's review of Longfellow's *Waif,* was again charged with plagiarism and acquitted in the way and even in the words that Longfellow had been. Margaret Fuller was lauded for "high genius" and for the integrity of her review of Longfellow's *Poems*:

The review did her infinite credit; it was frank, candid, independent —in even ludicrous contrast to the usual mere glorifications of the day, giving honor *only* where honor was due, yet evincing the most thorough capacity to appreciate and the most sincere intention to place in the fairest light the real and idiosyncratic merits of the poet.

In my opinion it is one of the very few reviews of Longfellow's poems, ever published in America, of which the critics have not had abundant reason to be ashamed.

56. *Godey's Lady's Book,* XXXII, 288.
57. *Ibid.,* XXXIII, 144.

Mrs. Osgood was praised as "ardent, sensitive, impulsive; the very soul of truth and honor; a worshipper of the beautiful, with a heart so radically artless as to seem abundant in art"; and, despite her light fame at the moment, "universally respected, admired and beloved." Miss Lynch, one of the committee who had come for Mrs. Osgood's letters to Poe, "has her hobbies ... (of which a very indefinite idea of 'duty' is one,) and is, of course, readily imposed upon by an artful person who perceives and takes advantage of this most amiable failing." Mrs. Ellet, although alluded to in this manner, remained conspicuously absent from the series.

What cannot be mentioned only in passing, however, is Poe's sketch of English that appeared in July. His resentment of English for his role in the Ellet affair bared his real feeling of contempt for a man whom, hitherto, he had been guilty of using.[58] The sketch, divested of its elaborate sarcasm, accused English of plagiarism and deficiencies in English grammar, and concluded with the statement that he was not personally known to the writer. English rallied to the attack at once by sending his reply to all the New York papers, if we are to believe Hiram Fuller,[59] but—as far as can be determined—only the *Morning Telegraph* and *Evening Mirror* published it—on June 23. English's "Card" was prefaced by Fuller as follows:

The War of the Literati.—We publish the following terrific rejoinder of one of Mr. Poe's abused *literati*, with a twinge of pity for the object of its severity. But as Mr. Godey, 'for a consideration,' lends the use of his battery for an attack on the one side, it is but fair that we allow our friends an opportunity to exercise a little 'self-defence' on the other.

58. Poe admitted to having patronized English, but "I solemnly say that in no paper of mine did there ever appear one word about this gentleman—unless of the broadest and most unmistakable irony—that was not printed from the MS of the gentleman himself" (Philadelphia *Spirit of the Times*, July 10, 1846). Carl Schreiber in "A Close-Up of Poe," *Saturday Review of Literature*, III (Oct. 9, 1926), 166, says of this statement: "This is the whole truth. I have carefully followed Poe's criticisms of *The Aristidean* [the monthly that English edited] from their beginning. These reviews Poe wrote tongue in cheek, keeping, however, always within a safe limit."

59. Fuller asserted in the *Evening Mirror*, Feb. 18, 1847: "We were assured that it ["Mr. English's Reply to Mr. Poe"] was to be published in every newspaper in the city on the day that it appeared in the Mirror." English's reply was also reprinted in the *Weekly Mirror*, IV (June 27, 1846), 186.

And "Mr. English's Reply to Mr. Poe" began:

A Mr. Edgar A. Poe has been engaged for some time past in giving to the public . . . sketches of what he facetiously calls the 'Literati of New York city.' These he names by way of distinction, I presume, from his ordinary writings, '*honest* opinions.' He honors me by including me in the very numerous and remarkably august body he affects to describe. Others have converted the paper on which his sketches are printed to its legitimate use—like to like—but as he seems to covet a notice from me, he shall be gratified.

The fact that Poe disowned acquaintance with him, English continued, was due to the "severe treatment he received at my hands for brutal and dastardly conduct. . . . Unfortunately, I know him; and by the blessing of God, and the assistance of a grey-goose quill, my design is to make the public know him also." He said that he knew Poe by a succession of his acts, which he proceeded to recount. His elaborate charges, stripped of scurrilous language and insinuation, were: (1) Poe had obtained a sum of money from him under false pretenses[60] —a fact, he said, he could support by Poe's written acknowledgment which he had in his possession. (2) Poe by his conduct had virtually admitted to the truth of an accusation of forgery leveled against him by a "merchant of this city." (3) Poe had "accepted an invitation to deliver a poem before a society of the New York University," but, unable to "compose a poem on a stated subject," drank until intoxicated, "as he always does when troubled," and remained intoxicated during the entire week. Thus, when the "night of exhibition came, it was gravely announced that Mr. Poe could not deliver his poem, on account of severe indisposition." (4) Poe was guilty of similar but more discreditable behavior at the Boston Lyceum:

Want of ability prevented him from performing his intention, and he insulted his audience, and rendered himself a laughing-stock, by reciting a mass of ridiculous stuff, written by some one, and printed under his name when he was about 18 years of age. It had a peculiar

60. According to English's deposition, as reported in the *New York Tribune,* Feb. 18, 1847, ". . . Mr. Poe solicited of him the loan of $30 to get the Broadway Journal in his own hands, and promising to get Mr. E. a share of the profits; that Mr. E. lent him the money, taking his note, but Mr. P. never afterward offered to transfer an interest in the Journal, and deponent understood that the paper had not yielded any profits."

effect on his audience, who dispersed under its infliction; and when he was rebuked for his fraud, he asserted that he had intended a hoax. Whether he did or not is little matter, when we reflect that he took the money offered for his performance—thus committing an act unworthy of a gentleman, though in strict keeping with Mr. Poe's previous acts.

(5) Poe, "having been guilty of some most ungentlemanly conduct, while in a state of intoxication, I was obliged to treat him with discourtesy":

He told me that he had villified [sic] a certain well known and esteemed authoress, of the South [Mrs. Ellet], then on a visit to New York; that he had accused her of having written letters to him which compromised her reputation; and that her brother (her husband being absent) had threatened his life unless he produced the letters he named. . . . In a day or so, afterwards, being confined to his bed from the effect of fright and the blows he had received from me, he sent a letter to the brother of the lady he had so vilely slandered, denying all recollection of having made any charges of the kind alleged, and stating that, if he had made them, he was laboring under a fit of insanity to which he was periodically subject. . . . The letter being a full retraction of the falsehood, he, to whom it was addressed, stopped further proceedings, and the next day Mr. Poe hastily fled from town.

English concluded his indictments by accusing Poe of using billingsgate and of being not only "thoroughly unprincipled, base and depraved, but silly, vain and ignorant—not alone an assassin in morals, but a quack in literature . . . ; while his cool plagiarisms . . . excite the public amazement."

In his "Reminiscences of Poe,"[61] English said that if his own language was scurrilous at times, it was only that it fell in character with Poe's. But the reply must have struck quite a few readers as extremely brutal. Even Griswold, a month after English's reply had appeared, wrote Duyckinck that he "would sooner have cut off my hand than used it to write such an ungentlemanly card, though every word were true. But my indignation of this treatment even of an enemy exceeds my power of expression."[62] There were no public allusions to

61. *Independent,* XLVIII (Oct. 15, 1896), 2.
62. Letter dated July 24, 1846 (quoted by Bayless, *Griswold,* p. 143). In his Memoir in *The Literati,* p. xxiii, Griswold repeated his indignation at English's card in almost the same terms and added that "every one acquainted with the parties" knew that Poe's sketch of English "was entirely false in what purported to be its facts."

English's "Card," at least none that I have encountered, and even Lewis Clark, on the lookout for quotable material with which to malign Poe, ignored this item.

Poe, under such an attack, which, in his contempt for English, he called a bagatelle, bestirred himself and sent a reply to Godey for publication in his magazine. He felt he had a distinct advantage over English in this quarrel, for *Godey's Lady's Book,* according to Poe's estimate (which assumed four readers to a number), had a circulation of at least 200,000, whereas the *Mirror* had a circulation of only a few thousand. But Poe was mistaken in assuming that Godey would publish his reply. Godey was apprehensive: he was still publishing the *Literati* papers that were exciting importunate letters and sales (he was to die a millionaire); there were other fish to be netted, perhaps the largest of which was Lewis Clark, who might retaliate as English had; and he was aware that if he lent his magazine gratuitously to give a slander currency, he might become a defendant in a libel suit.[63] Preferring to be a noncombatant, he sent Poe's reply to a sportsman's paper of small circulation, the Philadelphia *Spirit of the Times,* edited by John Stephenson Du Solle, paying ten dollars to have it printed and charging Poe with the cost. Poe, of course, was indignant. He wrote Godey that he regretted his action: he would have "found no difficulty in getting it printed here, in a *respectable* paper, and gratis"; that he was rather ashamed for Godey, who, knowing his poverty, demanded ten dollars from him; that the reply would clear him; and, finally, that he had referred English's charges to an attorney, who, when the matter was brought before a court, would mention the ten dollars as an item.[64]

Godey apparently wrote to Simms, whether to explain his refusal to publish Poe's letter or his rejection of further *Literati* papers is not clear; and Simms on July 30 wrote Poe: "But how can you expect a Magazine proprietor to encourage con-

---

63. According to an explanation in the *Philadelphia Public Ledger* of July 4, 1843, of what constituted culpability for libel. See William Henry Gravely, Jr., "An Incipient Libel Suit Involving Poe," *Modern Language Notes,* LX (May, 1945), 308–311.

64. Letter dated July 16, 1846 (Ostrom, *Poe's Letters,* II, 323–324).

tributions which embroil him with all his neighbors?"[65]—a rather peculiar question considering that Godey had published and would continue to publish the *Literati* sketches, though under no compulsion to do so.

With these delays, "Mr. Poe's Reply to English and Others," though dated June 27, made its belated appearance on July 10. Addressing the public, Poe said that he attached little importance to the *Literati* sketches, however much others might, for he regarded them as "loosely and inconsiderately written—aiming at nothing beyond the gossip of criticism—unless, indeed, at the relief of those *'necessities'* which I have never blushed to admit and which the editor of 'The Mirror' has, in the same manner, never blushed publicly to insult"; and that the "spasms of one or two enemies have given the articles a notoriety far surpassing their merit or my expectation," for which notoriety, he added, he could hardly be held accountable. He then turned to a consideration of English's reply, and, in so turning, he promised he would "not permit any profundity of disgust to induce, even for an instant, a violation of the dignity of truth." Yet, though aware that his assailants—among them Clark, Mrs. Ellet, Hiram Fuller, and English himself, not to mention the scores who had exchanged gossip about the Boston Lyceum and Mrs. Osgood affairs—were in possession of the facts, however distorted they may have become by this time, he rebutted only two of English's five charges. Of the remaining three, he evaded two entirely and merely palliated the other.

Poe's answers, reduced to their essential elements and presented in the order he presented them, took this form (the numbers in parentheses have reference to the order of English's charges): (3) An explanation of his "irregularities" which, hitherto, he said, he had not been the coward to deny or even to extenuate—irregularities which "were the *effect* of a terrible evil rather than its cause"—and which now, "in redemption from the physical ill I have forever got rid of the moral."[66] His

---

65. Oliphant *et al.*, *Simms's Letters*, II, 176.
66. In a letter dated Jan. 4, 1848, almost a year after Virginia's death, Poe explained this passage in answer to George W. Eveleth's inquiry. He said that the evil responsible for his irregularities was the fact that his beloved wife con-

failure to make his scheduled appearance at New York University he ignored,[67] as he also ignored (4) the Boston Lyceum affair. (5) A claim that he suffered an attack of amnesia while at English's apartment, so that he could "pretend to no remembrance of anything which occurred—with the exception of having wearied and degraded myself, to little purpose, in bestowing upon Mr. E. the 'fisticuffing' of which he speaks" (the same seizure of amnesia he earlier alleged to have suffered when the committee came for Mrs. Osgood's letters). In respect to Mrs. Ellet, he was blatantly evasive: "The 'celebrated authoress' is a mystery. With the exception, perhaps, of Mrs. Stephens, Mrs. Welby, and Miss Gould... there is *no* celebrated authoress in America with whom I am not on terms of perfect amity at least, if not of cordial and personal friendship." (1, 2) An assertion that the charges that he had taken money under false pretenses and that he had committed forgery were "criminal, and with the aid of 'The Mirror' I can have them investigated before a criminal tribunal." He defied English to produce the acknowledgment he named in proof of the first of these two allegations, and he cited a letter from the bearer of the second allegation to prove that it was baseless rumor.[68] He concluded with a blast at Hiram Fuller "who

tinually ruptured a blood-vessel, and that, with each rupture, he experienced "all the agonies of her death." He became insane, he said, with protracted intervals of "horrible sanity"; that during such seizures he drank, he did not know with what frequency or in what quantity; his enemies, he said, "referred the insanity to the drink rather than the drink to the insanity." He had all but abandoned hope of a permanent cure for himself when he "found one in the *death* of my wife. This I can & do endure as becomes a man—it was the horrible never-ending oscillation between hope & despair which I could *not* longer have endured without the total loss of reason. In the death of what was my life, then, I received a new but—oh God! how melancholy an existence" (Ostrom, *Poe's Letters,* II, 356). While this explanation would account for the "irregularities," it would hardly explain the recovery mentioned in his reply to English, for Virginia was still alive, though dying, when he wrote that reply.

67. According to the evidence presented by Hervey Allen, *Israfel: The Life and Times of Edgar Allan Poe* (New York, 1934), p. 520, Poe was guilty as charged in failing to meet his obligation at New York University.

68. The rumor that Poe had committed forgery had originated from an unnamed source, and the rumor had actually been repeated to Mrs. Osgood by an Edward J. Thomas, the "merchant of this city" to whom English alluded and whose letter Poe quoted to disprove the rumor. Mrs. Osgood, in turn, conveyed the report to Poe. For the sake of delicacy, Mrs. Osgood's name was left unmentioned by English, Thomas, Poe, and by the court. Poe, sometime before July 5, 1845, wrote to Thomas to ask him whether he had originated the allega-

(also with a thorough knowledge of the facts, as I can and will show) prostituted his filthy sheet to the circulation of this calumny...."

English wasted little time in writing a reply, and Fuller, unlike Godey, lent his journal again to "A Card" from English, which appeared in the *Evening Mirror* on July 13, 1846, under the title, "In Reply to Mr. Poe's Rejoinder." In it English pointed out that Poe's rejoinder, though dated June 27, was printed on July 10, from which he inferred that Poe "had some difficulty in obtaining a respectable journal to give currency to his scurrilous article." Then, listing the opprobrious words and phrases appearing in Poe's reply and saying that he could not respond to such vulgarity, he proceeded to accept Poe's challenge, noting in the process Poe's evasions:

> Actuated by the desire for the public good, I charged Mr. Poe with the commission of certain misdemeanors, which prove him to be profligate in habits and depraved in mind. The most serious of these he admits by silence—the remainder he attempts to palliate; and winds up his tedious disquisition by a threat to resort to a legal prosecution. This is my full desire. Let him institute a suit, if he dare, and I pledge myself to make my charges good by the most ample and satisfactory evidence.

He then exposed the "charlatanry of Mr. Poe's reply," particularly "his proclamation of recent reform, when it is not a week since he was seen intoxicated in the streets of New York," and "his attempt to excuse his drunkenness and meanness on the ground of insanity...."

Soon after this card appeared, Poe, on July 23, through an attorney, Enoch L. Fancher, filed suit for libel in the New York Superior Court against Hiram Fuller and Augustus W. Clason, part-owner with Fuller in the firm that published the *Mirror*. The declaration read in court on that date stated:

> ... the said defendants ... greatly envying the happy State and condition of the ... plaintiff and contriving and wickedly and maliciously intending to injure the ... plaintiff, in his ... good name, fame and credit, and to bring him into public scandal, infamy and

---

tion. Thomas proceeded to investigate the rumor and found that "it undoubtedly arose from the misunderstanding of some word used"—a fact he acknowledged in a letter dated July 5, 1845.

disgrace . . . to vex, harass and oppress, impoverish, and wholly ruin him . . . falsely, wickedly, and maliciously did print . . . a certain false, scandalous, malicious and defamatory libel over the name of one Thomas Dunn English. . . .[69]

A preliminary hearing was scheduled for August 4, 1846, in New York City Hall. At that time, the defendants, through their attorney, William H. Paine, pleaded not guilty to the charge of libel, and the trial was set for the first Monday in September, then unexplainably postponed until the first Monday in February, 1847.

During this protracted interval, rumors concerning Poe's insanity became rife. The public quarrel with English not only spread the gossip that Poe was a slanderer of a lady and a coward to boot who would resort to any subterfuge, even to a pretense of insanity, to save his skin; it also lent substance to that gossip, largely because of Poe's evasiveness. Poe was aware of these defamations but helpless to stop them, because of his own admission of insanity—an admission which he had written and delivered to Mr. Lummis and which that gentleman, in turn, had given to his sister.[70] Poe wrote to Willis:

> Of the facts, that I myself have been long and dangerously ill, and that my illness has been a well understood thing among my brethren of the press, the best evidence is afforded by the innumerable paragraphs of personal and literary abuse with which I have been latterly assailed.[71]

Clark, it will be recalled, quoted the *Evening Gazette and Times,* which had stated that Poe was "in a state of health which renders him not completely *accountable* for all his peculiarities," and Hiram Fuller had satirically put Poe in the

69. For many details of this suit, I am indebted to two articles by Francis B. Dedmond, "The War of the Literati: Documents of the Legal Phase," *Notes and Queries,* CXCVIII (July, 1953), 303–308, and "Poe's Libel Suit Against T. D. English," *Boston Public Library Quarterly,* V (Jan., 1953), 31–37.

70. Mrs. Ellet wrote Griswold's third wife in 1853 that she had not written the alleged letters to Poe and that she "possessed written evidence of the falsehood of such an assertion, in Mr. Poe's retraction of and apology for a slander of the kind once uttered by him, as he alleged, in a fit of lunacy" (Bayless, *Griswold,* pp. 278–280 n. 19).

71. Letter dated Dec. 30, 1846 (Ostrom, *Poe's Letters,* II, 338–339). Griswold, in his Memoir in *The Literati,* p. xxv, asserted with his gift for distortion that this letter was "written for effect. . . . There was no literary or personal abuse of him in the journals. . . ."

Bloomingdale insane asylum. But Poe's enemies were not alone in circulating the story. Well-intentioned friends, living outside the confines of New York and reading the gossip about Poe which they regarded as true, if only because of the frequency of its repetition, innocently repeated the most notorious of the rumors, that Poe's mind had collapsed. Simms, for example, wrote to a friend on May 15, 1846: "I see by one of the papers that it was gravely thought to send P. to Bedlam." And in his favorable review of the *Literati* appearing in the *Southern Patriot* on July 20, he announced that Poe was "sick, according to a report which reached me yesterday, of brain fever."[72] Joseph Evans Snodgrass, editor of the *Baltimore Saturday Visiter* and a friend of long standing, reported on April 18 that "Edgar A. Poe, according to a New York letter writer, labors under a mental derangement to such a degree that it has been determined to send him to the Insane Retreat at Utica."

If Poe could barely eke out a livelihood before, he became impoverished now, for few editors wanted his articles, even if he were well enough to write them. Even the do-gooders who, without Poe's knowledge or consent, sought to raise funds for the Poes in their sickness and poverty, helped only to defame him the more. The Philadelphia *Saturday Evening Post,* for instance, wrote that "Edgar A. Poe is lying dangerously ill with the brain fever" and that he and his wife "are without money and without friends. . . ."[73] The New York *Morning Express* of December 15 carried this item:

Illness of Edgar A. Poe.—We regret to learn that this gentleman and his wife are both dangerously ill with the consumption, and that the hand of misfortune lies heavy upon their temporal affairs. We are sorry to mention the fact that they are so far reduced as to be barely able to obtain the necessaries of life. This is, indeed, a hard lot, and we do hope that the friends and admirers of Mr. Poe will come promptly to his assistance in his bitterest hour of need. Mr. Poe is the author of several tales and poems, of which Messrs. Wiley &

72. Oliphant *et al., Simms's Letters,* II, 163 and 174 n. 145.
73. Quoted by George W. Eveleth without date in his letter to Poe dated Jan. 19, 1847. See Thomas O. Mabbott, ed., *The Letters from George W. Eveleth to Edgar Allan Poe* (New York, 1922), p. 9.

Putnam are the publishers, and, it is believed, the profitable publishers. At least, his friends say that the publishers ought to start a movement in his behalf.

And Willis, good friend of Poe though he was, devoted much of his editorial plumping for a "Hospital for Disabled Labourers with the Brain" to Poe, partly to raise funds for him and partly to defend him against his calumniators; but for all the harm it did, it might have been written by Poe's worst enemy:

The feeling we have long entertained on this subject, has been freshened by a recent paragraph in the *Express* announcing that Mr. Edgar A. Poe, and his wife, were both dangerously ill and suffering for want of the common necessaries of life. Here is one of the finest scholars, one of the most original men of genius, and one of the most industrious of the literary profession of our country, whose temporary suspension of labour, from bodily illness, drops him immediately to a level with the common objects of public charity....

In connection with this public mention of Mr. Poe's personal matters, perhaps it will not be thought inopportune, if we put on its proper footing, a public impression, which does him some injustice. We have not seen nor corresponded with Mr. Poe for two years, and we hazard this delicate service without his leave, of course, and simply because we have seen him suffer for the lack of such vindication, when his name has been brought injuriously before the public.... We refer to conduct and language charged against him, which, were he, at the time, in sane mind, were an undeniable forfeiture of character and good feeling. To blame, in some degree, still, perhaps he is. But let charity for the failings of human nature judge of the degree.

He related how he had discovered, when Poe was his associate on the *Mirror,* that a single glass of wine made Poe talk "like a man insane," though he showed "no symptom of ordinary intoxication," and that, under such influence, Poe was "neither sane nor responsible."

Now, very possibly, Mr. Poe may not be willing to consent to even this admission of any infirmity. He has little or no memory of them afterwards, we understand. But public opinion unqualifiedly holds him blameable for what he has said and done under such excitements; and while a call is made in a public paper for aid, it looks like doing him a timely service, to [at] least partially to [*sic*] exonerate him.[74]

Clearly, the gossip involving Mrs. Ellet and Poe's plea of insanity had reached, ridiculously, such a wide audience that

74. New York *Home Journal,* Dec. 26, 1846.

Willis needed only to allude to the episode rather than detail it. It is indication enough of the position to which Poe had been reduced that he could tell Willis that this editorial was "kindly and manly."[75]

But English was not done with Poe yet. Learning that Poe had filed suit, he, who had publicly pledged "to make my charges good by the most ample and satisfactory evidence," fled to Washington, D. C., to avoid involvement in the criminal action. Because of his absence, the case, called to order as scheduled, on the first Monday in February, was again post-poned—this time for two weeks. When the court reconvened, the judge ordered that a commission be directed to receive English's deposition, which was done. Among other things, that deposition repeated what English had said earlier, that "the general character of said Poe is that of a notorious liar, a common drunkard, and of one utterly lost to all the obligations of honor"—statements that seem to have been widely copied in the papers.[76] In the meantime too, English's novel, *1844, or The Power of the "S.F.,"* which had begun appearing anonymously and serially in the *Weekly Mirror* of July 25, 1846, abruptly introduced on September 5—several months before the trial for libel took place—a new character by the name of Marmaduke Hammerhead, which was an obvious satire of Poe. "Hammerhead is presented as author of a well-known poem, 'The Black Crow,' and of a volume, *The Humbug and Other Tales*. We are told that he had written criticism on the *Literati* of the country and that he considers himself the 'great Mogul of all the critics.' He refers to his friend M. Dupin, and constantly to his severe articles on Longfellow."[77] In addition,

75. See n. 71 of this chapter.
76. As reported by the *New York Tribune* and *Evening Mirror* on Feb. 18, 1847.
77. Leonard B. Hurley was the first to make this discovery. This quotation and the summary that follows are taken from his article, "A New Note in the War of the Literati," *American Literature*, VII (Jan., 1936), 376–394. The passages pertinent to Poe appeared irregularly from Sept. 5 to Nov. 7, 1846, when the serial concluded. Parts of the serial also appeared in the *Evening Mirror* from Sept. 9 to Oct. 31, 1846. Despite the show of candor in his series, "Reminiscences of Poe," English made no mention of this satire or his subsequent outright smears of Poe in the *John-Donkey*.

Hammerhead is depicted as going insane at the time he writes his criticisms of the literati. In the passages relating to Hammerhead, the familiar charges are repeated *ad nauseam:* habitual drunkenness and sponging; pedantry; hatred of Longfellow, the Transcendentalists, and Boston; plagiarism; susceptibility to women (he was also accused of flogging his wife); constant threats to annihilate his enemies by criticism. The serial, we are told, "attracted no little attention as a *feuilleton* in the New York Mirror," and in book form was "probably destined to still more general circulation."[78]

On February 17, 1847, Poe won his libel suit and was awarded $225.06 in damages, Fuller and Clason being assessed that amount together with court costs of $101.48. Despite the number of Poe's enemies, the degree of their animosity, and the frequency of their attacks, the defense could not produce a single witness to testify under oath either against Poe's conduct or his character (English was still in hiding), whereas Poe's attorney produced three—the merchant Thomas, who cleared Poe of the charge of forgery, and Judge Noah and Freeman Hunt, who never "heard anything against him except that he is occasionally addicted to intoxication." But to Poe the news that his name had, at least, been cleared in court, was anticlimactic: Virginia had died only eighteen days earlier. Broken in health and spirit, he was not even in attendance at court.[79]

The verdict, instead of clearing Poe once and for all, detonated instead a spate of newspaper articles which reviewed the affair in a way unfavorable to Poe. Hiram Fuller in the *Evening Mirror* of February 18, 1847, for example, remarked that the "facts in the case are well known to our readers, and

78. *Literary World,* I (June 5, 1847), 423. Duyckinck was no longer editor of the magazine at this time; Charles Fenno Hoffman, Griswold's friend, had taken over that position.

79. These facts are reported by the *Tribune,* Feb. 18, 1847. Hunt edited and owned the *Merchant's Magazine,* and Poe, when he discussed him in the *Literati* papers, remarked that he "is a true friend, and the enemy of no man. His heart is full of the warmest sympathies and charities. No one in New York is more universally popular." Mordecai Manuel Noah was prominent in law, politics, drama, and journalism. His most recent journalistic venture had been editing the *Sunday Times and Messenger,* in which, on Oct. 26, 1845, he had defended Poe against attack during the Boston Lyceum affair.

also the parties, who by resorting to low personal abuse of each other, have lost more in character than they have gained in money or fame." He had hardly expected Poe to resort to a libel suit, he confessed, since, with the possible exception of Bennett, he "has probably written and published more libellous articles than any other man in the whole country." He added that he had offered the plaintiff free use of his columns to vindicate himself, "an offer which he at the time accepted, but was probably advised differently by counsel, who hoped to find something worth picking from this 'bone of contention.' " And in another article in the same issue, he complained: "We gave a certain *Poe-t* $15 a week for three months, at a time when we neither needed his services nor could afford to pay for them, and have during the present winter contributed our mite to relieve his distresses, who in return gives us a viper's gratitude."

Greeley too reviewed the events leading up to the trial in the *New York Tribune* on February 19:

Genius and the Law of Libel.—Mr. Edgar A. Poe, well known as a Poet, having of course more wit than wisdom, and we think making no pretensions to exemplary faultlessness in morals, still less to the scrupulous fulfillment of pecuniary engagements,[80] wrote for Godey's Lady's Book a series of Literary Portraits of New-York notables. . . . They were plain, sincere, free, off-hand criticisms—seldom flattering, sometimes savagely otherwise. Of this latter class was an account of Mr. Thomas Dunn English, which seemed to us impelled by personal spite. To this birching Mr. English very naturally replied, charging Mr. Poe with gross pecuniary delinquency and personal dishonesty, and the *Evening Mirror* was so good-natured as to give him a hearing. Mr. English is a disbeliever in Capital Punishment, but you would hardly have suspected the fact from the tenor of this retort acidulous upon Poe. Mr. Poe therefore threw away the goose-quill (though the columns of the Mirror were impartially tendered him for a rejoinder,) and most commendably refrained from catching up instead the horse-whip or the pistol; but he did something equally mistaken and silly, if not equally wicked, in suing—not his self-roused castigator, but the harmless publisher, for a libel!

80. On Oct. 24, 1845, Greeley had signed a sixty-day promissory note made out to Poe to the value of $50, which, endorsed by Poe, was given to John Bisco on the same day as a down payment for purchase of the *Broadway Journal*. Greeley never collected the loan, and after Poe's death he remarked that he had an autograph of Poe which he was prepared to part with for far less than the amount it cost him (Horace Greeley, *Recollections of a Busy Life*, New York, 1868, pp. 196–197).

Poe wrote to Greeley on February 21, enclosing this editorial article, lines of which he had underscored—the passages referring to his failure to meet his debts and his throwing away the quill. With an obtuseness hard to understand, he said that the only personality in his sketch of English was contained in the words, "I have no acquaintance, personally, with Mr English"—meaning, he explained, that he wished to decline his acquaintance in the future. Under such slight provocation, Poe continued, English had libeled him with what he must have presumed would be impunity "on account of my illness and expected death. . . . I sue; to redeem my character from these foul accusations. . . . The jury returned a verdict in my favor—and the paragraphs enclosed are the comments of *the 'Tribune!'*" He acknowledged that he owed Greeley money, but he had been "ill, unfortunate, no doubt weak, and as yet unable to refund the money—but on this ground *you,* Mr. Greeley, could *never* have accused me of being habitually 'unscrupulous in the fulfillment of my pecuniary engagements.' The charge is *horribly false*—I have a hundred times left myself destitute of bread for myself and family that I might discharge debts. . . ." He added that he did not throw away the quill, but arose from a sick-bed to write a reply which was published in the *Spirit of the Times.* He admitted that the columns of the *Mirror* had been offered him, but only "with a proviso that I should forego a suit and omit this passage and that passage, to suit the purposes of Mr Fuller." In closing, Poe begged Greeley "to do by me as you would have me do by you in a similar case"—to disavow his damaging statements,[81] but that request Greeley ignored.

English was not silenced by the libel suit. In the *John-Donkey* that he edited and co-owned, he continually smeared Poe until the seven libel suits filed against the magazine by various complainants forced him to discontinue publication. The most telling of his smears, perhaps, was that the Germanesque style in the short story was "accessible to every impudent and contemptible mountebank who may choose to

81. Ostrom, *Poe's Letters,* II, 344–345.

slander a lady and then plead insanity to shelter himself from the vengeance of her relatives."[82]

Nor did the matter end there. Charles Frederick Briggs, better known as Harry Franco in his day, was ready to pick up the cudgels the moment that English had dropped them. He, like English, had reason to dislike Poe. Poe had edged him out of the co-editorship of the *Broadway Journal*[83] and, to compound the injury, had attacked him in the first instalment of the *Literati* papers. In that sketch Poe observed, among other things, that Briggs's novels were insipid imitations of Smollett's and that Briggs "has never composed in his life three consecutive sentences of grammatical English." Thus, even as English's *1844* was drawing to a close, Hiram Fuller promised his readers that a "new novel of very great interest, but of a very different character, written expressly for the *Mirror* by one of our most popular authors" would be serialized.[84] Briggs was the popular author in question and his picaresque novel, *The Trippings of Tom Pepper, or The Results of Romancing,* was the work to be serialized. On February 27, 1847—ten days after Poe had been awarded damages in his libel suit—there appeared an instalment that was designedly a smear of Poe and that had special reference to the Poe-Ellet scandal. Briggs in that instalment openly announced his satire of Poe, even while disowning any intention of "wantonly exposing the private conduct of any person to the public," because, as he said, alluding to Poe and his *Literati* papers, he had "always looked down upon those authors who write histories of their own contemporaries from mercenary motives, with abhorrence," and that "such a person['s character] shall form the only episode in my autobiography."

In this satire Lizzy is a central character—a girl who sends

82. I (Jan. 1, 1848), 3. For similar smears in the *John-Donkey,* see Feb. 5, p. 96; Feb. 12, pp. 99–100; Feb. 26, p. 140; March 4, p. 155; March 18, p. 182; April 15, p. 245; and June 3, pp. 364–365.

83. For details see Briggs's letters to James Russell Lowell in Woodberry's two-volume life of Poe, II, *passim,* and in Quinn's *Poe, passim.*

84. As quoted by Miller, *The Raven and the Whale,* p. 177. Miller states that the serial began in the *Weekly Mirror* on Nov. 14, 1846 (which would be the week after English's *1844* was concluded), and "proved so popular that it could also be started in the *Evening Mirror* on January 6, 1847."

"her compositions to the magazines signed with her full name" —clearly, Elizabeth Frieze Ellet. Wanting to have a "conversazione," Lizzy takes advantage of the absence of her family to invite a number of artists, among them the "celebrated critic, Austin Wicks, author of the 'Castle of Duntriewell,' a metaphysical romance, and a pscychological [*sic*] essay on the sensations of shadows. . . ." Here again Wicks-Poe is shown to be shallow and pretentious, a man whose "highest efforts in literature had been contributions to a lady's magazine." He imbibes but a single glass of wine and begins "to abuse all present in . . . profane and scurrilous terms." He calls one man an ass who cannot write English, and, after a brawl from which he is rescued, the party disbands in great disorder.

At this point Briggs rakes over the Mrs. Ellet affair. After the party, he continues:

Mr. Wicks sent her a letter, lamenting his destiny, praising her poetical abilities, and asking for the loan of five dollars. The kind-hearted Lizzy was so shocked at the idea of so great a genius in want of so trifling a sum, that she made a collection among her friends . . . and sent him fifty dollars, accompanied by a note so full of tender compassion for his misfortune, and respect for his genius, that any man possessed of the common feelings of humanity must have valued it more than the money. [This is the first time anyone conceded that Mrs. Ellet had sent Poe letters.] Wicks had no such feelings, and with a baseness that only those can believe possible who have known him, he exhibited Lizzy's note to some of her acquaintances, as an evidence that she had made improper advances to him. The scandal had been very widely circulated, before some candid friend brought it to Lizzy, who, on hearing it, was thrown into an agony of grief and shame, which nearly deprived her of reason. She could not call upon her father to avenge the wrong that had been done her, but one of her married sisters having heard of it, told it to her husband, who sought for the cowardly slanderer, with the intention of chastising him for his villainy. But he had become alarmed for the consequences of his slanders, and had persuaded a good natured physician to give him a certificate to the effect that he was of unsound mind, and not responsible for his actions. Having showed this to Lizzy's brother-in-law, and signed another paper acknowledging that he had slandered her and was sorry for it, he was allowed to escape without a personal chastisement. But shortly after, being employed to write for a fashionable magazine, he took an occasion, in a series of pretended biographical sketches of literary men and women who had been so unfortunate as to become known to him, to hold poor Lizzy up to ridicule....[85]

After this novel had run its course both in serial and book form, Briggs, like English, continued to attack Poe. When he edited *Holden's Dollar Magazine,* for example, he printed a poem by "Motley Manners, Esq.," which, modeled on a *Fable for Critics,* contained this passage:

> With tomahawk upraised for deadly blow,
> Behold our literary Mohawk, Poe!
> Sworn tyrant he o'er all who sin in verse—
> His own the standard, damns he all that's worse;
> And surely not for this shall he be blamed—
> Far worse than his deserves that it be damned!
>
> Who can so well detect the plagiary's flaw?
> "Set thief to catch thief" is an ancient saw!
> Who can so scourge a fool to shreds and slivers?
> Promoted slaves oft make the best slave drivers!
> Iambic Poe! of tyro bards the terror—
> *Ergo* is he—the world his pocket mirror.[86]

And on Poe's death, Briggs wrote: "His merits as a critic were very slender, he was a minute detector of slips of the pen, and, probably, was unequalled as a proof reader.... One of the strange points of his strange nature was to entertain a spirit of revenge towards all who did him a service. ... he rarely, or never, failed to malign those who befriended him."[87] Years afterward, in 1877, he again reviewed Poe's character. Poe's dissipations, he declared,

which were not intentional—for he was extremely temperate both in his diet and drink unless he was subjected to strong temptations— were not the repulsive traits of his character. What rendered him so obnoxious to those who knew him intimately were his treachery to his friends, his insincerity, his utter disregard of his moral obligations, and his total lack of loyalty and nobleness of purpose. He aimed at nothing, thought of nothing, and hoped for nothing but literary reputation; and in this respect he gained all he aspired to, and his friends should be satisfied to know that he accomplished all

85. This serial was subsequently published in two volumes, the first volume appearing in 1847 and the second in 1850. The quotation here is from the book. This passage is to be found in the first volume, pp. 157 ff.
86. *Holden's Dollar Magazine,* III (Jan., 1849), 22.
87. *Ibid.,* IV (Dec., 1849), 764–765.

that he labored for, and not endeavor to compel the world to award him a character which he never coveted and held in supreme contempt.[88]

Nor did the story end with Poe's death. To damage Poe's posthumous reputation, Griswold retold the Ellet episode, basing his "facts" on Briggs's satire or, possibly, on Briggs's personal account, for he and Briggs were very close friends.[89] According to Griswold:

Poe borrowed fifty dollars from a distinguished literary woman of South Carolina [Mrs. Ellet], promising to return it in a few days, and when he failed to do so, and was asked for a written acknowledgement of the debt that might be exhibited to the husband of the friend who had thus served him, he denied all knowledge of it, and threatened to exhibit a correspondence which he said would make the woman infamous, if she said any more on the subject. Of course there had never been any such correspondence, but when Poe heard that a brother of the slandered party was in quest of him for the purpose of taking the satisfaction supposed to be due in such cases, he sent for Dr. Francis and induced him to carry to the gentleman his retraction and apology, with a statement which seemed true enough at the moment, that Poe was 'out of his head.'[90]

Typically, editors like Clark—more concerned with Griswold's portrait of Poe than with Poe's works, and not loath to introduce racy reports into their columns, if with a touch of sanctimony—repeated the Griswold version of Poe's dishonorable conduct: "Two of the most painful things mentioned in his subsequent history is [sic] the slander of a well-known literary lady, who had befriended him when in need, and which slander he was obliged to retract under the threat of personal chastisement from the lady's brother on the plea of temporary insanity."[91]

---

88. *Independent,* Dec. 13, 1877, quoted by Woodberry, *Poe,* II, 426. In various places, including the *Dictionary of American Biography,* it is said that Briggs wrote a sketch of Poe for the *Encyclopaedia Britannica.* Careful search has failed to uncover the article, and the records of *EB* do not show that Briggs ever wrote about Poe for that work, either under his own name or that of Harry Franco.

89. Bayless, *Griswold,* pp. 125, 126, 253.

90. Memoir in *The Literati,* pp. xxiii–xxiv. From Mrs. Ellet's letter to Mrs. Griswold (cited in n. 70 of this chapter) written some three years after the publication of this Memoir, it appears that Griswold knew the facts in the case and was guilty of deliberate distortion. Mrs. Ellet in that letter accused Griswold of having told several persons that she *had written* letters to Poe.

91. *Knickerbocker,* XXXVI (Oct., 1850), 371.

What were the reasons for Poe's private affairs becoming public knowledge and his weaknesses common copy? For his criticism to be discredited and his career virtually ended? The answer lies in his journalistic career and in the literary battles he fought against the coteries, publishers, and editors that were dominating American letters for their own commercial ends. As we have seen, Poe as a critic had many glaring faults. He did not always fight his battles on purely literary grounds. He did not reserve his powder for coterie-sponsored authors but as freely "used up" authors who were not members of cliques. He praised a number of writers who were hardly better than those he gibbeted. He did not always analyze books but, like the very critics he derided, quoted specimens from them to exhibit their good and bad points. He had a separate critical standard for female authors, forgivable, perhaps, in the light of his gallantry, though it was a gallantry he could forget when a female author attacked him. And he was too eager to make a journalistic splash at whatever cost to himself or others.

Nevertheless, with all his faults, Poe appeared on the literary scene at a crucial point in history. The public had taken the place of the patron. Coterie art had given way to works aimed at masses of people. Books were judged by publishers who, as businessmen, were far less concerned with artistry than with salability. With literacy being the only qualification for authorship, writers were rushing into the market place. And, with competition in the book market becoming severer by the day, publishers and authors, banding with their new-found allies, the editors and reviewers, sought to trick the public into buying certain books and avoiding others.

Having a high regard for the literary profession, Poe for the most part sought to resist its being disgraced by dilettantes who would not or could not master the craft. Having a vital concern for literary taste, he tried, on the whole, to keep public taste from becoming degraded by a regimen of bad books and to protect the public from a system of puffing that would, in their eyes, transform poor works into great ones and literary dabblers into geniuses. And having in general sound literary values, he condemned the prevailing notion that popularity and sales were measures of a book's worth by insisting there were standards of judgment other than those of the market place.

The efforts that Poe made to safeguard a tradition whose value it is impossible to exaggerate were absolutely necessary, but a less militant man would not have devoted a career to the task. Whatever his motives, for he was by no means entirely altruistic, his militancy is attested by the fact that for almost his entire career he single-handedly fought the two most powerful cliques in America—those in Boston and New York—which were undermining that tradition. Whatever his motives, his devotedness to that tradition is attested by the fact that he persisted in his assaults (the lapses that occurred during his breakdown notwithstanding) despite the very real danger of ruin—a ruin to which he was finally reduced.

Though Poe was not an "ideal" critic, his struggles with the coteries led him to develop critical principles and practices that, for America, were unprecedented and brilliant—brilliant enough for him to be called our first great critic. Had he been an "ideal" critic—serene, unimpoverished, not forced to write against the clock—there is every reason to question whether he would have remained in the profession or have made himself felt as a force. From the beginning to the end of his career, there were those among his contemporaries who encouraged him to be ruthless in his analysis, scathing in his comments, and merciless in his judgments to offset forces that were extremist in an entirely opposite way—in a way calculated, either through indifference, ignorance, or chicanery, to prevent the free play of talent—and who lauded him when he was.[92] And no

92. In 1839, for instance, James E. Heath wrote to Poe: "In the department of criticism . . . I know few men who can claim to be your superior in this country. Your dissecting knife, if vigorously employed, would serve to rid us of much of that silly trash . . . with which puerile and conceited authors, and gain-seeking booksellers are continually poisoning our intellectual food" (quoted by Harrison, *Poe's Works*, VIII, xi). And after Poe's death, a writer in the *Democratic Review* (XXIII, Feb., 1851, 164) remarked: "He determined the profession should not degenerate in his hands, and mapped out in his own mind a course of earnestness and a critical standard, which he followed with design and defended with ability."

doubt Poe's temperament and his sense of journalism were such that he relished the role of literary crusader.

But whatever quarrel one may have with Poe as a critic, one must finally concede what is of ultimate importance, that he did range himself on the side of the artist; that he did call for support of worthy authors; that he did urge a free, outspoken, and responsible criticism; and that he did struggle to provide an audience for deserving works.

The price Poe paid for his militancy was enormous—poverty for the most part and defamation for the rest. As Griswold reminds us, Poe worked at a time when a man could "not write a purely literary criticism without encountering for it streams of personal abuse drawn from all the sinks and sewers of slanderous blackguardism."[93] It was also a time, as we have seen, when a man was bound to be starved or hooted out of the critical profession if he kept insisting there were other standards than commercial ones and if he clashed with those coalitions whose watchword, despite their lofty slogans, was profits. And this is precisely what occurred. Threatened by Poe's continual attacks, the coteries indeed destroyed Poe as a critic. They so damaged his reputation that his critical judgments became discredited; that he himself became the target, as Lewis Clark said, for " 'Punchy' writers . . . to take up their pen and impale . . . for public amusement"; and that finally led to his being hounded out of the profession. There is no question that Poe abetted his enemies by the life he led, and only an error of charity would impel anyone to make a special plea for his weaknesses—his drinking, his relations with women, his defense of his Boston Lyceum performance, his quarrel with Thomas Dunn English.

One last word is in order. It is impossible to assess the full value or power of Poe's critical work unless one understands that Poe was fundamentally a literary reformer, a rather lone figure on the American scene who, wanting to maintain a high literary tradition, waged a career-long war against those com-

93. In an undated letter to Abraham Hart postmarked Oct. 15, 1847 (quoted by Bayless, *Griswold*, p. 133).

mercial forces that today have become all too conspicuous. The attempt has been made here to present a significant record as fully as possible—not to whitewash Poe but to give him his due.

Index

The only items indexed under Poe are his works. For his relation to persons (such as Longfellow), to events (such as his Boston Lyceum performance), to ideas (such as "The Heresy of *The Didactic*"), and to periodicals (such as the *New York Mirror*), see under persons, events, ideas, and periodicals concerned. With this exception and that of Longfellow, the titles of whose works appear under his name, authors and titles are indexed separately, except where obfuscation might occur. Titles of works are followed by identification of the author; titles of periodicals are followed by their places of publication when this information is not already contained in the titles themselves. When a subject is mentioned in text and footnote on the same page, the footnote has not been indexed. Works more or less contemporaneous with Poe and those mentioned in the text have been indexed; other works mentioned in the notes have not.

Symbols

DATE DUE